CONSTANTINOPLE

to

KENSINGTON

Geoffrey & Dan

CONSTANTINOPLE

to

KENSINGTON

The Reminiscences of Geoffrey William Whittall
1906 – 2003

Edited by John W. Whittall

Matador
9 Priory Business Park,
Wistow Road, Kibworth Beauchamp,
Leicestershire. LE8 0RX
Tel: (+44) 116 279 2299
Fax: (+44) 116 279 2277
Email: books@troubador.co.uk
Web: www.troubador.co.uk/matador

ISBN 978 1780881 850

British Library Cataloguing in Publication Data.
A catalogue record for this book is available from the British Library.

Typeset in 11pt Baskerville by Troubador Publishing Ltd, Leicester, UK
Printed in the UK by TJ International, Padstow, Cornwall

Matador is an imprint of Troubador Publishing Ltd

CONTENTS

PREFACE

Following his retirement my father wrote copiously. Some of his articles were written to remind himself of periods in his life, some for pleasure and some for the Anglo Portuguese News and his local church magazine. He also carried out a great deal of research on the early family history and that of the other families in Turkey with whom the Whittalls intermarried. A list of his writings is attached at the end of this book. Copies of the majority of these will be lodged with the University of Exeter, University Library, Special Collections.

This book has been compiled from a selection of his essays and articles. My father assembled some of them into separate volumes and I have continued the work by adding chapters which give a more complete picture of his and my mother's life. This work has been a labour of love and has brought back many memories. My thanks are due to my sister, Maya Donelan, Betty McKernan and especially to our cousin Dolph van Rechteren for their work and advice on content, proof reading and general support and encouragement.

John Whittall
March 2012

Part I

BACKGROUND

...Then to call on all my Whittall friends. They have the bulk of the English trade in their hands, branch offices all down the southern coast, mines and shooting boxes and properties scattered up and down the S.W. coast of Asia Minor and yachts on the seas. They all have immense quantities of children. The sons, young men now in the various Whittall businesses, the daughters very charming, very gay. The big gardens touch one another and they walk in and out of one another's houses all day long gossiping and laughing. I should think life presents itself nowhere under such easy and pleasant conditions.
(Extract from the Letters of Gertrude Bell; Smyrna, April 4th 1907).

CHAPTER I

A British Community In Turkey

I was born on the 16th January 1906, in Moda, an Asiatic suburb of Constantinople, the sixth child and fourth son of William James Harter and Lilian Adeline Whittall, both of whom were born in Smyrna in 1871 and 1872 respectively.

The family's presence in Constantinople arose as follows: In 1860 Grandfather, J.W.Whittall, later to become Sir James William Whittall (1838 – 1910), was sent to Manchester from Smyrna to represent the family company C. Whittall & Co.'s interests in J.C. Harter & Co. He subsequently became a partner in this firm. In 1862 he married Edith Anna Barker, daughter of Samuel Barker of Budja, Smyrna and took up residence in Bowdon, Cheshire. The climate of England did not suit him and his doctor advised him to return to a warmer clime. In 1873 he left England and set off, accompanied by a pregnant wife and five small children, by long sea voyage for Smyrna, the journey lasting two weeks. With them went two goats to supply milk for the children. So as not to compete directly with his brothers in Smyrna, he decided to settle in Constantinople where, in October 1873, he founded the firm of J.W. Whittall & Co. in conjunction with Sidney La Fontaine, who was then agent for J.C. Harter & Co. in Constantinople.

Having decided to settle in Constantinople, he was faced with the problem of finding suitable accommodation for his wife and six children, so he bought several acres of land in the still sparsely inhabited hamlet of Moda on the Asiatic shore of the Sea of Marmara.

In due course, following on Grandfather's initiative, further members of the British and foreign communities settled in Moda, including some of the Charnaud, Maltass, La Fontaine and Barker families, long resident in Smyrna. What with Greeks and Armenians, Moda became very much of a non-Turkish suburb. In early days getting to town each day involved a quarter-hour walk to Kadikeui, and then hiring a small boat to row or sail to make the crossing. This was all right in calm weather, but if it was rough, or a strong South wind was blowing, one had either to abandon the journey or make the crossing over the calmer waters of the Bosphorus. One English family, the Thompsons, who ran a farm some way inland, used to ride into Kadikeui on horseback, before taking to the boats. Later on, with the opening of the Anatolian Railway and the progressive increase in the Asiatic population, a ferry service was inaugurated.

As the British community in Moda increased in numbers, the need began to be felt for a Church. Soon, with the help of a considerable endowment from Grandfather, the Church of All Saints was consecrated, and served by priests brought out from England, whose emoluments were paid for by the congregation. Most of these arrived as young bachelors, with many marrying local girls. These proved a blessing on their return to England, where they opened their large country vicarages to take in expatriate school children during the winter and Easter holidays.

Services at All Saints were always well attended, so much so that at one time the Church looked like becoming too small. There was never any lack of talent for the choir, and the organ was played by a spinster lady, hand-pumped by one of the household servants. After the service everyone foregathered in the street outside, to exchange news and no doubt to gossip, with everyone having the opportunity to keep in touch. Until the Crimean War burials used to take place in the Protestant Cemetery in town, but thereafter the beautiful cemetery at Haidar Pasha came into use.

Another need that soon came to be felt was for a club, and in due course the Kadikeui Rowing Club was founded, in premises by the pier in Moda bay. Initially ladies were not admitted nor any of non-British nationality, but in the course of time these strictures were removed with a resultant development of wider friendships and inter-marriages.

Some time later the Club's name was changed to the Moda Yacht Club, an indication perhaps of greater prosperity, for, by then indeed, many members owned yachts which were anchored in Moda Bay during the summer months, during which, unlike the winter, the anchorage was safe. In addition, to accommodate bathers during the summer, a two-cabined raft was also anchored in mid-bay in deep water, while children and non-swimmers made use of the fine sands at the far end of the Bay.

During the season regular sailing, swimming and rowing races were held under the Club's auspices, but most dramatic was the annual regatta, open to all comers. On this occasion the bay was filled with boats of all sizes and descriptions, including Bosphorus ferries bringing visitors over from town, all gaily decorated with flags and bunting to make an enchanting scene in the strong sunlight and the deep blue of sea and sky. Races included all the standard ones for sailing, rowing and swimming, but most colourful and most appreciated were those for caiques, local boats with crews drawn from all round the coast and ports, with fine looking men in colourful clothes, rowing to immense acclamation, and for well-earned and well worthwhile prizes.

Another requirement that arose was for a community meeting place, and with Grandfather's offer of a piece of land, the 'Institute' came into being. It consisted of a two-storied wooden building made up of a large hall with stage, and several smaller rooms, one housing a library and another used as a school for the younger generation, run by the clergyman. Here all community events took place, such as communal plays, some of these locally written with parodies of events and of everyday life, dances, parties and also the annual Christmas tree and party held on Boxing Day for children. Music was very much to the fore, with most ladies playing the piano. A popular form of entertainment was the 'ballad' evening, in which people gathered round the piano and sang popular and other songs to the accompaniment of cups of hot chocolate.

Every year too, a pantomime was presented by the children, and one year this led to an interesting incident. The British Ambassador was proposing to bring his children over to see the performance, when two men purporting to come from the Sultan, arrived at the Embassy and told the Ambassador that the Sultan considered that such shows as were put on in the Institute were indecent and immoral, and he demanded that they should be discontinued. (The then Sultan, Abdul Hamid, lived in a perpetual state of fear, especially of all gatherings of people, whether Turkish or foreign). This request aroused Sir Nicholas' anger, and turning on the men he told them he did not believe they came from the Sultan and then sent them packing with a reprimand for having dared come to him with such a tale. He then proceeded to ring up his fellow Ambassadors (Embassies were fewer on the ground in those days) and invited all their children to attend the show with his, and ferried them all over to Moda in his launch. Nothing more was heard of the matter.

To provide facilities for sport, a piece of land was bought near the river and laid out for rugby, association football and cricket. It may well be that this was the first place in which soccer was played in Turkey. Matches were played with other teams from town and there was an annual match with Smyrna which led to divided loyalties in our household, for though Father played scrum-half for Constantinople, Mother, remaining true to Smyrna, backed the side in which her brothers were playing. In due course tennis courts were laid out, while golf of a sort was played on the Ok Maidan, some fields up the Golden Horn. These fields also offered favourable pasturing grounds for the sheep of Albanian shepherds, and occasional disputes arose, until peace was restored with an edict from the Sultan allowing the British 'to play ball' on the site.

The community was divided between those who loved the sea with its sailing and fishing, and those who preferred the land with its shooting. We children used to fish in the bay for small fry, and also watch the nets being drawn up of an early morning. The more experienced went further afield after bass and bream, using lines in preference to rods. Fishing in those days, before the era of pollution, was excellent, with the local boatmen knowing all the best places in which to try one's luck.

Yachts were used for cruising in the Marmara as also in the Aegean, but no one ever ventured into the treacherous waters of the Black Sea. In addition sailing and picnics up the coast, whether in large or small boats, were always enjoyed, especially in the summer months whenever bathing was practicable.

In Moda social life in the 'village' was free and easy, with people dropping in on each other at all times and usually without warning, to be greeted with a cup of coffee, a glass of cold water and possibly a teaspoonful of some sweet jam. Outside of this there was a more formal life of dinner parties, dances, teas and so on. Visitors from abroad were made especially welcome and Grandfather, who was in close touch with the Embassies, would meet them in town and then ferry them over in his yacht to Moda to land at his private jetty.

Communications with town after dark were difficult. Most entertainments had to be organised at home or in the village. Card-playing in the shape of auction bridge or four-pack bezique was popular as were gatherings at the piano in which all would sing ballads or other popular songs to the accompaniment of cups of cocoa.

One of the highlights of the year was a bazaar organised by Grandmother in aid of the Dorcas Society, which was held in her garden, and this was always attended by all Moda as also by large numbers from town. Trees in her large garden were decorated with bunting and white linen-covered tables with vases of flowers on them displayed goods for sale. A superb tea was also provided. Maids in white pinafores and bonnets weaved amongst them serving everyone with their needs, while the Montenegran men-servants rose to the occasion by donning their green and gold native costumes, with pill-box on head, strutting about and showing themselves off with pride. Of the articles for sale I remember little apart from large bottles of lavender and rose water, prepared at home, which were favourite toilet requisites among the ladies. With everyone in their best clothes it was a very gay occasion, offering a wonderful opportunity to meet members of the community from all parts. And, perhaps most importantly, we children were able to escape into the crowd and do full justice to the excellent fare provided.

Another occasion in summer was the annual picnic to Buliver's Island. This waterless, flat small island lying outside the main series of Prince's Isles, had been bought by Sir Henry Buliver when Ambassador to Turkey from 1858 to 1865. On this he had built a large house, somewhat after the style of Knebworth and to this he used to repair at weekends, and in it, so the story ran, to hold orgies in the company of girls introduced from town. In actual fact Sir Henry was, I believe, a very respectable man, but the story lent colour and glamour to the island, at any rate in our children's eyes, as we speculated as to what exactly took place in an orgy. When I last saw the island in 1914, the house was in ruins, and the only evidence of human habitation lay in the large numbers of purple irises in flower. Following on Buliver's retirement the island was bought by the Khedive of Egypt under speculation that this was a quid pro quo in return for the support Buliver had always given him. From then on the house was never again inhabited.

On the way we used to pass another small rocky island, and on this all the pi-dogs of town had been marooned to die of thirst and starvation after having been gathered up in 1911. In town these dogs had been very well organised into bands, each jealously guarding its own territory from interlopers. So much so that it was said that anyone going to live in a new area and owning a dog was well advised to introduce it to the pack to ensure its safety.

At home the 'Times' arrived regularly from England as well as a weekly journal, the 'Near East' (in those days Turkey, the Balkans, Persia and Arabia were considered to be the Near East. No one had ever heard of the Middle East), while locally there were published the 'Levant Herald' in English and the 'Journal d'Orient' and the 'Stamboul' in French. There was also an English bookshop in town. As for general reading I know that Grandfather and an Uncle had excellent libraries, and I made my first acquaintance with the works of Tolstoy and Ibsen from Mother's collection. French books were easier to obtain than English, French being the lingua franca and taught in excellent French schools. It was a great advantage having a common language, talked by anyone with a glimmering of education, as this facilitated social life with foreigners and led to the British becoming less and less exclusive, even to the point of inviting non-British to join the club. Sadly, owing to the seclusion of women, no normal social life was possible with Turkish families as such, although Father had his Turkish men friends and Mother her Ladies.

In households the women servants were invariably Greeks who also spoke Turkish, and the men servants Turkish who learned Greek. In those days and even during the Balkan wars, there was never any trouble or unpleasantness between the two peoples, either in the houses or out shooting in the country. At the same time there was no intermarriage.

The relationship between master and man was also interesting, as will be seen from the following incident. My Uncle Kenny, wanting to start fishing up the coast at daybreak, the best time, decided to spend the night on a deserted island to facilitate this, and set off with his man Hakki, a Greek. When night fell, Uncle turned in, leaving Hakki to his devices, which as it happened were concerned with a bottle of raki, the local strong drink. In the middle of the night a strong wind blew up and woke a somewhat befuddled Hakki, who thereupon decided he had better get home before the wind turned into a gale. So into the boat he got, and rowed home. Morning came and Uncle woke up to find no Hakki, no boat and no breakfast. What he felt like can be left to the imagination. In the meantime Hakki woke up in his bed, next to his wife, and, out of his previously confused state, suddenly remembered Uncle marooned on the island, to which he returned post haste, to be well and truly sworn at by Uncle, by now in a good fury. But, heinous as the offence was, there was no question of sacking. Hakki was an old friend and a good fisherman and his eccentricities had to be taken in good part, for after all he was only human. So Uncle, on his return home made a joke of the incident and related it to all with great glee. This was the attitude adopted by most men who came into close contact with both Turks and Greeks in their employ, and it made for a particularly pleasant and loyal relationship.

Turkish Art is in the main a discovery of more recent years, and in those early years few if any members of the colony showed any interest in it, except in the way of buying old carpets, silver and pots to decorate their houses. Apart from this there was a tendency to regard the Turks as having been semi-barbarian by nature and to ascribe all artefacts to the handiwork of Christians, Turkish architecture as nothing else than a derivative of the Byzantine. Of course this attitude was not a mere local manifestation but was widespread in Europe, as evidenced in the case of 'Rhodian' pottery This was for long regarded as Greek in origin, and purely because of an exhibition of this ware from a collection stemming from the isle of Rhodes. It is interesting how in contra-distinction the wares of the Kutahia pottery were regarded as pure Turkish whereas they were of Armenian origin.

It must be admitted in mitigation however, that at that period very little had been written about Turkish art, while a large corpus of the best specimens were hidden away and not available to the general public. Even I remember having to get special permission to enter Saint Sophia and the Kahrie Cami in the early twenties. Incidentally the Byzantines fared no better for apart from these two churches and the cisterns none of their former churches were known. People in general were far more interested in Greco-Roman remains.

Turkish architecture was by its very nature far more easy of inspection, but here again attention was riveted on the mosques of Sultan Ahmed (the Blue mosque) and that of Suleiman. No one ever visited Adrianople (Edirne) and only a few Broussa (Bursa) with their superb monuments. In effect it was left to generations following the First World War to realise the importance of Turkish and Seljuk architecture.

There are no records of how the colony was affected by the Russo-Turkish war of 1878, nor by the Armenian troubles of 1896 during which Grandfather was placed in charge of all relief work and for which he was knighted by Queen Victoria at Osborne in 1898.

The 1908 Young Turk Revolution also passed without notice, but things were otherwise during its counterblast of 1909. The first intimation of this came from the sound of shooting across the water, and then Father and those crossing over to work saw a string of bodies hanging from lampposts on the bridge spanning the Golden Horn.

Meanwhile our good friend and neighbour, Mahmoud Muhtar Pasha was in charge of the garrison at the War Office, and was one of the few to offer resistance to the revolutionaries. In view of this the Sultan, who was strongly suspected of having instigated the affair, issued an edict that he was to be taken dead or alive. Arriving home pursued by troops he climbed over the garden wall into Grandfather's garden and was given shelter in the house. Immediately the whole family compound was surrounded by troops and no one allowed in or out. The officer in charge then went up to the front door and demanded that the Pasha be handed over to him. Granny, who met him, flatly refused to do so, and pointed out that under the Treaty of Capitulations none of his troops had the right to enter the property. This was accepted by the Officer, while his troops remained in position. Some time later Grandfather returned from town accompanied by a porter carrying some purchases. He was allowed in, but on hearing of what had happened he immediately wrote letters to the British and German Ambassadors, describing what was going on, and these were delivered by his porter.

Immediately a Dragoman was sent to the War Office, but the Minister said he could do nothing as the order had proceeded from the Sultan. So a strong order, demanding immediate withdrawal of the troops was drawn up and sent for signature by the Sultan in his Palace. On arrival the messenger was told that the Sultan, being in his bath, could not be disturbed. The messenger did not leave, but continued to make further demands, until the document was signed, the Sultan evidently realising that this affair had the makings of a serious diplomatic incident from which he might emerge the chief sufferer. Anyhow the document quickly reached Moda, the troops were withdrawn, and that evening the Pasha in disguise was smuggled onto Grandfather's yacht and placed on a ship on its way to Malta.

1909 witnessed a counter Revolution and this was followed in 1910 by the war with Italy over Tripoli (Libya). This, being distant, did not affect people much, and in the same year there was a huge fire in town. This in its turn was followed by the Balkan War of 1912. This latter was a different matter and has left memories of bands of three or more men, circulating the streets, and shouting out the numbers of those classes called to the colours, to the accompaniment of the beating of a big drum. Rightly or wrongly we knew these bands as 'daoulia'. Later in the war we woke one morning to hear the sound of distant gunfire, as the fighting approached Constantinople. As usual with any trouble in Turkey there were alarms over cholera and suitable dietetic measures had to be imposed. This war came to an end with the loss of most of Turkey's European possessions, to be followed by threats of war in Europe.

The war over, two British warships arrived on a visit, the ill-fated *Hampshire* and the *Zealandia*, and these, to our delight, gave a magnificent children's party with all manner of delights, and new ribbons, bearing the names of the ships, to put round our sailor hats. Sadly a short time later we woke up to find two German warships anchored off the bottom of Granny's garden, the *Goeben* long and low in the water, and very menacing, and the *Breslau*, tall in the water and with four funnels. These had eluded the British fleet in the Mediterranean and were now threatening the city, to help lead Turkey into the war on Germany's side.

We were all evacuated to England when war broke out in 1914 but my great-aunt Maria and Father's old nurse decided to stay on in Granny's house. On hearing of this the German General in local command arranged for an officer to call at the house once a month to ensure that the old ladies were well and lacked for nothing.

CHAPTER II

Constantinople

The city into which Grandfather settled in 1873 was much smaller than that of to-day, its population in 1876 being 800,000. In one way it was changing in character, for, having hitherto played second fiddle to Smyrna in the way of international trade it was now catching up to such an extent that many members of the British colony in Smyrna such as the Barkers, La Fontaines, Charnauds and Maltasses changed their place of work.

In those days the town was known to all foreigners as Constantinople, whereas to the Turks it was Istanbul (or Istambol), a name derived from the Greek *Ist-in-polin*, "to the town" (a derivation hotly contested by the Turks of today). Interestingly at the same time it was known to the Arabs as *Kon-stantiniyey* while all coins minted in the town until 1926 bore the inscription "Darabafa Constantiniye", "struck in Constantinople". The alternative name of Istambol was corrupted to Stambouland. This name was applied to that quarter of the town comprising the old Byzantine city, situated on the Western bank of the Golden Horn, that narrow inlet of deep water which effectively split the town in two and offered the original settlers a superb harbour. This quarter was mainly inhabited by Turks, except for a few enclaves, such as that of the Orthodox Patriarchate, in which lived Greeks. It contained the Sultan's Palace as well as the main Government Offices, as well as the main Byzantine and Ottoman "sights" and the quiet bazaars. In addition the main commercial offices were sited on its lower reaches alongside the Golden Horn, surrounding the General Post Office, the Stock Exchange and the Sirkedji Rail Station.

From this part of the town a bridge over the Golden Horn acted as a link with the quarter of Galata across the water, which from Byzantine times onwards had been the main seat of foreigners, originally mainly Venetian and Genoese, living and working in the town. But at this time it was mostly connected with shipping offices, warehouses and quays, abutting on the usual sleazy, crowded, dirty and neglected housing of a typical Eastern Mediterranean port.

The bridgehead was surrounded by shops, and from it ran a broad road lined with foreign banks which led past the Pera Palace Hotel and the British Embassy up to the quarter of Pera on the hill-top. This could also be reached by an underground funicular, the Tunnel, dating back to 1873 and by Step Street, the Yildirim Sokak. This lived up to its name and passed through a very low quarter, the story running that in those days it was dangerous for a lone man to climb the street as the young ladies from adjoining houses tended to run out, and seize a hat, to return in haste hoping that the owner would follow them into their lairs.

No foreigners of any repute lived in Galata, leaving it to the very mixed port population, who preferred to live in Pera, a quarter making no claims to either beauty or interest, mainly consisting of narrow streets lined by tall ill-kept houses and generally by no means clean. At its upper end, by the open space of Taxim, there were better class houses, also on the hillside facing the Bosphorus, from which magnificent views were obtainable and which benefited from the cool afternoon wind in summer.

The main road, the Istiklal Caddesi, more commonly known as the Grande Rue de Pera, ran from the tunnel to Taxim, to form the main shopping centre of the town, in which more or less everything was obtainable. Along it stood Talatlian's, the rival hotel to the Pera Palace, as also Leban's patisserie, in which everyone used to meet. Another favourite was Baker's, an English run store for household goods. The original Baker had come out as gardener to the Embassy in 1846 and later started importing and selling goods from England, with considerable success. One son moved to England where he set up a factory colour-printing household textiles, with such success that an exhibition of the firm's products was later held at the Victoria and Albert Museum in London. He, however, became better known for his interest in the wild flowers of the Near East, and had many of his discoveries named after him.

The British Community in Turkey enjoyed certain very considerable privileges, following on from a treaty entered into in the days of Queen Elizabeth, and generally referred to as the 'Capitulations'. Under these Britons paid no taxes and their persons and property and houses were inviolate to the police and the armed forces, without their getting prior approval from the Consul. In addition, all children born to them and registered at the British Consulate retained their nationality, as in my case. I am of the fourth generation to be born in the country. In addition a British Post Office was sanctioned, and used British stamps, overprinted Levant, and a British Legal Officer, entitled, among other things, to settle any disputes not involving the Turkish Law Courts. These Capitulations endured until 1924, in which year they were abolished.

The British Community was roughly divided into four groups residing in town, up the Bosphorus, in Moda and finally in San Stefano, where the modern airport now exists. The community in San Stefano was too small to be represented in sport, but the other three were able to raise teams for football, cricket and tennis and so to allow regular tournaments.

Socially, the main trouble lay in the difficulties in getting about, so that in general members of the different communities either met in town or on special occasions such as dances, sporting events, weddings and funerals. Grandfather was better placed in this respect for his yacht could pick up guests and land them in his garden. He entertained on a grand scale, for, much involved in Ambassadorial circles, he met all important newcomers and visitors to the town and was a participant in all activities.

Communications with the Asiatic shore became much easier with the construction of the Anatolian railway, with its terminus at Haidar Pasha. Landing stations were constructed, and a ferry service inaugurated, with the use of paddle steamers brought out from the Clyde, serving Haidar Pasha and Kadikeui, and later Moda, the Coast and the Princes Isles. Subsequently trams were introduced into the town, but even with these facilities the various communities tended to 'stew in their own juice.'

Adequate water supplies came from a series of dams and aqueducts, dating back to Byzantine times and mostly situated in the Forest of Belgrade to the North of the city, while lighting was mainly by gas. All drainage was discharged into the sea, which in those days remained clear. It is a very different story now that the population has increased fivefold.

The climate of Constantinople has always been more continental in type than that of Smyrna, with cooler summers and colder winters, often accompanied by heavy snowfalls. On occasions in the past the Bosphorus has been completely frozen over and in 1929 it was blocked by ice-floes descending from the Black Sea. One result of climate and geography is that the town is on one of the main migration routes for birds. Very conspicuous is the daytime movement of storks, which first appear as a small cloud in the distance, becoming a long line of birds flying at no great height.

Ever since our forebear settled in Smyrna in the early nineteenth century all who could afford it sent their sons to England for education, and this persisted until my time. Girls were mostly educated at home or locally until after the First World War when most were sent to England. In Constantinople there was a High School for Girls with an interesting history. After the Crimean war the Sultan presented both the French and the British communities with land and a building to serve as a school. The girls' school was organised but a difficulty arose as, according to Turkish law, no foreigner could own property in the city. This gave rise to considerable anxiety, which was only allayed when some bright individual found that, under existing Turkish law, all women of whatever nationality residing in the town could be regarded as Turkish citizens. So the school was immediately inscribed in the name of the Ambassadress, Lady Stratford de Redcliffe, until the law was changed in 1870. There is no indication as to how safe it was for girls to travel to and fro alone. Certainly Turkish women never went out alone unless accompanied by a man, although this may only have applied to the upper classes. A British High School for Boys was founded later in the early nineteen hundreds. Before that they either had to be sent to England or to attend a local French School, of which there were a number. In general most boys were educated in England.

Following the Crimean War, a competition was held over the design of a proposed Crimean Memorial Church. This was won by that great Victorian architect William Burges, but sadly when it came to building, his design was considered to be too expensive, and an alternative one by G.E. Street was selected. With the fall in the number of resident Anglicans it was deconsecrated in 1978 and re-consecrated in 1991. For medical care, there was a resident British doctor who, amongst other things, looked after the British Seamen's Hospital, now also gone.

Until the opening of the railway, Constantinople could only be reached by sea, unless one wanted to brave the slow and tedious journey overland, involving much discomfort. Even then, the rail passage through Thrace was slow, for the German engineer in charge of construction had been paid by the mile, which resulted in the lines being carried over huge and unnecessary loops to increase this mileage. Nevertheless rail travel, once it started, was faster and more convenient, especially for the towns of Central Europe, but it missed out in one respect as the view of the city from the sea in the early morning light as a ship approached was one of almost unsurpassable beauty.

In those days the quays and the harbour were alive with ships, with those anchored at sea discharging their cargoes into lighters. Numerous shipping lines offered regular services to neighbouring countries, Romania, Greece, Italy, France and Egypt among others, with British and other merchant lines making regular calls. In addition, there were the regular Turkish lines serving the Aegean and the Black Sea coasts. In the days of sailing vessels, if there was a North Wind, they used to congregate at the mouth of the Bosphorus, awaiting the favourable South Wind which would carry them into the Black Sea against the prevailing current.

Apart from the occasional sight-seeing visit to Saint Sophia with its neighbouring relics and to the Bazaars, few residents ever wandered further afield. And yet the old quarters of Stamboul were fascinating with their narrow streets lined by rows of low, grey wooden houses. These were broken in places by a high wall, interrupted by a tall and important looking gate, probably concealing within a large house and garden, which shut off as they were, gave a touch of mystery as one speculated as to what went on within the enclosure. One was rarely able to get a glimpse of the interior to have one's visions of luxury and beautiful houris destroyed by the all too visible air of general neglect.

Otherwise the grey monotony was here and there broken by an ornate fountain or tomb, or by a mosque, usually set in a tree-clad open space and adding a touch of the picturesque. Here and there a large open area gave an indication of a former fire, not an infrequent event, seeing that the dry houses would burn like tinder. It was said that fires were most frequent in the aubergine season, during which, whilst frying them, paraffin stoves standing on the floor were easily knocked over. Other open spaces marked the sites of former Byzantine water reservoirs, one of which I saw on my last visit had been converted into an excellent football ground.

But of all places the bridge over the Golden Horn with its seething crowds offered the best panorama of life in the town. On it one saw all manner of men, ordinary men about town, their usually sombre clothes relieved by the brilliant scarlet of the fezzes they inevitably wore, Christians without that touch of gaiety, and numerous Greeks and Armenians who copied Moslems in that respect. Then there were smartly clad officers in uniform, often accompanied by grey-clad soldiers, and grey-bearded dignitaries in flowing robes and white turbans, setting off beggars plying their occupation in all manner of rags. Porters (hamals) carrying seemingly impossible loads balanced on their bent backs and water vendors clinking their glasses as they sold their precious liquid for a farthing or two. Other passers-by were gypsy women, with face uncovered who were, apart from Christians, about the only women to be seen on the pavements. These wore the brightest of colours, with small jackets, and ballooning trousers clasped round the ankle, and often carrying a sickly looking baby in their arms or to the breast.

The carriageway was likewise crowded with vehicles of all descriptions and many beasts of burden, mainly horses and donkeys, well laden and either ridden or driven. Some of the carriages carried women, veiled to the eyes, safe in the company of the male driver, for Turkish women in general never went out alone or unaccompanied. In addition there were men from all parts of the Turkish Empire and from neighbouring countries, Arabs, Egyptians, Albanians, Montenegrins, Circassians and many others, all dressed in accordance with their national customs and adding a yet still further touch of variety. One could in effect spend hours just regarding the scene.

Sadly today all this is over. Stamboul is pierced by wide streets; the old wooden houses are giving way to bricks and mortar and animal drawn vehicles to the motor car, and the former comparative peace and quiet to unbridled noise. Also gone are the cheerful clothes and the fez.

Part II

PARENTS

CHAPTER I

William James Harter Whittall (1871 – 1930)

Father died in 1930, some sixty years ago, consequently, with memories having faded, it is difficult to write in detail about him. Also the circumstances of life were such that I saw comparatively little of him, and, maybe, never got to know him really well.

He was born in Smyrna in 1871, and subsequently spent his boyhood in Moda, prior to being sent to school in England in the company of several cousins. This school was situated in the Isle of Wight, and was run by a Mr. Le Bouvier, who had had some connection with Smyrna.

On finishing his schooling he joined his father (Sir James Whittall) and brother Edwin in the family firm in Constantinople. His job entailed quite a lot of travel in the interior, on horseback where no public transport was available, the bad roads rendering carriage travel most uncomfortable. It is of interest that in those days written contracts were unheard of and not necessary, for complete trust existed. In these ways and with shooting all over the local countryside, Father made innumerable friends amongst the local village population, and in later life it was always a delight to me to see how well he was received wherever he went.

At the start of the century Father had had a house built in the country at Alemdagh some fifteen miles inland. In this house the entire family would spend a month or so in the spring, while for the rest of the time it was used as a shooting box, as a country depot for poultry and cows and as kennels for the shooting dogs. Whenever Father was in residence all his friends from the surrounding villages would drop in to see him. We boys got used to the presence of these frequently ill-clad and rough-looking men and, quickly losing all doubts, soon got to feel at home with them and to like and trust them, feelings which have never altered.

In winter he played scrum half in the Constantinople rugby football team and tennis in summer. In 1896 he married his cousin, Lilian Adeline Whittall and they lived in the small cottage standing in Grandfather's garden, prior to taking over Aunt Leila Barker's house, which became our permanent home. Of his early married life I know nothing except that he used to play bezique with Mother, who, in a fit of exasperation, once threw the pack of cards at him.

Children came in pairs, first two boys, Hugh b. 1896 and Vernon b. 1898, then two girls, Monica b. 1899 and Edna b. 1901, followed by two more boys, Osmond (Osie) b. 1904 and myself b. 1906, with Willie coming some five years after me as a sort of afterthought.

In the household Father always took first place in Mother's consideration, and his routine of life had always to be respected. Normally he woke up between the hours of five and six of a morning, then he would perform his exercises in the hall for some twenty minutes and proceed to run round the gardens for a further twenty. A cold bath would be followed by a rub-down with a rough glove and towel, after which he would have breakfast at about seven o'clock. This usually consisted of two boiled eggs so lightly cooked that he used practically to drink them down, accompanied by cream crackers and honey. During this meal Osie and I used often to come down in our night-wear to join him, silently standing at his side, and hopefully awaiting our reward, a biscuit spread with butter and honey which, to avoid drips, were mixed together to form a fairly solid paste.

Father was a constant sufferer from indigestion, and I have no doubt that in these days he would have been diagnosed as suffering from an ulcer. He kept to a strict diet although this was not helped by his heavy smoking of pipes and cigarettes.

He would leave for the office between 7.30 and 8.00 to return at about 5.30 or 6.00. Then, after a change into easier clothes, he would either pay Granny a visit or, during the warmer weather sit in an armchair in the bow window of the dining room (in the company of two pots of aspidistra on stands and of Sonny, the cat) and from here gossip with all passers-by on the Drive, teasing all and sundry. In winter he would be found sitting in front of the fire with his legs cocked up against the mantle-piece, once again in the company of Sonny.

Weekends in the season were usually spent shooting, but in the summer he used to take us children out fishing or sailing. I remember him teasing us by hiding silver piastres for us to find. He would at times put on waders and carry us out to sea at the bottom garden, and set us on one of the projecting rocks, to our delight and simultaneous anxiety lest we be forgotten. Otherwise I cannot remember much about him at this age, but his interest in us boys certainly increased as we became able to take up shooting. He never really liked the sea although in those days he owned a sailing boat, the *Viking*.

Shooting was his great joy in life. In these parts of the world this was essentially rough in character and entailed the use of dogs and long hours of walking over scrub-covered hills, with usually only the prospect of a small bag at the end of the day. In his younger and impecunious days Father, on his return from the office on Fridays, would walk ten miles or so up country, to spend the night in a village house, and then shoot all day Saturday and on Sunday morning to walk back home in the afternoon. He was not a brilliant shot, as was Uncle Edwin his brother, but he excelled at the snap shooting which was vital when shooting woodcock in thick scrub. In his eyes a day's outing in the country and a long walk almost always made up for the possible absence of game. From a purely shooting point of view this was not an ideal way of getting a good bag, and it may be that he was so much more successful with woodcock than with other game as the thick cover in which they lay slowed both man and dog. In such coverts the dogs were fitted with bells so as to keep in touch and to signal pointing at a bird by their silence. Naturally when we went out with him the pace was slowed, but in later years when much older we used to have great difficulty in keeping up with him on rough and precipitous hills.

It was very largely in connection with shooting that I got to know him much better. As soon as Osie and I were large enough to hold and handle a gun Father started teaching us how to shoot. He was a stickler on gun safety and the only occasion I ever saw him angry was over Osie pointing a gun at someone. Over shooting lessons he showed unusual patience, took infinite care and introduced us to a quite different Father to that in Moda, much greater simplicity and approachability. These lessons also brought us into close contact with his village shooting friends, whom we learnt to like and respect.

Father's dressing room always intrigued us, as did the loaded revolver he kept hanging by his bed. Most attractive however was the large stock of boxes containing packets of Nestlé milk chocolate he kept stored in his cupboard, while a small chest fitted with many small drawers held a fascinating array of small objects including a ball of opium. On his person his waistcoat was adorned by a gold watch and chain to which was attached a gold ring and a round spring-fitted box containing gold pounds.

During the first year of the war when we were in England, I saw little of Father, but in 1915, Mother, Willy and Marina, Willy's nurse, and I joined him in Greece where he had rented a house for us in the Athenian suburb of Kiphissia, which in those days, like Piraeus, was separated from the town by open fields. He used to do his morning exercises on the terrace in front of our house in full public view, to become locally known as the "Mad Englishman". Here he introduced me to a new pleasure, that of going for long walks with him, for, outside my natural pride at being chosen to accompany him, I found him to be extremely interesting in his knowledge of birds and other aspects of the countryside. He did not spare me and even took me to the top of Mount Pentelicon, from which we got a magnificent view over the plain and the bay of Marathon. Father would also climb to the top on hot days to appreciate the cooler air. He never wore a hat and his bald head was tanned a dark brown.

Later on he moved to Salonica when, with the possibility of local trouble attending the abdication of King Constantine, we moved over to Rome. Here he joined forces with an old friend, a Mr. Saltiel, to set up the company of Whittall, Saltiel and Co. In addition he also supervised a large enterprise devoted to growing potatoes for the British troops. (Mr. Saltiel came into our lives in later days, when on passing through Marseilles on our way home on holidays, he always met us with a large box of chocolates.) In Salonica Father lived with old friends, the Jacksons, whose son Herbert subsequently married my sister Monica. His spare time in winter was spent shooting ducks and geese on the local marshes.

Once we had settled in Rome, Father occasionally dropped in on us, when, to my great joy, he would take me out for walks, this time in the Alban Hills which were reached from town by a tram. Such walks covered the entire ground, passing through the villages of Grotta Ferrata, Rocca di Papa, Nemi, Albano and Genzano and usually ending on the summit of Monte Cavo. On these occasions we took sandwiches of mortadella and pecorino cheese with us and ate these sitting in an osteria, in which, for the first time of my life, I was allowed to drink a mixture of wine and water. I also felt important as I had to act as interpreter.

Back in Salonica Father had found an old friend, a Mr. Mountain, dying of consumption and more or less unattended. Father proceeded to look after him, but sadly caught the infection which was later to lead to his death. But before this had happened I had left Rome for school in England.

Once the war was over civil authority in the Turkish countryside broke down. With the peasants living in a state of poverty, conditions arose which led many men, both Greek and Turkish, into the time-honoured pursuit of brigandage and this made it dangerous to sleep in villages or to go shooting far afield. Father was in a more fortunate position than most, for he was so well known over the countryside that none of the locals would have touched him. But there was always danger from those who had filtered into the area from outside.

In consequence Father rented a house at Hamamli, on the far side of Chamlidja Hill within walking distance of Moda, and this he used as a base where he felt safe both to sleep and to entertain guests over the weekend. He never hesitated to go further afield, to Samandra for a day's shooting, returning before dark, and on such occasions used to invite British Officer friends to join him, for the Allied forces were still in military occupation of the area. At the same time he remained on good terms with the local brigands or whatever you like to call them. Meeting a band on one occasion, they exactly described Mother's movements over the last few days, and told him that they had kept an eye on her to see that she did not come to trouble when out walking alone. Whereupon having told him all this they asked for some waterproofs as the rainy season was approaching, which Father supplied. Another time the leaders of one band told him that they had on occasion seen him and Mother walking out alone, and each time had followed them to ensure their safety. Father rather sympathised with the local peasantry over their difficulties, but was in somewhat of a quandary as the Officer in charge of the local Gendarmerie, whose duty was to pursue such men, was a cousin of his.

On another occasion, Osie and I got separated from the main body when out shooting, and were at once excited and somewhat alarmed to see a couple of men on horseback approaching, each with a rifle and belts of cartridges slung over their shoulders. But all was well, for they had no evil intentions, as having heard that Father was out shooting they wanted to pay their respects to him. One of these was the notorious Milti, a resident of the village of Pashakeui, and one of the most renowned in his calling. I remember meeting him in company of father, an amicable occasion marked by an interchange of news. He was later caught and paid the penalty. But one happy result from the situation was that others were frightened to go shooting and so the field was left to Father.

Life at Hamamli was sufficiently settled for Father and friends to spend the weekend there and shoot over neighbouring territory, and as usual he gathered round him a number of men who slept in the lower floor of the house. Of some of these Mother violently disapproved, and especially of one Husseyn, whom she regarded as a drunken sponger, which in essence he no doubt was. But Father liked him and enjoyed his company, as he did that of his other companions such as Yorgi the Yalandji, George the Liar, another old drunk but a superb cook although his methods might not have been tolerated by hygiene experts. In the shooting world Husseyn always knew of places in which there was an abundance of game, and of these he would give graphic and tantalising descriptions. Sadly, on every occasion his advice was taken, by some extraordinary quirk of nature all birds had disappeared by the time we turned up. Husseyn was never dispirited, and two days later, having survived everyone's anger and joking, he would make mention of another such game paradise.

Once peace was effected and the Allied forces had moved out, the country quickly returned to normal. With brigandage ceasing there was no point in keeping up the house at Hamamli as better shooting was available at Samandra where Father could always stay in the houses of either of his two great friends, Kara Mehmet or Ahmet Chaoush.

Here Father was in his element for nothing gave him more pleasure after a hard day's shooting than to follow supper with deciding on the next day's programme, and then to talk at large to his hosts and to any men from the village who dropped in to see him. Conversation would then cover local affairs, the state of the crops and such-like matters, but would then inevitably turn to the day's shooting, when, what with raillery and exaggeration, every mishap and failure to shoot straight was resurrected and made fun of to the sound of general laughter. Only Father was exempt. He did not talk much but what he had to say was treated with silence and respect, and he only had to raise his little finger for anything he wanted to be done immediately. On such occasions I felt very proud of Father as I saw the respect and affection in which he was held, without the least trace of sycophancy, the innate dignity of these peasants rising well above any such bent.

With us, at the time youngsters, these men never had any hesitation in pointing out the error of our ways and in correcting us, and this we never minded as, knowing how they felt about Father, we knew that these feelings were extended to us his children. Their natural manner gained our full respect and at the same time we felt so lucky and privileged to know such men and to be able to consort with them. In this way Father taught us a very valuable lesson in the way of regarding others.

Sadly, as time went on, Father became weaker and weaker as his disease started to take a firmer hold, and periods of treatment in Switzerland and the Tyrol in 1924 and 1925 were of no avail. I last saw him in September 1927 in Moda, prior to going to hospital in which I was fully involved with only short holidays for the next three years. It was in the early weeks of 1930 that I heard that he had died. He was buried in the British Cemetery at Haidar Pasha, with his old friend Kara Mehmet down from Samandra to throw a bunch of wild flowers into the grave.

Father was not a man of any intellectual attainments and made no pretences about this. He enjoyed light reading, at one time showing a preference for French novels, but these were about his limit. The only book of his I remember went under the name of 'We Three and Troddles', a copy of which I have sought for ever since, without success. On the other hand he showed a lot of ability in the way of business, he and Uncle Edwin having put the somewhat ailing firm well onto its feet in their early years, Grandfather at that time had not been too successful. The two brothers worked together in the closest of harmony and understanding, which was well shown at a time when Father was too ill to do much. Some extremely promising shares came onto the market in which Uncle invested heavily, at the same time buying a considerable number in Father's name and paying for them himself. He then told Father what he had done, saying that the opportunity was such that he could not leave Father out in the cold, and that he need not worry about repayment until it was convenient. This was eventually effected and it was largely due to this very profitable investment that Mother was able to continue to live in comfort after Father had died.

That Father was highly respected and considered in the way of business is shown by the following event. An uncorrected typing error in an offer made to a Japanese firm could have led to a considerable loss, which gave Father a great deal of worry until he received a letter from his opposite number to say that clearly a mistake had been made, and that in view of the very happy and straightforward relations always enjoyed with him, his letter was being returned for amendment. It is also interesting that some of the most appreciative letters Mother received after Father's death came from firms he had dealt with in Japan.

Immediately after the War Father went to Moscow, presumably to discuss matters connected with the stocks that had been confiscated by the new regime. Nothing came of this but Father was subjected to an attempted burglary, fortunately without any loss.

A visit to America was of a different nature, and in New York he was put up in the guest flat of some millionaire complete with private servant and a seat in the Metropolitan Opera. This was in connection with a conference on opium, on which Father was an authority. Anyhow it makes me smile to think of Father at the Opera for he had no ear for music at all, the only song I ever heard him sing ran somewhat as follows:

The Animals went in two by two,
The elephant and the kangaroo.
One more river, there's one more/river to cross
One more river, there's one more river to cross.

In Constantinople Father was one of the most respected men in the town both on account of his total honesty, plain speaking and his unfailing readiness to help people in all walks of life. Years later I was to hear nothing but praise of him from old Machray, a man of somewhat doubtful commercial reputation, whom Father had got out of difficulties on one or two occasions. He told me later that there was no one like Father in the town.

Frank Collas also related how he had had to have a business interview with Father, of such a nature that he left Father with anything but kindly feelings towards him. A short time later Lucy, his wife, fell very ill and had to be sent to hospital, leaving Frank very worried both about her and about how to meet the bills. But when she came to be discharged there was no bill waiting and it was only later that Frank found that Father had paid the hospital. And so it was with others.

Another story was that Father in the past paid for a young man to emigrate to America, and forgot all about it. Thirty years later a well set up man came to the office and asked to see Father, who had not the least idea who he was, when to his surprise the man told him that thirty years ago Father had paid his fare to America and that he had now returned to pay off the debt with interest.

On another occasion, during the Balkan War, Father took into care a young Turk, Yusuf, who had had both legs blown off below the knee, and in the absence of any prostheses had to shuffle about as best he could. He remained at our home till he was either fixed up or until we all left on the occasion of the War.

Some twenty years after Father's death I was staying at Alemdagh on my own when, out walking, I met an old man driving a cart and stopped to talk to him. In the course of our conversation he asked me what nationality I was, and on my saying English, immediately asked if I knew the "Buyuk Chelebi", as Father was known. On hearing I was his son he told me how Father had been loved and how greatly missed throughout the countryside he was. I too was delighted to feel that he had not been forgotten locally.

In London, Father was quite out of place and visited it rarely. He usually stayed at the old Langham Hotel, where one day he received a packet of letters addressed to W.J.H. Whittall, none of which had anything to do with him. He reported to the office where he found that there was another W.J.H. Whittall staying in the hotel. The two met up, but found there was no family connection.

What he enjoyed in London was shopping for clothes and equipment for shooting, including the latest gadgets. His custom was to buy things in quantity so as never to run short in Turkey. Cooking utensils for camping, sleeping-bags and boots all came his way, especially the latter, for boots heavy enough to stand up to local conditions were not available at home. His shooting room was a source of the greatest fascination to us boys; particularly admired were two very heavy and very long overcoats, lined with very thick fur, possibly wolf or bear, and which would well have suited a Siberian winter. They had been bought in Russia.

One day he was out shooting with an old Turkish friend, Nazim Bey, when coming to a hill they separated, each taking one side. With no sign of his friend at the far end, Father went to investigate, to find Nazim lying dead with his gun and his dog at his side. How much more suitable an end this would have been for Father.

CHAPTER II

Lilian Adeline Whittall
1872 – 1959

Mother never talked much about her life as a girl in Smyrna and little of her life there prior to marriage had come down to us. I do not know how well she got on with her mother, but she greatly loved her father and also her elder brother Dick. Another brother was Osmond, who died young and of whom a portrait hung over the washstand in her bedroom. She was also very friendly with Harry Giraud, a friendship which lasted through life, though they did not see much of each other after marriage. That her family life was happy I know for certain, although I have no details.

She was educated locally and also taught the piano, to become quite a proficient player. Otherwise all I know is that she must have been good-looking, for, when on a naval visit a ball was given, the then Duke of York particularly asked to be introduced to her. Interestingly, in character, of all the family Mother most took after her Grandmother 'Dudu', having the same strength of mind and purpose in which respect she was outstanding among her brothers and sisters.

At one time she became engaged to a Mr. le Bailly, whom in later years I often used to meet when staying in Hull with Uncle Jim. He was a delightful old boy, but the mere idea of Mother marrying the likes of him filled me with horror.

As a child in Moda I did not see much of her, for what with governesses and nurses, and the nursery being at the top of the house, we children led a somewhat secluded life, although we took all meals except for supper en famille. But Mother never failed to come upstairs of an evening to hear us say our prayers and to kiss us goodnight. From an early age she related Bible stories to us, so that we soon became acquainted with the likes of the Infant Samuel, Jonah and David and Goliath. In times of illness or trouble she never failed us, although we did not appreciate the doses of castor oil she liked to administer.

She was a strict disciplinarian who never hesitated to use the slipper when occasion demanded. Contrary to the teaching of modern psychological pundits, such physical damage left no permanent after-effects. Mother could on occasions be impossible, but we learnt to escape her when such was the case. Out of the house and in the gardens, we were given complete freedom to do as we liked, provided we did not fall foul of grown-ups or damage flowers. This latter crime was by far the most serious in her eyes. She was at best a very handsome woman, and when all dressed-up she was superb. I have never forgotten her appearance in a rather close-fitting, long-skirted green silk dress, trailing behind her and set off by an aigrette in her hair. As for jewellery I cannot remember whether she wore much.

With the onset of World War I things took on a different complexion when we had to leave for England. At this stage the family financial situation must have been tricky with the firm in Constantinople closed down. Hugh and Vernon were still at Rugby, although Hugh was about to leave and join the forces, while Osie soon went on to Eagle House prep school. Willy's Greek nurse Marina accompanied us to England and the girls were under the care of a governess, Cousin Kathleen La Fontaine, alias C.K.

We first stayed in Esher and subsequently in London. Later the girls were left in London with C.K. while Mother, Willy, I and Marina set off to join Father in Greece. Here we spent a year in the suburb of Kiphissia of which my happiest memory is that of the shouts and screams that arose when a mouse ran up Mother's leg. And of her we saw much more, for, our house being on the edge of open country, we constantly went with her for walks and picnics, with flowers, mushrooms and wild asparagus shoots to be picked in season.

Political trouble involving King Constantine made it advisable to leave Greece and settle in Rome. It was here in Rome that I started really to appreciate her as an individual and a personality, for in some ways it was here that she really came into her own. Hitherto Mother, who had been born with a good brain and a potential for many interests, had had her development frustrated through having to live in a largely unintellectual atmosphere both before and after marriage, leaving her with only books and music to fall back on. In addition there were limitations imposed on her activities through being a woman living in a Moslem country.

Here in Rome she was surrounded by ubiquitous and enduring evidences of history and architecture, covering both Roman, early and later Christian periods. Freed from all restraints she had opportunity to develop her interests, not only in the city but also in all that lay outside the city area and in the surrounding country. In those days there was little building to be seen outside the walls, and the Campagna lay still unmarred by man.

So Mother went out to make the most of her opportunities and the whole family was introduced to a programme of regular sight-seeing. She, ever enthusiastic and tireless, led us in all directions, not only in the town but also outside to Hadrian's Villa, Tivoli and to villages like Frascati on the Alban Hills. Her appetite for sight-seeing was insatiable and each excursion was followed by a visit to Piale's bookshop in the Piazza di Spagna to buy photographs.

Outside of sight-seeing she had music at her disposal in the shape of opera at the Costanzi theatre and concerts at the Augusteo. In view of the state of finances she thought nothing of sitting in the gallery and made full use of occasions when prices were 'populari' or 'popularissimi'.

In the warmer weather Mother loved to go on walks and picnics, and in those days the nearest approach to open country lay in the fields of Parioli, today the smartest quarter of Rome, but in those days full of flowers. The Alban Hills were a favourite resort – covered in narcissi, anemones and cyclamen in spring. From these she would return with bunches of narcissi and cyclamen among other flowers. Her enjoyment spread itself to others and I still have a picture in mind of her sitting on the grass, a sandwich in her left hand and gesticulating with her right as she pontificated. From time to time Father would turn up for a few days, and then her happiness was complete, but one anxiety persisted and that was over Hugh at the Dardanelles.

Her energy for sight-seeing was inexhaustible, and naturally there were set-backs to her programmes. The major one of which was over a visit to the Etruscan Museum, housed in the Villa Giulia, which she persisted in calling the Villa Papa Giulia (actually it was named after Pope Julius). For a time, every visit planned received some set-back, until eventually she succeeded in entering its portals, to return with an air of satisfied triumph, which was so typical of her.

Father was the first to arrive back in Moda in 1919 and on arrival found that he had been preceded by Kiamil, who had deserted from the army to clean and prepare the house for his coming. This had been rented to the Austrian Consul throughout the War and had been left in some state of disorder. Mother later had to come to England to Maples to make up for deficiencies in the way of equipment and furniture.

Constantinople had meanwhile been occupied by Allied Forces, and with the presence of British army and naval units social life for the younger generation became very full, and after five years of gloom all were out to enjoy themselves.

War, and possibly age, had affected Mother rendering her much more calm and subdued, and no longer subject to such furious outbursts as heretofore, at least that is how it struck me when coming back home on holidays. But she had to accept modern ways such as the girls going out unchaperoned and drinking spirits in the form of gin in the cocktails, which were now all the fashion. She never got to feel quite at home with the idea of mixed bathing, despite the voluminous bathing dresses still worn by ladies at that time.

Following the end of the war Mother was subjected to shock after shock. Firstly her beloved Father and her brother, Dick, died of the Spanish influenza which raged soon after. Their death was followed by that of Uncle Vem van Heemstra, who had married Mother's sister Maud, who I think died of a heart attack in our house. Then in 1921 Smyrna was sacked by the Turkish army, and everything in Granny's house, including Uncle Dick's fine collection, was looted. The same thing happened to the van Heemstra farm, leaving Granny, with Aunt Estelle and Aunty Maud and family to come to Moda, to live near Mother who was left to look after their well-being. Aunty Maud, with her four daughters was almost penniless, but Granny had been left comfortably off. Of these three Granny had all her wits about her, whereas Estelle was quite helpless.... she had always been somewhat simple-minded, and was unable to look after herself. Aunt Maud seemed to live in an idealistic dream-world, but in spite of this managed her affairs perfectly well, with the aid of Ailsa her eldest daughter.

On our arrival for the holidays, Osie and I were made a great fuss of by Mother which aroused the ire (or was it jealousy) of the girls. But how marvellous it was to be back home again and in the company of Mother and Father and of all our friends from all walks of life. Mother went all out to give us as good a time as possible while with Father we went out shooting to see him at his best.

Mother's attitude to shooting was interesting. Whether it was the result of having spent most of her life amid shooting circles, she felt that there was something lacking in the virility of any boy who did not enjoy the sport, and how delighted she was when on the first occasion Barbara and I took the children to see her, John immediately asked for a gun. I also fully believe that in her mind the only truly valid excuse for escaping from Church on Sunday was that of going shooting. And of course Mother preferred men to women, and I well remember sister Monica's indignation when schoolboy Willy was given a key to the front door and she was refused one. I also have a suspicion that in early life, Mother did not much like small children, but if so this altered in later life for one of my happiest memories of her is seeing her sitting on a bench chatting to small Feyhan, her great niece, with every sign of pleasure on her face.

As time went on the tuberculosis Father had contracted in Salonika began to take a firmer and firmer hold as he began to weaken. When the girls got married and left home, Willy and I were in England and both Osie and Vernon were causing problems. The outlook in Father's case was hopeless, and knowing this full well Mother had to nurse him and gradually watch him growing weaker and weaker. To all this she stood up patiently and without complaint. Fortunately she was greatly helped by her friends, Gladys Madge, Janet La Fontaine and Aunt Alec Whittall, who were a perpetual source of comfort to her. The end came in 1929, after which Mother was left to her own devices.

What really saved her during this period was her love of gardening. While on trips to England she had seen a number of gardens and these had inspired her with the desire for a grass lawn, with an apple tree growing in its middle, under which she could take her afternoon tea. So, on every trip to the country the car returned laden with flat stones and, with the garden's old Victorian layout being revolutionised, these were used for crazy paving for paths surrounding the central lawn from which the apple tree soon started to emerge. The final result was a real triumph, and, when in full flower, I have seldom seen its match. From England I sent her seeds of new plants and cuttings from new roses which she successfully grafted and all this took her mind off what was going on in the house. In a way it is remarkable how at her advanced age she was able to totally alter her conceptions of what a garden should be like. Incidentally her grass lawn was probably the first to be laid in Constantinople and was widely copied.

After Father's death Mother was left with only Hugh and Vernon still living in Moda. The latter was little comfort, for with his marriage breaking up, he had taken to the bottle, and after his wife had left him he moved into Mother's house, in which Hugh and Mercy, his wife, were already installed. Here, what with his drinking and his jealousy and animosity towards Hugh, there were incessant rows during which he shouted and raved, upsetting everyone and particularly Mother. Eventually the position became such that it was decided to ship him to England on a pension, but even on the voyage he fell into trouble, somehow finding himself penniless in Barcelona. Anyhow from now on Mother had peace.

From 1933, when I settled in practice, I was only able to see Mother on rare occasions, and in consequence my timing of events is uncertain. She certainly came to my wedding in 1936 and we visited her the following year.

Then came the Second World War and Mother was left on her own as Hugh rejoined the Army and Mercy went with him to Egypt. She took in some young people as paying guests. At one time, when the Germans threatened to invade Turkey, she was evacuated to Alexandretta for some months, an experience which she enjoyed. With the end of the war Hugh and Mercy took on a flat of their own, while Granny celebrated her hundredth birthday with a party and cake, decorated it is said with a hundred candles. The story goes that in the course of the party she tried to play a Strauss waltz on the piano. Anyhow after her death Aunt Estelle was taken in by Mother as well as another old friend and relation, Mercy's mother, Nelly Lawson. Although life-long acquaintances, these two were totally different to Mother in character and in outlook, which resulted in Mother finding them somewhat trying. On one occasion I found her sitting in her little room upstairs. When asked why she was not downstairs in the lounge, she answered "I cannot stand those two old women", a not surprising answer, for although both were younger than her, she was far younger in spirit.

Mother remained devoted to her garden, and this was of the greatest comfort to her. One stroke of luck came her way as men working on the road running along the back, uncovered a well in which there was plenty of water, and the opportunity being too good to miss, lengths of iron piping were obtained, and the men 'persuaded' not to turn up one morning, when a pipe was let down into the water with an underground connection into the garden, the whole being subsequently hidden away as the road surface was re-laid. And so with the aid of an electric pump Mother had a copious and free supply of water for the garden.

Life went on, but with the passage of time Mother grew older and feebler and doubts arose as to whether it was advisable to allow her to go on living in her cold and large house, although in it she was well attended to by her faithful Osman, and a former maid of Estelle's (who was not above stealing what she could). So Aunt Estelle was sent to England, and, I believe, Cousin Nelly Lawson had in the meantime died, and a modern flat was bought. Mother did not want to leave the house in which she had spent most of her life, and three weeks before the move took to her bed. Edna flew out from England to help look after her, as she lay apparently contentedly in bed, ending in a more or less semi-conscious state, in which she never lost her normal determination to have her own way. Edna bought her a new nightgown, the others being in a poor state, and having put it on her left the room. On her return shortly after, she found Mother lying quietly in bed, unclothed, with the nightgown lying on the floor beside the bed. Mother then died peacefully, one week before the move was due to take place, having had her own way even to the end. And how much happier it was for everyone to feel that she had died as she would have wished, in her own bed and in her own home.

I will now complement this brief account of Mother's life with a few reminiscences.

She was somewhat of an original character in whom determination and strength of will were combined with great generosity of spirit. Her moods varied, and while at times she could show every consideration to others, there came moments, fortunately rare, in which she could prove very difficult. This side of her character may have been more evident in her dealings with women, for she greatly preferred men, and the girls I know had some tough times with her. For my part I never experienced any difficulty with her except for the one occasion when I was properly told off for using the word "damn" in her presence.

Her relations with servants were another matter and I never quite understood them. On occasion I have felt furious over the way she addressed them, while in what we called her 'fourias' she could be impossible. And yet she was never without servants. Surprisingly she never had any difficulty in either getting or keeping maids, and in general they only left because of some family or other trouble, and were always willing to return should they be in need of work at a later date. They never hesitated to seek her help and advice over any troubling matter. All of them continued to keep an interest in our family affairs and liked to be kept up to date.

I can only explain this by the fact that she treated them fairly and honestly on every occasion, and with great consideration (when not in one of her moods) and they appreciated this. On their side servants of this period showed an almost bovine patience and tolerance, and when Edna on one occasion had been made to suffer, a maid told her: "But, Miss Edna, why do you worry so? Your Mother means no harm; it is just her way and her nature." The thing about Mother was that although she was a difficult character at best, she was totally honest and above board and ever willing to help anyone who had been involved in the household. This was a comparatively rare state of affairs in the Turkey of those days.

Only on one occasion have I heard of Mother treating an employee unfairly and that was in the case of Mehmet, our gardener-chauffeur. But I was not present at the time and know no details. On the other hand she put up with Sarandi, her cowman gardener who in the course of 50 years association regularly infuriated her by going his own way and, with a considerable exercise of skill, ignoring her orders. During his latter years, he and Mother were in regular disagreement, he always going his own way and she furious as he never did what she wanted. On one occasion he was told to kill two specified chickens for the table, which led to violent protests, for apparently these were two old favourites of his, which he had even endowed with names. Mother, as could be expected, reacted strongly until finally Sarandi agreed to comply with her wishes. That evening two chickens arrived in the kitchen, plucked and dressed, but next morning, strangely enough, his two old friends were still running about, alive and well.

At the end of fifty years of employment when approaching or already past his eightieth year, Mother thought the time had come for him to retire, and told him that he need no longer come to work, but should call in once a week to collect his wages which she would continue to pay him. Sarandi thanked her, but next day was back at work again. Mother then explained to him that he need no longer work, to which he replied: "Madame, I have happily worked for you nearly all my life, and now you want to throw me out because I am getting old. I have decided, however, that while you continue to pay me wages I am going on working as long as I can whatever you say." He also said that he could not face the prospect of having to be in his wife's company all day long. So he carried on working until the fragility of old age made him stop and leave his beloved cows and chickens.

Mother's knowledge of cooking was almost negligible; she hardly knew how to boil an egg. And yet the food served in the house was always superb, and I do not think I have ever eaten so consistently well as at home. And it remains a mystery how Osman, a mere village boy, learnt his superb art in our house. Mother always did the carving and served at table, and it was always a fine sight to see her determinedly tackling a large joint, carving knife in hand. When my brother-in-law, Kapa Nebolsine, was once in Turkey he was enormously impressed by the way she carved a turkey.

She had her own ideas about finance. For example, in the days she kept cows she used to sell any surplus milk to other members of the family and friends who preferred drinking fresh and clean milk which did not have to be boiled. Once a year she would settle down to work out a balance sheet which always showed a profit, which she proudly announced to all the family. Father, on such occasions, would try to get in a word to the effect that he had paid for the hay and for this and that, and that Mother had not taken these expenses into consideration, but any such interpolations were swept aside as being immaterial. Mother had made a profit and that was that.

She also had the faculty of completely ignoring anything that she did not want to hear and her ideas of economy could be adapted to suit circumstances. Thus, she would think nothing of hiring a car to take her the fifteen miles to the village of Samandra in order to be able to buy eggs at a penny each cheaper, and then extend the journey to pass by the village of Bashi Buyuk, where honey was also cheaper than in town. Of this latter addition to the journey I must say I always fully approved, as the honey, based on thyme and wild lavender, was unsurpassed. On her return home she would delight in relating how she had bought cheaper eggs.

As she grew older, Mother became more and more forgetful, in consequence of which Hugh looked after her finances. Every month he used to give her her allowance, some of which she would place in her handbag, while the remainder would be hidden away for security reasons. When her purse was empty, she would accuse Hugh of not having given her her full allowance, making her 'bankrupt' before the month had come to an end. No, she had no hidden resources, Hugh had just not given her her full due. So Hugh would make up for his 'lapse' with a further donation to tide her over the remaining days. Life would then proceed quietly until one day, Mother would come downstairs jubilant, having found some money in one of her drawers, which was clearly a gift from heaven, and had nothing to do with her housekeeping or with anything Hugh had given her. And so, feeling she was entitled to spend the money as she liked, she would hire a car and go off for a drive in the country, picking flowers and buying cheap eggs, delighted with herself and giving pleasure to the one or two cronies invited to accompany her.

Once when taking coffee one day with Osman in the kitchen, he came out with the statement that Mother was getting very difficult. I asked how this was and he told me that on the preceding day he had asked for a couple of lemons, at which Mother flared up to say that he had been given two lemons the day before and that his extravagance would ruin her. Then, that morning, the fish man had turned up with lobsters, only available at a very high price, and of these Mother, without turning a hair had bought two. I immediately burst out into laughter, this kind of behaviour being so typical of Mother, and in this I am glad to say Osman joined me. Talking to him, I realised that despite her vagaries he was devoted to her. In a way this was strange in a male Turk for to the end of her days, Mother remained upset when, outside Western precincts, we boys would be served before her.

On the first occasion I took Barbara to Moda in 1937, she woke me one morning to say that she was alarmed about Mother, for there was an awful noise coming from the back garden with much shouting from Mother and some men, and I was told to go down and see what was happening. This I did, to find that some charcoal Mother had ordered had arrived in sacks, each, according to the man, weighing so much. Mother did not take his word and insisted on each sack being individually weighed. This led to the man shouting that he had personally weighed the sacks and that on his honour the weights were as he stated. Unfortunately as it turned out each sack was deficient by a matter of five kilos or so, and this fact led to even greater excitement, with the man shouting and claiming that the scales were wrong, and with Mother trying to make herself heard above his loud protestations. Anyhow things settled down, and I was able to reassure Barbara that there was nothing amiss and that all that had been going on was nothing more serious than the straight-forward purchase of charcoal.

Shopping with Mother was always good fun, for more often than not there were arguments (enjoyed incidentally by both parties), with Mother standing firm and refusing to give way. In Moda all the shopkeepers knew her and always greeted her with open arms, she was very much respected, not least for standing up for herself. In England on one occasion she horrified Edna, with whom she had gone to Bradley's to buy a fur coat. In those days Bradley's, although situated in Westbourne Grove, was world-renowned and the best fur emporium in London. Anyhow, once there, Mother found what she wanted, and asked the price, at which she offered to buy the fur she had chosen at ten per cent less. Poor Edna nearly fell through the floor in horror at the very idea of this sort of thing taking place in Bradley's of all places. The floor-walker went off to make enquiries and returned to say Mother's offer would be accepted, and she left the shop very pleased and replying to Edna's protestations with a "What are you worried about? I got the coat ten per cent cheaper didn't I?" Judging by the expression on her face when Edna related this story in after years, the idea of taking Mother shopping again must have given her nightmares.

One day, when Mother, half blind, was poking about in the garden she came across a hole in the ground, concealing a sort of stopcock, and so idly and without thinking, she turned it off and went about her business. Some hours later uproar arose in Uncle Reggie's former house, now occupied by Turks, as their drains were not running away. Mother was mildly interested and no more, and carried on as usual, and the commotion only ceased when one bright spark found the stopcock and opened it up, leaving Mother completely oblivious to the trouble she had caused.

On yet another occasion she presented Aunt Alec with the seeds of a beautiful and rare plant and gave her full instructions as to how to treat it. Aunt Alec planted the seeds, to return to Mother in the greatest of joy to tell her that those priceless seeds had grown into fine cabbage seedlings.

My happiest and most vivid memories of Mother are mostly connected with her presence in the countryside, picking flowers or mushrooms, especially in connection with the latter, when, old as she was, she would suddenly start to run to a stand she had seen to get there before anyone else, to return with booty in hand and a triumphant look on her face just as though she had conquered the world. The same story could also be told over her collecting eggs laid by our chickens. But above all I remember her at Samandra, where she had gone to buy eggs. There, seated on a stool in the yard of Father's old friend Kara Mehmet, in a dark and rather untidy dress, with a flat grey hat on her head, her legs encased in loose-fitting dark stockings and with aged shoes on her feet, she would talk to the women in her execrable Turkish, and at the same time give sweets to the children, while above her head, sitting on their large nest, a family of storks would from time to time clack their beaks.

Sadly those days are over, and the last time I saw Mother was about a year before she died when I realised that Mother was getting very old. Hugh wanted her to sign a power of Attorney and so he and I explained to her what it was all about, and she said she fully understood. So off I took her to the Consulate to do the necessary. But once in the Consul's presence he asked her whether she understood what she was about to sign, only to get the answer, "I haven't the least idea." Dismay and confusion followed in my mind, but fortunately the Consul asked me what it was all about and knowing the family so well signed it, and I took Mother back home.

As I was leaving for the airport, she, frail, old and small, stood at the top of the marble steps to wave me goodbye as I left her, grief stricken for I knew that I would never see her again. I reached the airport feeling somewhat more composed and then all my feelings returned for, in front of me, an old monk pulled up his gown to get at something carried underneath, and this brought Mother back to me, for this is what she would do to her skirt to get at her keys which she carried on a belt over her petticoat. After this it was somewhat of a relief to reach home and family, but that last impression of Mother has remained vividly in my mind.

I wish I could write in greater detail about Mother's personality and character, but, in life I find that the fonder one is of a person the more difficult it becomes to describe idiosyncrasies and characteristics, these becoming so familiar as never to arouse second thoughts. She had such a lively and alert mind and was always liable to come out with the most unexpected remarks and comments. In a way she never grew old for she remained a personality to the end while at the same time maintaining a determination to do as she liked or as she thought fit, with a distinction between the two which was rather difficult to evaluate. She also retained her physical energy remarkably well into old age, usually being on the move or getting up to something, and at the same time finding pleasure in even insignificant activities and happenings.

In her younger days, during which she had to cope with a large family and a large domestic staff, she was the Mistress and tended to chivvy those coming under her aegis into doing things according to her lights, while outside this circle she never hesitated to tell people how to do things and how to manage their affairs, and it is testimony to the love in which she was held by all that no one ever took offence but on the contrary enjoyed her sallies with teasing and laughter. It always amused me how on occasion I was asked for my medical advice, while on another occasion I was dismissed as an ignoramus, she knowing better than me.

She never talked much about the past in her later years, and this I ascribe to the fact that to do so might bring back memories of Father, who was never out of her mind, but she was always alive to the present and in my case she loved to hear me talk about my family.

In my time I never remember Mother reading very much, but she must have at one time for I owe a deep debt of gratitude to her library. Browsing through this one day I found a book named 'Peer Gynt' and having heard the music I picked it up to find out what the original was about. This was after lunch, and lying on my bed I could not relinquish the book even to go down to tea. Out of this grew my love of Ibsen and also of Tolstoy, for this experience tempted me to sample his works which lay alongside on the shelf.

I will end with two further stories about her and my brother Willy. On one occasion she punished him for some minor misdemeanour as a small boy, when as he walked away in disgust, he was heard to mutter: "And to think I was in love with that woman". During his early days in Rhodesia, not having heard from him for some time she sent off a telegram: 'Wire news', to get back the reply: 'What news?'.

Shakespeare of Cleopatra wrote:

'Age cannot wither her, nor custom stale
Her infinite variety.'

And in many ways I think this could be said of Mother.

With her I always felt completely at home and enjoyed her company, finding her at her best when out in the country, in search of eggs, mushrooms, flowers or blackberries, and never will I forget that look of almost childish pride and pleasure on her face when she had found a new hoard and could better her companions. Whatever the occasion or the state of her mood life with Mother was never dull, she was always full of fun and originality. At the same time there was a great simplicity in her pleasures and in her demands on life, leaving behind in my life none but the happiest and most loving of recollections.

Thinking of her always brings to mind a poem of Ernest Dowson's, which to some extent covers my feelings:

They are not long the weeping and the laughter
Love and desire and hate
I think they have no portion in us after
We pass the gate.
They are not long the days of wine and roses;
Out of a misty dream
Our path emerges for a while, then closes
Within a dream.

CHAPTER III

Other Family – Reminiscences

Uncle Edwin (1864 – 1953)

In the early days of the firm, Grandfather was going to Carlsbad for his annual cure, and leaving the firm in the hands of Uncle Edwin and Father, he gave strict instructions that they should lay off a certain commodity. But no sooner was Grandfather away than the two started buying heavily, so much so that on Grandfather's return he was in absolute despair at the prospect of bankruptcy. The market then changed suddenly giving rise eventually to very large profits, from which, it is said, Grandfather took all the credit.

Uncle was an old friend of Calouste Gulbenkian, the oil magnate, who had been Head Clerk to him in Constantinople, and when Uncle had refused to buy a parcel of shares in an oil company, bought them for himself to make his fortune. In after life, Uncle, when asked whether he regretted not buying the shares, answered, "No", for the possession of such money would not have allowed of a quiet and/or peaceful life. Throughout his life, Uncle Edwin used to correspond regularly with Calouste. So whenever he came to London I used to phone Nubar, Calouste's son, who would call on Uncle and pay his father's respects.

Uncle Edwin was the complete gentleman in every sense of the word, and the only one of the family to have what one might call an aristocratic appearance. Barbara was a great admirer and considered him much the "best" of the relations. The first time we were in Moda after our marriage, he invited us to a long weekend on his yacht, giving us a fascinating time, and I have always thought how good it was of him. In the '30s he was very friendly with Sir George Clerk the British Ambassador, who used to come over to stay both in Moda and at the country house at Alemdagh. Barbara was very fond of the two, and when we were in Moda took to joining them over elevenses in the garden. Sir George was very fond of his champagne, both at this hour and at others.

He was a keen fisherman, but always used lines as he found rods not suitable in those waters. His son Kenny was likewise a fisherman and he did things in comfort. When staying with him in his house up the coast, we men would get up at five and go off in his boat, the *Bati*, to the fishing grounds, where we would disembark into a rowing boat to fish, while the *Bati* returned home, to return later with the ladies on board, hooting as it approached. So, up came our lines, and we would join her, to find breakfast already served on the table (and a very good breakfast at that). Then, after a suitable interval, fishing would recommence, until the *Bati* hooted again, when, on boarding, we would find drinks all ready and iced. We would now set off either for home, or for the shore if we were having a picnic, to enjoy a rest after a hard morning's work.

Uncle was also very fond of shooting and on one occasion I got into hot water with his man, Hussein Pehlevan, an awful old rogue. When out with my gun and the dogs I put up a pair of pheasant and got a right and a left, to return in triumph (pheasants were very scarce birds). Hussein on hearing of this was furious. He had already located these birds and was keeping them for the Ambassador, in the hope of getting a large tip.

Uncle was staying in Norwich at one time with the Corbould Warrens and was invited to a shoot. As he had never shot at high-flying pheasants, he was told not to expect too much, as, without previous experience, he would find these birds very difficult. The gamekeeper who was standing nearby took a rather superior attitude to this guest, which changed when at the end of the day it was found that Uncle had done better than anyone else, getting something like 90% of kills. He was a first-class shot.

Later in life he contacted me from Turkey and asked me to fix up an appointment for him with an eye specialist, whom he went to see on arrival in London. That evening I got a phone call: "I saw your Uncle to-day, Geoffrey, a most extraordinary man in his demands, for, well on in his eighties, he told me that when out shooting he could not see woodcock very well, and so would I please give him a pair of glasses to overcome this defect."

During the war the Whittalls were sending parcels to P.O.W.s, and one day received a letter of thanks from one, who said he was a Whittall from Australia and was there any connection. On investigation it turned out that he was a descendant of Percy Whittall who had emigrated to Australia from Smyrna in the late 19th century.

At a later date two of these Australians came to Europe and Uncle invited them to stay. One was a lady who had spent her life running a hostel for backwoodsmen somewhere out in the wilds and she could never get used to Uncle's gentle and polite ways. One day there was talk of getting up a party to go somewhere into the interior, and she asked whether she could go, to which Pat Tweedie (Uncle Edwin's son-in-law) answered "No, you talk so much that you would drive us all silly. Your coming is quite impossible." She pleaded and eventually was accepted and enjoyed the trip enormously. At a later date she was talking to Mother and said how wonderful it was to be talked to in the manner which she was used to in Australia.

Some Aunts

Aunt Lily (his wife) was my Godmother, but I never got to know her well, she was of a very retiring nature and never, for that matter well, presumably after the effort of having 14 children. Barbara first met her when we went to Aunt Gertie's in London for tea, Barbara's first encounter with some of the Aunts (sisters of my father). Aunt Florry was lying at full length on a couch, in a state of prostration. She had arrived in England so debilitated that she had to travel from Dover to London by ambulance. That evening lying on her bed in a state of complete exhaustion, she was offered a seat at a window in Regent Street the next day to watch some Royal procession. She was at her window at 9 am and sat there until 1 pm, returning full of the joys of life. Aunty Gertie told us all about her health misfortunes, with Aunt Florry intervening from time to time with hers – both making a very good meal. Sitting on the floor was Cousin Adeline Whittall, aged 83 and smoking cigarettes compounded of a mixture of tobacco and mixed herbs. She lived in a cottage in the country alongside two other old dears from Turkey. She told me all visitors to a meal at the cottage automatically thought they would be having roast pork by reason of the smell from her cigarettes. On our first visit to her in the country we had to taste her spring water before being allowed in. The only silent one was Aunt Lily, who really looked ill, and said nothing about herself. Barbara remarked on this as soon as we had left, while I reminded her that my delicate Whittall-born Aunts mostly managed to attain their nineties, despite a lifetime of ill-health.

Aunty Gertie was very interested in Byzantine art etc. and when a British troop came to dig in the vicinity of the former Palace, she watched them with interest, but made herself most unpopular by telling them that they were digging in the wrong place for what they wanted. After several failures they turned to her and rather angrily asked her where she thought they ought to dig. She pointed out the place and they got straight onto their objective.

Cousin Adeline as a girl tried to swim across the Bosphorus. Feeling tired halfway across she clutched onto the nearest floating object, and with its aid reached dry land, where she found that en route she had been embracing a dead donkey.

Brother Hugh's main distinctions were to meet the Queen at Gallipoli and to lunch on the Britannia, and to sit at lunch next to the Archbishop of Canterbury when on a visit to the Greek Patriarch. Once when fishing in the interior, an intruder entered the camp but only removed the airmail numbers of the Daily Telegraph – for use as cigarette papers, which, under state monopoly, were very expensive to buy. At one time he bought some lobster pots, which a fisherman up the coast saw to. To start with these yielded a frequent supply which, however, gradually grew smaller, finally to cease altogether. So Hugh went up to investigate to find his fisherman entertaining a group of friends to a lobster meal.

During the 1920 war, my brother Vernon was in command of a small force of British troops in Angora (the present day Ankara). One day he received a message from the Turkish High Command to say that they were proposing to enter and take over the town on the following day, so to avoid incidents could it be arranged for the British to leave beforehand, with at the end of the missive an invitation to dinner that night. Vernon made all the suitable arrangements, and that evening enjoyed a very happy dinner with the Turkish officers.

Sister Monica, when engaged to Herbert Jackson, son of one of Father's old friends in Saloma, decided on a runaway marriage. So they came to England and approached a priest who was an old family friend, but he shattered their hopes of a quiet wedding by inviting a number of relations including myself.

Part III

HOUSES

CHAPTER I

Moda 1910 – 1914

The large plot of land which Grandfather bought in the hamlet of Moda on the shore of the Marmora sloped gently down from the main road to the cliff-top overlooking the sea. It offered two advantages, one being a view of the whole extent of the city across the water, and the other that shooting was available within a half hour walk. On this he had built a large, white stone house, which, in true British style, was given the name of "The Tower", in distinction to the local habit of calling houses after the names of their owners or tenants. Later on the main road was paved and given the official name of Moda Caddesi, although to most foreigners it was known as the 'Grande Rue de Moda'. This road communicated with the big house by a Drive.

Then, as business prospered and the family settled down comfortably, the boys were sent to school in England while the girls were educated locally. As the elder children matured and married, the problem of accommodation was solved by either building houses for them on Grandfather's land, or by buying adjoining properties. By the time I arrived on the scene, some six such children were living in immediate contact with the Big House, to form the Whittall compound. Of the remaining five children, two had settled in England, one in Bordeaux and the remaining two had houses elsewhere in the village.

A pair of iron gates, flanked by two cypress trees, cut off Grandfather's garden from the Drive which ran straight down to the front door of the house under a canopy of tall fir trees, giving onto its first floor, the roadway being raised to allow this. To its left a path ran down past stables and poultry run to the kitchen door, on the lower ground floor. At the entrance to this stood a mulberry tree, which was much appreciated in due season, while on the far side another path led past the fruit and vegetable areas to the front garden, facing the sea. This path was bordered by an evergreen lonicera hedge, which was always searched by the servants for edible snails after rain.

Neither of the grandparents showed any interest in gardening, and so what one might call the social part was entirely formal and mainly consisted of gravel paths running between beds of ivy, out of which rose tall fir trees leaving a large open space, free of encumbrance, running along the cliff top. Here a semi-circular built out projection was shaded by a large terebinth tree, this making a favourite sitting out place for the elderly in summer.

Beyond the cliff edge a series of zigzag paths led down to the 'bottom garden', a piece of flat land, possibly once reclaimed from the sea, from which it was protected by a stone wall, which allowed access to a boat house and a jetty, much used in the days when Grandfather had a yacht. The paths running down to the area were lined with gooseberry bushes which never, as far as I knew, ever gave any fruit, and the open spaces were filled with vines and fig trees.

This bit of land lay open and uncultivated, and so very suitable for play, especially as it offered several clumps of bamboos which, cut down, made excellent hobby horses. The sea was however out of bounds, as all the house-drains entered somewhere here, and the most we could do was to pick up mussels and break them open in the hope of finding small pearls.

Uncle Edwin's garden, which adjoined that of Grandfather, also ended in a bottom garden, although this was covered in trees, and the cliff face was shored up by a brick wall, to which was attached the framework of a disused lift shaft. This land was approached from above by a dark tunnel, in which we never lingered for fear of meeting 'baboulis', ghostly creatures our maids told us of. In addition an electrical generating engine emitted strange noises, which did not encourage any delay.

In those days our house was rented from Aunty Leila Barker, to whom it had been given on marriage. Built of wood, it was reputed to be earthquake proof (a predecessor on the site had been knocked down by one such event). The front door was approached from the Drive, and in summer was flanked by two pots of jasmine, whose flowers we used to pick and thread onto twigs of pine needles to make sweet-smelling gifts. From the door a set of marble steps, surmounted by stags' heads, led up to the hall which, in Turkish fashion, stretched across to the staircase on the far side which, in turn, was backed by a large window which gave light to both this hall and the one above.

On entering the house the first room to the left was the drawing room, of which I remember little at that period as it was out of bounds to us children, except when we were invited in to a formal tea. On one such occasion Osie got in first and ate up all the butter balls before the arrival of the guests, much to Mother's dismay. What I do remember is the grand piano, on which Mother used to play and the girls practised their scales. Outside two sets of French windows gave onto a broad, covered terrace, which ran the whole length of the house, and on which we used to play in wet weather.

Adjoining this room and at the bottom of the stairs lay the schoolroom in which we used to have lessons and took our tea and supper. This had a central table on which we used to play cards and other games when kept indoors and it also had doors giving onto the terrace. By the wall a green sofa which later found its way to Alemdagh, to be still later carried off by brigands.

The large dining room lay across the hall on the other side. This boasted of a bow window, opening onto the Drive. It was furnished in good, solid Maple oak with large engravings of Napoleon in Russia hanging on the wall. The sideboard was covered in polished silver, and outside of this there was a serving table and the large central, expandable table at which we sat to meals. In summer two leather armchairs stood in the bow window, and here Father liked to sit on his return from the office, to talk and gossip with passers-by along the Drive. Here also stood a couple of pots of aspidistras on stands. In winter Father preferred to sit in front of the fire, with his legs propped up on the mantlepiece surround. Everything had to be large as we would sit down eleven or more to table at weekends. Parquet flooring had been laid down in all these reception rooms.

From the dining room a hatch connected with the pantry, which in its turn was connected to the kitchen below by a hand-operated lift. Beyond the pantry there was a large cupboard to hold the crockery, and then the maids' bedroom, outside of which there was a cloakroom. The telephone was attached to the wall.

The stairs led up to the broad hall on the first floor, against the walls of which stood a series of commodious cupboards which housed the domestic linen etc. Otherwise apart from a sofa against one wall, over which hung a clock which regularly struck the hours, there was no further furniture. Six bedrooms gave off this hall, Kathleen La Fontaine's (the English governess), Osie's and mine, the girls', Father and Mother's together with Father's dressing room, the spare room and Hugh and Vernon's. These last three gave onto a balcony, corresponding to the covered terrace below, and offering a grand view over Grandfather's garden to the sea.

All the bedrooms were furnished in the manner of the age with mirrored dressing tables, fitted with a number of small drawers, marble-topped washstands with pottery jugs, basins and slop pails, and minor containers for toothbrushes, soap etc. On this floor the solitary bathroom served the family perfectly well, without giving rise to disputes.

Our nursery occupied most of the top floor, but outside this there was room for the German governess's bedroom, the sewing maid's room and Father's gunroom. There were also extensive attics to which we were not allowed access. And, of course, the great advantage of this arrangement was that at play we could make a lot of noise without causing disturbance downstairs.

Apart from the pantry, the services occupied the basement, which stood at ground level, although on account of the slope, the back door had to be approached down a few steps from the garden. Round the central hall, in which the servants took their meals, there were washing and ironing rooms, the men's bedroom, and the storeroom which was always kept locked (in later years Mother used to wear a belt under her skirt from which was suspended her bunch of keys. I have often wondered whether this was the case in her smart days). A further room off the hall was Kiamil's preserve, and here were kept all the butter-making paraphernalia and the ice box, to which a supplier delivered a huge bar of ice daily. Here were prepared the superb ice-creams we enjoyed. The kitchen, which gave onto the back garden, was of course out of bounds, but from it or from the hall we enjoyed stealing pieces of the grey kitchen bread, which was not served at table.

Cooking was carried out on a coal-fired range which also heated the water, with the occasional help of charcoal braziers, which were especially used for grilling. These were also used for heating the irons used on clothes. In more palmy days the cook was assisted by a youth, who was called a marmiton. The coal cellar lay underground immediately opposite the back door and was filled through a circular hole above, just as in London houses.

In winter the house was cold, the only constant heating coming from the 'calorifere' a perpetual-burning stove in the downstairs hall. So we depended on coal fires, which were only regularly lit in the downstairs rooms and the nursery, the bedrooms being warmed only in times of illness. So with a house of this size and the customary cold winters the house was never too warm. We also had a good stove in the nursery. In a wooden house, fire was an ever present source of alarm, especially as the fire brigade of those days was useless. An alternative form of heating was offered by tandours. In these a charcoal brazier was placed under a deal table, and the whole covered with a thin eiderdown. To this chairs were drawn up, and with the eiderdown covering one's lap, and with legs almost under the table one could talk or play cards in comfort, in even the coldest weather.

The house was lit by gas, electricity only being supplied after World War 1. We enjoyed mains water, but in summer this was liable to vicissitudes and to be cut off at short notice. Given warning of such an interruption every suitable vessel in the house was filled. We did not drink the tap water, preferring spring water brought down in large demijohns from up country.

Our garden was square in shape and covered about an acre. It was bounded by the Drive in front and a service road at the back, and by Grandfather's and Aunty Gertie's at the sides. At a later stage Father bought a further rectangular plot, which was turned over to chickens and cows. The garden consisted of three parts, the farmyard, flower garden, and back garden. A high wall separated the flower garden from the service road, across which lay the large houses and property of Mahmud Muhtar Pasha, a member of the Royal Family, with at its end a large French school, and under this wall Mother grew her beloved violets. The rest of the garden centred round a large palm which, in winter, was always wrapped around in bamboo matting to keep it from the cold, and round this radiated flower beds and curved gravel paths, with the whole garden ablaze with colour in the summer.

The farmyard was approached through a small gap in the wall, by which stood a greenhouse surmounted by a pergola carrying a vine, whose fruit always fell victim to the wasps. I remember this was always full of ferns and cyclamen and the like. Beyond this there was another walnut tree which at a later date, and I know not when, was felled.

Most of the area of the farmyard was devoted to the chickens, but the stable building had stalls for four cows and over it were a couple of bedrooms for the men. In another corner there was a shed for hay, and by this the wall separating us from Grannie's garden was so low that we could easily climb over it and help ourselves to her peaches, taking care to avoid the eagle eye of Aleko, her gardener, a good friend of ours, who would cuff us hard but never reported us to higher authority. Things did not go so well with our apricots however, for I thought up the ingenious idea that if my friend Denis picked them, Mother would not punish him, and we would get away with it. Sadly Mother did not see eye to eye with my reasoning and I suffered in the usual way.

What we called the back garden extended from the Drive to the service road to which a gate gave access and by which stood a further stable, used at a later date for the girls' horses. This plot was just a tract of hard brown earth, from which grew a solitary plane tree outside the kitchen and a walnut tree by the stable. It was cut off from the flower garden by a wire fence and from the neighbouring garden by a tall brick wall, at the foot of which grew a number of bushes of white spiroea, which we always alluded to as May. On the other side of this wall Uncle Harry employed a gardener called Andoni, and we used to delight to sing to him:

"Andoni, Andoni, min fass poli poponi
Tha katourisis to pantaloni".

High grade poetry, which on translation runs:

"Andoni, do not eat too much melon,
Else you will wet your trousers."

In this garden, clothes were hung up to dry, and carpets were beaten of their dust, while the 'chopdji', or dustman, used to call daily to remove all rubbish etc. on his horse-drawn open cart, the contents of which, lying exposed to the sky proved a delight to the flies. (After the First World War municipal hygiene greatly improved with modern machinery, greatly reducing the number of flies arising from garbage, and water control altogether did away with mosquitoes, which used to necessitate sleeping under nets in summer).

Work for the staff started early, with the earliest sound that of the maids brushing the stairs. Early morning is also associated with the sound of the girls practising their scales on the piano, but at what hour they started I cannot remember.

In summer one of the first tasks was to open all windows and shutters to let in the cool air. These were tightly closed, and the curtains drawn to keep out the heat later on in the morning, with the situation reversed in late afternoon. Hence my later memory of the drawing room is mainly one of gloom. Saturday was an exceptional day for it was always the occasion of what the maids called "savatanya". On these occasions Mother supervised the maids over a thorough cleaning of the house, starting up in the nursery and gradually working downwards. Saturdays always gave rise to considerable anxiety, for if Mother became angry or excited, or as was popularly known in a "fouria" she could be very dangerous on approach. And so, at the first sign of her voice rising, it was wiser to get out of the house and not make an appearance until lunchtime.

Interestingly the maids were never upset by Mother's goings on, accepting it, as one of them told me, that to get excited was in her nature.

Mother always saw to it that the food in the house was of the finest standards and was made up in general of a combination of English, French and Turkish cuisines. At one time in those days we had an Austrian chef, who from all accounts was superb. One sweet of those days I remember, though whether he was responsible or not I do not know, consisted of a purée of chestnuts covered in a caramel glaze, into which were inserted orange segments, also glazed, the whole served and decorated with whipped cream.

Clothing offered no problems for apart from what was bought in England, there were quite good local dressmakers and tailors, while in addition the sewing girls were perfectly capable of running up simpler garments. There was not the same choice of materials as in London, for example, but good ones were available and the local Bursa silk was of good quality. Men had their best quality suits made in England, but otherwise relied on the local market. In summer Father always wore suits of a light brown colour made up from heavy cotton, which were both cool and easily washable. Most men changed of an evening but not into formal wear. Shoes could be made to measure locally.

There was a Scottish doctor, Dr McClean, in charge of the British Hospital in town, but locally there was Dr Antipa, a Greek resident in the village, who more commonly looked after us. The choice of remedies in those days was simple, cupping, tisanes, especially camomile and lime flower, ammoniated quinine, camphorated oil. Castor oil used to be given us in Turkish coffee, which put me off that beverage for many years. I remember being told that a good remedy for a sore throat was to wrap a dirty sock round the throat, though whether Mother ever allowed of this I do not know. In general all the family led very healthy lives, and most lived to a good old age, great care always being taken over hygiene, especially in times of epidemics.

The sea crossing acted as a deterrent to entertainment in town, especially at night, in consequence of which Moda did tend to stew in its own juice and not take part in the more intellectual pursuits of town. As is so often the case with communities living in foreign countries, every effort was made to preserve British characteristics, a factor here abetted by the total impossibility of leading a social life with the Turks. This exclusive state of affairs gradually broke down, and despite the fuss arising from Uncle Kenny's engagement to a Serbian lady, all initial feelings of dismay disappeared in a very short time, both she and her brothers and sisters becoming accepted into the family.

We children did, in retrospect, lead very pleasant lives, for although subject to strict discipline in the house, once out of doors we were allowed full freedom, provided of course, that we did not get into the way of the older generation, a point to which we paid full attention.

Life in this part was always interesting in view of the constant coming and going of tradesmen and others. Among these were gypsy women, always dressed in brightly coloured garments and usually carrying a sickly looking baby at breast. Apart from cadging for food and money they used to tell the future, and in fact one in July 1914 prophesied that we would soon be away from home for a long period, words which were remembered later. Other visitors included dancing bears, which used to rise on their hind legs and shuffle about ponderously in what was called a dance. (These used to be caught as cubs in the mountains above Bursa). Then of course there were the usual deliveries of coal, wood and charcoal, the arrival of donkeys laden with coops tightly packed with chickens or ducks, while from time to time pleasant smells would arise from coffee being roasted or jam made.

Winters could be very cold and we often had heavy falls of snow. Such cold weather brought the woodcock down, to Father's satisfaction, and also the wolves into the outskirts of the town in search of food.

In May the whole family would move to Alemdagh, but this is described elsewhere. On our return we would find the bathing season in full swing. Non-swimmers would then be rowed across the bay to the sandy beach at Kalamish which in those days was beautifully clean. For swimmers a raft, with a couple of changing rooms, was anchored in mid-bay, offering superb deep water swimming. When out bathing 'simits' were always bought to sustain us in mid-morning. (A simit was a form of biscuit, presented in large rings and covered in sesame seed).

Of an afternoon the wind would always arise to the satisfaction of those wanting to go sailing. Father was not keen on the sea, and instead we used to go fishing under the care of Dimitri, our boatman. The fish we caught were small but gave us a lot of fun. Occasionally we would go out to watch the nets being pulled up, before doing which large stones were thrown into the water on either side, presumably to scare any loiterers into captivity.

In the village there was a rink for roller-skating and an open-air cinema at

Muhurdar. Here I saw a film of Les Miserables, and remember seeing little Cosette cowering under a table, but this might have been immediately after the war. Excursions to Chamlidja were another favourite amusement, for there we used to picnic under a circle of stone pine trees, and collect their nuts. Here in the very large property there was ample room for games and in addition a house built up a tree. Fruit trees grew everywhere and in summer there was a large patch of strawberries to which we were allowed to help ourselves. Otherwise I remember large clumps of hollyhocks and the pomegranates both in flower and in fruit. We loved this garden and even though it lay within a half hour's carriage drive, the atmosphere there was quite different to that of Moda. (The garden was about 250 yards square in area.)

One excursion we loved was one to the mosaic hill. Here on the hill top, out in the wilds, a small church or shrine must have existed in Byzantine times, for searching around one could find small coloured glass or stone mosaic cubes which we greatly prized, those still adhering to plaster being especially valuable. We were comfortably brought up amongst relics of the Byzantine era, there being ruins in every direction, so the antique became part of our lives from an early age. It was interesting that even after a hundred years of living in a foreign country, children were still brought up to traditional English rhymes and games, as for example, hunt the slipper and postman's knock and musical chairs at parties.

We started going to Church at an early age, first to Children's Services and then to Mattins, sitting in our family pew. On these occasions Granny (Moda) and Aunt Maria used to arrive by carriage and walk in state up the aisle to their pew at the front. There was a hand-pumped organ played by Mildred Barfield, Aunty Gwen's sister, while Vassili, Uncle Reggie's gardener worked the pump. In summer there was some entertainment derived from watching the reactions of uncles and others to flies settling on their bald heads and when so disturbed choosing a similar site on someone else's head.

Thanks to our German governesses the great feasts were celebrated in true German style. Thus at Easter, apart from the coloured eggs, small nests containing sweets or miniature eggs together with chicks and small rabbits were hidden about the garden for us to find. At Christmas the tree was set up in the nursery from which we were excluded until all was ready on Christmas Eve, when we would rush in to find it lit up with candles. Then we would all hold hands in a ring and walk round the tree singing 'Stille Nacht' and 'O Tannenbaum', and then await Father Christmas's arrival, all in red and with white beard, and carrying a huge sack on his shoulders. This he would then place on the floor and hand out the presents, finally turning it upside down and pouring a cascade of oranges, apples, nuts and sweets all over the floor as we scrambled about, each intent on gathering up as much of the loot as possible.

Bed followed soon after, with early awakening to see what was in the stockings hanging at the foot of our beds. I have failed to mention the waits who used to go from house to house on the Eve. These consisted either of members of the colony or of boys from the Greek Church who had learnt our carols and by singing them collected money for the Church.

Christmas lunch was traditional following on Church in the time-honoured way, with the largest of Mother's turkeys appearing on the board. A rest followed and then we would be off to Granny's for her tree, which always stood in the hall and was also lighted with candles. Here we met all our fellow grandchildren, after which early bed was the routine.

Naturally we also got presents on birthdays, which were duly celebrated, Osie and I usually having a combined party as our birthdays lay so close together. Outside these occasions the only ones on which we expected and got presents was after losing a tooth. This would be carefully kept, to be placed in the evening under a loose corner of lino in the upstairs hall (downstairs was no good as it was all parquet) from where a kind mouse would take it away and leave a present behind, usually a silver coin.

After a lapse of close on eighty years it is of course difficult to throw one's mind back to one's childhood days, but today nothing is left in my mind to suggest that I had anything but a very happy childhood. True, what with Mother's ways, those of the governesses and to say nothing of a bevy of elderly Aunts and relations who never hesitated to speak their minds, we were well disciplined when in their company. Mother, contrary to modern ideas, never hesitated to use the slipper when we were naughty or disobedient, but, despite these unfortunate incidents, we always remained assured of parental love, which gave us that sense of stability and security which is so essential to a healthy growing child.

At the same time, in the nursery and especially out of doors, we enjoyed complete freedom in our play, and especially so in Granny's garden in which we were allowed to do what we wanted, within certain bounds of course. But never was this freedom and our links with the parents as close as when staying at Alemdagh.

It is also interesting how we were able to cope with a multiplicity of languages, apparently with no difficulty, for outside the solid basis of English in the family we learnt French and German from the governesses and had to talk Greek to the maids and the majority of the local population, while we boys were subjected also to Turkish when out shooting. In 1914 I left Turkey with a fine vocabulary of swear-words, whose meaning I happily did not get to know until many years later. I can only hope we did not make use of them at awkward moments.

An important aspect of our lives was that of our relations with the local world of servants, tradesmen and the like. In general, in Turkey, children are greatly loved and made much of, and in this way we were generally welcomed wherever we went, and genuinely so and not because we were Father's children. And so we regarded our household staff as friends and extended this feeling to the staff in the houses of surrounding Uncles and Aunts. Outside of these there were other personalities such as the Moda carriage drivers, Nikoli, Yorgi, Christo and others who, in the days before cars, used to drive us about everywhere. Then there were the local boatmen and fishermen such as Beddo, Mihali (our man) and Panayoti who served on Grandfather's yacht, and of course all this was extended to local shopkeepers and others. In consequence wherever we went in the locality we felt secure and that we were among friends. Since then I have often wondered to what extent these circumstances have played a part in my at times still thinking of Moda as home.

All the memories left me of my childhood in Turkey are ones of happiness, as also of ever increasing love and affection for Mother and Father. I have no doubt that there were occasions when I went to bed hoping that something unpleasant would happen to me to make Mother sorry for having treated me so badly, but these have gone, leaving no trace.

CHAPTER II

Alemdagh Pre-1914

Were I ever to have the chance of reliving any part of my life in Turkey I would unhesitatingly opt for a few days in the Alemdagh of old, the seat of some of my happiest memories of that country. Moda in pre-war days was very much of an adult stronghold, with us children well disciplined by parents and governesses, who were, as it appeared to us, aided by the potential and freely expressed disapproval of numerous (and to us elderly) Aunts and female Cousins. It is true that we were allowed the freedom of the gardens, provided we did not trespass on flower beds or vegetables, did not make too much noise and generally did not disturb the grown ups. At Alemdagh things were entirely different, for there we were free to run wild, to play anywhere around the house or in the open land in front of it, and could make as much noise as we liked without disapproval.

There Father and Mother were both free of the anxieties of business and of running a large household so were more relaxed and had more time on their hands to devote to us children and to share with us the joys of country life. Gardening, Mother's chief pleasure in life was too advanced for us and anyhow impracticable in Alemdagh, but we happily joined her in her other favourite pursuits of walking and looking for wild flowers and picnicking. With her too we also used to love picking such things as blackberries, wild asparagus and mushrooms. Some of my happiest memories are connected with the latter, for example getting up early in the morning and gathering them on the hills and then frying them with bacon for breakfast. This pleasure of hers lasted well into old age, when, rather tottery on her old legs, she would run to pick some she had seen before anyone else could get at them, and then show her trophies off proudly with a look of happy triumph on her face.

Father's pleasures were more robust. He particularly loved walking for its own sake and there was nothing he loved more than to set off with a couple of dogs and a gun to walk at full speed for hours on end, returning with the dogs exhausted but not he. Naturally I was too small to accompany him on such occasions at Alemdagh, but later on in Greece and in Rome we often had such days together, taking a picnic lunch and walking for miles.

Another factor at Alemdagh, which probably had an unconscious effect on us, was our close involvement with all manner of animal life. Firstly there were all the domestic beasts constantly around the house. There was frequent talk of wild boar, deer, wolves, foxes and jackals, and at times their dead bodies were brought to the house. Bird life teemed, with hawks and kites circling overhead, with an eye on the chicks, and such brightly coloured ones as 'blue jays' (rollers), golden orioles, hoopoes and bee-eaters. Insects also abounded and one could not move without disturbing grasshoppers of all sizes with brilliantly coloured wings, cockchafers and 'zeenas', brilliantly green scarab beetles. And if one were unfortunate enough to squash a 'stinking bishop' the air literally did stink. More exciting was the periodic arrival of a carpet of caterpillars, some square feet in area, which would attempt to climb one of the oak trees, and which had to be burned with paraffin to prevent defoliation of the trees. Lizards abounded, some long and brightly green, while on every walk one heard the knocking of two tortoises fighting and trying to turn the opponent onto his back, to lead to a certain death. Empty tortoise shells of all sizes were also found, and occasionally a broken one, which we assumed had been dropped from a height by a raptor bird. In fact nature brought itself to our notice at every step.

The family connection with Alemdagh started when early in the century Father and Grandfather were out shooting, and stopping for a minute above the village of Ermenikeui to admire the view offered by the Alemdagh hills rising above the forest, Father happened to say: "This would be an ideal place in which to have a house". To this Grandfather replied: "Well, why not build one here then? This land belongs to me and you can have it." Father wasted no time and in a few months the square, red wooden house we loved so well had been built.

From then on it was used as a shooting box in winter, but in the spring the whole family migrated there for a month or so, and we children used to look forward to the day of departure with ever mounting excitement. Mother, who had to organise the extensive preparations necessary for transporting a large household, must also have welcomed that day, but in her case with relief. The village had little to offer in the way of supplies, only boasting a small shop, and although milk, butter, eggs, poultry and meat were available from our own resources, everything else had to be brought up from Moda by weekly cart.

The family departure was preceded by that of the servants who took with them all necessary stocks of food, linen etc. and cleaned the house in preparation of our arrival. Then on the morning of the appointed day the carriages arrived. These were of two kinds, Victorias and Talikas. The former, drawn by two horses offered two comfortable seats for adults at the back, with two uncomfortable let down ones for children in front of them, with a much prized seat by the driver on the box. The drivers of these carriages were all old friends who had known us since birth: Yorgi, Mihali, Nikoli and Christo. The Talikas offered cushioned and rather uncomfortable seats for four, facing each other, and approached by a small door at the back. Roof and sides were decorated with highly coloured curtains and awnings, alive with tassels. The driver sat in front just behind the horse which, periodically, set us children giggling by making rude noises, which the more decorous grown ups affected not to notice.

Everyone being packed in, the convoy of carriages set off on the fifteen mile journey which usually took four hours. The early stages ran through built up areas to Chamlidja, where the high walled properties with their heavily portalled gates, reputed to belong to a Princess of the Royal Blood, intrigued us with their mysterious possibilities. This route via Chamlidja was always taken in my time, but formerly alternatives via Sherif Ali or Kaish Dagh used also to be used. At Moijirkeui the so-called metalled road started, but as this, in true Turkish fashion, was never repaired and full of potholes, it was at times wiser to avoid it by using the earth tracks running alongside it across fields. After a time and a lot of encouragement from the "Dee Dee Dee" of the drivers the horses brought us to the small village of Dudrulu where we halted at a café for refreshment under a huge plane tree while the horses were watered, inspired to drink by the whistling of the drivers. After half an hour or so, we would set off again to pass through flattish, semi-cultivated country, leaving on our right the tree up which our man, Bekir, had once been marooned by wolves, and on the left the village of Sultan Chiftlik, to reach a wooden bridge at the entrance of the forest. This was a point of great interest as on one occasion we had seen a large snake coiled round one of the posts, and ever after we always stopped to see if it had returned, which it never did. So on past the "Palace", of which more anon, and then back into the open as we ascended through the village to be greeted outside our stables by a concourse of men gathered to welcome us. Then as we jumped out of the carriages there was a rush to see what changes had been effected and to savour the lovely scent of the house, a mixture of untreated wood, polish and Alemdagh air.

The house stood alone on the top of a hill, backed by a spinney of tall oak trees. In front lay open scrubland, oak, cistus and heather, descending into a valley and rising again on the far side to the forest, above which emerged a long line of rounded hills, Alemdagh proper. Immediately opposite the house on the far hillside lay the "Clearing", an open patch, once cultivated and planted with fruit trees and now invaded by broom which afforded a brilliant display of colour in the spring. This, like so many other odd pieces of land, belonged to Father, though how he came to acquire it I do not know.

The house itself stood in a fenced-in compound of about an acre, surrounding the oak spinney. Built of wood, it was of the utmost simplicity, basically consisting of four rooms upstairs and four down, giving off central corridors, the kitchen being housed in a sort of excrescence. The front door, which was somewhat elaborate, lay in a most awkward position on the far side of the house, giving onto a vine pergola, beloved of the turkeys which roosted there and of the wasps which ate the grapes. In consequence the back door was the preferred mode of entry into the house.

The sitting and dining rooms faced the front, the former having a huge fireplace, with a brass cowl, in which the largest of logs could be burnt. It also boasted of a French window, the unwitting cause of great excitement on one occasion when a large snake glided into the room when everyone was having tea. The tea always came from small square, brown and green tins, supplied by Melrose. This tasted much better in Alemdagh than in Moda. (Recently when in Edinburgh, I saw to my joy that this tea is still marketed, though now in cartons only). The dining room has few memories, apart from its large table.

Off the staircase landing lay toilet and bathroom, the former modern and comfortable but flushed with slops in view of the absence of running water. The bath consisted of a round, flat, spouted tin vessel to which hot and cold water had to be carried up from downstairs. In the absence of any permanent water supply every drop had to be brought to the house by cart, to be stored in a huge tank. Drinking water however, always came in demi-johns from the springs at Tashdelen.

Cooking was on charcoal, which occasionally required stimulation by fans made of feathers. Water was heated in a large copper pan on a wood fire, of which there was always a large pile outside. Food was kept in a small storage room which was kept locked from our depredations. Ceilings, floors and furniture were all of unpainted and unvarnished deal, and all the walls were plastered white. Each bedroom (six in all) was furnished with two iron bedsteads, a wash-stand, table, chest of drawers and a fitted cupboard, the latter a favourite haunt of hibernating red admiral butterflies and red underwing moths.

Facing the hill was a balcony on which Osie and I used to have lessons from the German governess of the day. How effective they were I do not know, for, apart from the dullness of German grammar and indignation at having to have lessons at all, there was so much to distract attention; the smoke of a charcoal burner's kiln rising lazily into the air, a creaking cart slowly passing by, guinea fowl wandering about the scrub whose every movement was followed in case it led to a hidden nest, large hawks circling overhead threatening our chicks, and finally simple day-dreams about what to do when free. In the lovely spring weather it is more than likely that our unfortunate governesses felt just as we did.

To one side of the compound lay the poultry runs, stables and men's quarters. During the day the birds ran about freely, chickens, ducks, turkeys, geese and guinea fowl, all having access to a large manure heap, which no doubt favourably flavoured their eggs and meat. Two small water basins served the ducks. These however were disdained by the geese, who being more independent wandered far afield, always to return at night. These we held in considerable respect, but not so the turkeys whose noisy gobbling, we soon learnt, concealed very faint hearts. The guinea fowl tended to lay their eggs in the scrub outside the compound, and one of our tasks (and pleasures) was to look for these as Father loved them for breakfast. Often a bird would elude our searches to reappear proudly one day shepherding a family of chicks. The chickens were better trained and usually laid their eggs in the boxes provided. Collecting these of an evening, basket on arm, was an enjoyable experience, although coloured at times by the fear of being pecked if a hen sat tight, and a hand had rather anxiously to be slipped under her.

As can be imagined, with all these birds about, the place was not exactly silent. Ducks and cocks started their music early in the morning to be joined later in the day by the others and especially by the hens clucking over the laying of an egg, or calling to their broods of young. But the sound which I loved best and to this day reminds me most of Alemdagh was the "come-back, come-back" of the guinea fowl, which I last heard to my great joy in the wilds of Rhodesia.

On a morning the cows were taken out to the fields, and the sound of their bells as they returned of an evening was a warning of impending bed-time. At times they were tethered in the yard, but never in winter since a calf was once killed by wolves. On one occasion our bull chased Mother and me across some fields, and so having become dangerous it was decided to doctor it, an operation which we were highly sorry not to be allowed to watch.

Several more acres of adjoining scrub, mostly oak and heather, also belonged to Father. Attempts at cultivation had not proved very successful, but near the house there were a number of fruit trees and also a potato patch. Digging this up was always interesting as in addition to potatoes the soft white eggs of a serpent or tortoise would often be exposed. In this area also lay the snow pit, a large hole in the ground which, tightly packed with snow during the winter, and then covered with straw, acted as our refrigerator during the early summer. When empty it was regarded with some suspicion as the possible home of snakes, though what they would be doing down there is not clear. Nearby stood a haystack, a source of great pleasure as a slide.

Two men looked after the property. One was a Turk called Bekir, who was held in great respect, for not only had he been a professional smuggler, but had also been marooned up a tree one snowy night by a pack of wolves. In addition, to add to his glamour, there was a current suspicion that he had once killed a man. His opposite number was a mild, small Greek called Sarandi, endowed with a drooping bushy moustache. He was very much appreciated by us males for he always addressed us as "Pasha". In all he remained in the family service for over fifty years, moving down to Moda after the war, to act as cow and chicken man.

Some of the Armenian villagers were also well known to us. At the home of one Karabet, we once attended a wedding to be regaled with masses of sticky sweets. Another was Heretik, whose cart we always used to use. In later years I was told that he once tried to do Father in by only delivering half the hay crop for which he had been paid. Another was Artin, a simpleton, who used to give amusement by stripping to the waist and giving exhibition wrestling matches with other villagers. He should have been a lucky man for a stork had nested on his chimney, but this happy omen did not prevent his being driven away into exile and almost certain death during the War.

There were usually other visitors or temporary residents, mostly shooting friends of Father's. His shooting expeditions led him to range far and wide over the countryside, sleeping in the villages and making innumerable friends among the peasants, who in time of trouble invariably came to him for help, to be as invariably assisted in one way or another. Many of these, on hearing he was staying at Alemdagh, used to visit him, some from miles up country, and I have often thought that Father was perhaps at his happiest when surrounded by a group of these men, sitting on their heels and discussing shooting prospects and local affairs.

I was too young to get to know any of these men, and incidentally to appreciate their sense of humour and it was only in later years that I realised how Father was loved and how devoted they were to him. For example, one Sali, at this time an old man, walked seventy miles on one occasion to Moda, to find out how Father was as news had reached him that he was ill.

At times Mother used to become somewhat restive over certain of Father's friends whom she suspected of sponging on him, and after the War this particularly concerned one Hussein, whom she called an old drunk (which he was), but who was a highly amusing raconteur of improbable stories, which Father delighted to hear and which kept him well amused. But in spite of his defects Father liked him and that was enough, and Mother's protests were disregarded.

In this sort of atmosphere we children grew up to accept the presence of these men, dressed as they might be in rags, and with whom speech was difficult, but who always greeted us with that kindliness which Turks invariably show towards children. We instinctively treated them with full respect both as Father's friends, and also as their great natural dignity deserved and I cannot remember us ever transgressing in this respect.

Perhaps our greatest cross in Alemdagh was the presence of Uncle Edwin's immaculately white house, which was built some time after ours, and just below it. We felt very strongly that the Edwins were upstarts, with no right to imitate us or in fact to be at Alemdagh at all. They spoilt the tone of the place by their bourgeois attitude to country life (not that we had ever heard of the word at that age) for in place of simplicity their house contained all manner of highly unsuitable luxuries, such as curtains, drapes, smart furniture and even a proper bath and running water. While to add injury to insult, they being older and bigger, usually beat us at games.

Days passed quietly but all too quickly. Games featured quite a lot in the routine, and of these I remember Chillik-Chilmak (tipcat in English), flags, in which each side had to cross the frontier to capture the opponents trophies, hide and seek and statues. Old photos show that our house was often filled with young people in large numbers, invited to stay by Mother, but as most of these were much older than myself, I do not remember much about these gatherings.

In the afternoon we were made to lie down on our beds, and in the semi-darkness we would listen to the wind rustling in the trees outside and long to be up and about. Meanwhile we would watch the dust particles floating in the beams of sunlight let in by cracks in the solid wooden shutters, while now and then a fly would lazily buzz about or the voice of someone outside would distract our attention, and so time passed slowly till sleep descended and we lay lost to the world until woken for tea.

After tea we usually went for a walk with Mother and with Father if he was there, for often he only came up at weekends. From these walks we usually returned laden with bunches of flowers: pinks, anemones, orchids, love-in-the-mist, irises, tulips, cornflowers, cyclamen and almost inevitably "cambanakia", the greater quaking grass, whose bells rang silently for us as we shook them. These were dried for winter decoration. A favourite walk was down the hill opposite the house, then along the valley, past some ponds in whose mud and waters buffaloes delighted to wallow, then across some fields in which the tulips grew, back up the hill again, past a group of "rustling birches", whose restless leaves shone silver in the wind and so to the small grey Karakol, the local police station, after which running over rolls of bright red, naked clay we once more reached the house.

Another favourite walk was to the "Palace". Here Sultan Abdul Hamid, having heard of the health-giving properties of the Alemdagh air, had built himself a large three storied house, in the French style, elaborately decorated with parquet floors, porcelain door fitments and marble bathrooms, together with a metalled road from Chalidja, the one we had taken to get to Alemdagh. In addition there was a complex of gardens, kiosks, stables and accommodation for staff and troops, all beautifully laid out and planted. He spent one night there never to return, terrified by the loneliness. Everything was then left slowly to decay. We used to go there to pick lilac in May and enjoyed watching and hearing the frogs and turtles plopping into the water of the ponds on our approach, while occasionally there was the added excitement of a snake swimming in the water.

Beyond the Palace ran a stream, a good place for paddling and by which we often had picnics. In its higher reaches near a clearing in the forest known for some reason as the "Salon", a tributary served to water some vegetable gardens. Our delight was to dam this stream and so cut off the water supply to the gardens, whereupon the gardener would come rushing up swearing and cursing and brandishing a hoe or some such garden implement while we took to our heels. He would then break down the dam, and we returned as soon as it was safe to do so to rebuild the dam if time allowed.

Just as Mother loved her flowers, Father loved his shooting, and as soon as we boys were old enough to hold a gun our lessons started, slowly graduating from a single-barrelled 36 bore, to a 20 bore, ending finally, when more mature, with a 12 bore. Osie and I used to go out with Onik, one of the villagers. I started on sitting birds, and very regretfully remember that the first bird I ever shot was a sitting blue tit. As we progressed larks became our main pursuit, and to lure these a bird shaped piece of wood studded with small mirrors was rotated on a swivel stuck into the ground by a long string, and the resultant flashes of reflected sunlight attracted the birds to offer good flying shots, any resultant bag being enjoyed for supper that night. This was fun until one day I mishandled the gun which kicked back onto my mouth and teeth.

Another major pleasure, perhaps enjoyed more by Mother than by us, lay in picnics. For these a site near a spring was inevitably chosen, and of these we had three within walking distance of the house. The most sophisticated of these was Tash Delen, whose waters were highly appreciated in town and were bottled at the spring for transport. It was therefore much frequented by carters and even boasted of a small café. Its great advantage was its situation in open forest which allowed us to play games. Malkeui Su, not far away, lay in thick forest and though its water was reputed to be much more palatable, it was impossible there to run about. The third, Ermali, lay in the chestnut forest and here in autumn we used to collect the nuts, or rather such as the wild boar had left us, to roast over the fire of an evening. In the early summer the forest was carpeted with bright yellow St. John's Wort, with cyclamen growing under certain beech trees. The largest picnic of the year was that held in the cemetery at Samandra when all those at Alemdagh joined those staying in Uncle Harry Pears' house in Yakakjik. I was too young to appreciate these occasions but from all accounts they were hilarious and thoroughly enjoyed by all.

Further afield lay the Polish Farm, which was reached either by horse or by bullock cart. The latter, although much slower, was generally preferred as being more comfortable. Such a cart, drawn by either two bullocks or buffaloes, consisted of two pairs of wheels on axles linked by a series of long poles. Being thus completely flexible and devoid of springs it could contort itself to suit the vagaries of any rough track, which it usually did to the accompaniment of a series of excruciating groans and squeaks. When used for pleasure mattresses and cushions were laid over the poles, allowing the lazy to sit or lie in comfort, progress being so slow one could jump off and on at will. Horse carts were more uncomfortable, being equally springless, and also seatless, upturned boxes being used for sitting. Travel in these was somewhat precarious owing to the Turkish driver's innate dislike of being passed by another vehicle. In the face of such a danger his horse would be goaded to further effort, the speed would increase and finally if the land were open enough both carts would race neck and neck at a gallop over fields and road alike, in constant danger of colliding or overturning with total disregard for passengers or cargo and for all cries of anguish or protest. Fortunately, Allah being kind, accidents were few in number.

Polonezkeui, or the Polish Farm as we called it, was a settlement entirely inhabited by Poles, who had retained their language and religion, which with its white-washed houses, church and cemetery, beset with crosses, stood in marked contrast to the average rather decrepit looking Turkish village. Known in Polish circles as Adampol, its history is interesting. After the Polish insurrection of 1830, Polish prisoners taken by the Austrians were handed over to the Russians, who forced them into the army and sent them to the Caucasus, where permanent war reigned until the second half of the 19th century. Many of these soldiers deserted to the enemy, counting on their friendship, but the good Georgian Christians sent them to the Turkish slave market. Prince Adam Czartoryski (nephew of the last Polish king and uncrowned head of the great emigration of 1830-31), hearing of their plight sent money to the Lazarist Fathers in Constantinople to buy them out of slavery and to lease 1200 acres of land on the Asiatic side of the Bosphorus for their settlement. This colony was organised in 1842 and the first soldiers were later joined by others from the insurrections of 1846 and 1848 and from Polish veterans of the Crimean War, in which Polish regiments were raised by the Turks. How the women got to Adampol is not clear, but these probably consisted of members of the men's families, or of émigrés who managed to get there. (I was at

Polonezkeui in 1975 when I found it unchanged, but developing into a considerable holiday resort, with a shop in Pera to sell its produce).

This settlement proved more permanent than a Jewish one, founded by the Rothschilds at the Yaoudi Chiftlik near Samandra, which soon foundered. Another interesting foreign community in Turkey was that of the Doukhobors, a strange Christian sect, who left Russia as a result of persecution. A group of these settled in two lakeside villages in Anatolia where they carried on their former occupation of fishermen. Here they led a peaceful life, retaining their Russian habits and language, but although strict teetotallers used to have periodic orgies on methylated spirit. Many of them returned to Russia after the Second World War, but the majority emigrated to Canada where they became well known for their engaging habit of taking off their clothes and walking about in the nude when protesting over any Government ruling of which they disapproved.

Of an evening the dogs were let out of their kennels to run about freely all night. Their release was the occasion of a mad rush as the fifteen or so animals, with tails wildly wagging and looks of intense pleasure on their faces, bounded out, almost knocking us over in their excitement. These were all shooting dogs, mostly pointers and English setters and crosses between the two. I also have vague recollections of a large brown dog, called I think Minik, on whose back I used to ride when very small. Several of these dogs had been given to Father by his old friend George Marshal, who lived at Sulina on the mouth of the Danube, where among other things he was Lloyd's agent and represented several insurance companies.

A possibly apocryphal story is told of him. For some reason or other he was once made redundant whereupon he wrote to his employers, deploring their action and lack of wisdom, ending as follows: "I am afraid you will come to regret your action, for do not forget I AM THE DANUBE." Some time later a ship went aground, as often occurred on the shifting sands of the delta. The salvage vessels were summoned, but did not turn up and the ship lay there stuck fast. Soon after the same fate befell another ship and once again the salvage vessels refused to come to its aid. By this time there was imminent danger of two total losses on the insurers' hands, so Marshal was hastily recalled and in a couple of days both ships were free. Truly he does seem to have been the Danube.

He was a keen shot with a wonderful scope on the Danube marshes. Amongst other dogs he presented Father with was the incomparable Jibbo, a black and white pointer setter cross, who became legendary by his virtuosity. During the war he was cared for by an old shooting friend, Yorgi the Yalandji (George the Liar), who once told me that, happening to be in our house when Father returned in 1919, Jibbo was so excited at seeing him that he jumped from a first floor window to greet him. Father also said that the dog never recognised him, but that was a way with many of Yorgi's stories. Both before and after the War dogs played an important part in my life and to this day the mere recollection of their classic names: Jibbo, Boy and Lady, two superb English Setters, Minik, Mahdi, Samour, Gumish, Yell, Sari, Cedar and so on gives rise to wonderful memories.

Nights at Alemdagh were never quiet. With the onset of dusk the crickets started to chirp and the frogs in the pond in the valley to croak, while mice pattered about in the ceilings of the house. On moonlight nights especially, wolves and jackals would tend to start howling and they or the footsteps of some late passer-by would often set a dog barking. Other dogs in the village would then take him up and they would arouse dogs in neighbouring villages, and the chorus of barking would only settle down as the dogs became bored or sleepy. Early in the morning the cocks and ducks would start their crowing and quacking and with Father getting up to do his exercises a new day would open.

Other isolated events come to mind. On one occasion Fraulein Muller, our much loved German governess, unique in this respect, climbed the Alemdagh hill alone and on her return got a severe wigging from Mother as it was considered unsafe for women to go on long walks unaccompanied. In this connection Gladys Madge told me that once when staying at Alemdagh together with Aunty Gwen, Mother showed such persistent anxiety whenever the latter was lost to view that Gladys said: "Lilian, why is it you worry so much about Gwen, but never show any concern when I go off alone." "That is true Gladys, but things are different with you, for Gwen is such a beautiful woman."

On a similar occasion many years later, two ladies staying with Kenny at Pendik alarmed his man Mehmet by going for a walk on the hills alone, at a time when there were many soldiers about. Kenny pooh-poohed Mehmet's fears for as he said both ladies were old and ugly. To this Mehmet replied: "Yes Chelebi, that may be true, but do you think a bull looks a cow in the face before mounting her?"

Kenny played a part in two other incidents. On one occasion he was riding in a carriage with a number of others, when, seeing a hare he picked up his gun and fired. With the carriage lurching at that moment he only just missed blowing the head off our parson (Stephen Langston Day), while on the other he fell foul of a hornets' nest to come off a very bad second best. Then there was the incident of the crabs. These arrived from Moda as a treat and we had them for supper. Retribution came in the night when the whole family were roused by the symptoms of an acute stomach upset, with pain, vomiting and heaven knows what. But the unkindest cut of all was that Osie, who alone ate two crabs, was completely untouched.

CHAPTER III

Alemdagh Post 1918

Note:
After the end of World War I, I spent most of my life in England with only occasional brief visits to Turkey, in consequence of which there are gaps in my knowledge.

During the 1914-18 War our house in Moda had been let and we were very lucky that little damage had been done to it and its contents, but not so Uncle Edwin, whose larger house had been used as a hospital. Granny's house had also remained intact for Great-Aunt Maria and Father's former nurse Jenny had continued to live in it.

At the start of the war the Alemdagh house had been left to its own devices and in effect had been taken over by soldiers who left it in a lamentable state of dirt and disorder, but free from any structural damage, except for a little to the kitchen. Also, more happily and unexpectedly, they had left the house free from bed-bugs and suchlike vermin. But once things were taken in hand the house was soon rendered fit for occupation, with all gaps in the furnishings filled with the surplus stuff from Moda and after all this was done it was left under the care of our old friend Sarandi.

While the house remained virtually unchanged, the same did not apply to the village, from which all the former Armenian inhabitants had been deported, never to be heard of again, and replaced by Lazes, a dour and hard-working tribe from the Black Sea, who never gave us any trouble, but with whom it was quite impossible to enter into any friendly relationship.

This was bad enough, but a worse complication was to arise in the shape of brigandage, a not unfamiliar aspect of life in Turkey. Military defeat and its consequences had left the country in a state of confusion and poverty, which, together with an accompanying breakdown in law and order, had led many impoverished villagers to take to this pursuit in an effort to remedy their state of life. There was no novelty about this. For example, when the first member of the family moved out of the town of Smyrna, in about 1820, to settle in an outlying village, he retained two armed guards to protect his family and property. Later one of his descendants died while under capture and at the turn of the century two of my uncles had been taken and had had to be ransomed. One of my grandfathers also relates in his memoirs how he had helped an old friend of his while serving a prison sentence for this very offence.

The majority of such men were not professional cut-throats or miscreants, but men driven by misery to pursue this occupation as a sideline to their normal way of life. From such local brigands, Father was quite safe, for, in the course of his shooting activities, he had stayed in many villages and was highly respected and liked, in part as he had always proved ready to help anyone in trouble. Any danger to him came from men coming from outside the area who did not know him so that it was considered unsafe for him to stay overnight at Alemdagh. Day visits were however perfectly in order and these became more practicable after Father had invested in a car and chauffeur (Sefi).

During this period of uncertainty the only damage done to the house resulted from a burglary, in which quite a lot of its contents were removed. These included the familiar, green covered sofa which had formerly graced our school-room and the piano, which was later found abandoned on a hillside not far from the house.

At this time, immediately after the war, and before the signing of a peace treaty, all the land stretching inland from the Bosphorus on the Asiatic shore was under the control of Allied military forces, with the Gendarmerie under the control of our cousin George Whittall, who was faced with the unenviable task of overcoming brigandage in a land ideally suited to its purposes, most of it being covered by thick maquis. One of his subordinates, one Armstrong, subsequently wrote a book about these activities, but this was largely discounted by the family for describing our Alemdagh houses as “the summer palaces of the Whittall family”. Some palaces!

No mention is made in his book, however, of one amusing incident. Information had come to hand that a band of brigands had made its headquarters in the Karakol, the small police station standing some two hundred yards from our house at Alemdagh. A force of armed men was sent up to deal with the matter. On arrival they split into two groups, taking up positions on opposite sides of the building. All was quiet for a while until one section was suddenly subjected to heavy gunfire from the Karakol, and immediately replied in kind. The gunfire continued for some time and was then called to a halt, when, surprisingly, no more came from the house. This was then approached and found to be quite void of men, when it was realised that each detachment had mistaken the gunfire from its opposite number for that of an enemy which did not exist. At a later date I found a lot of cartridge shells lying about which may confirm the story.

Once peace was signed and all the Allied troops had left the country, conditions slowly returned to normal, and this in turn was greatly helped by the exchange of Greek and Turkish populations between the two countries, for a considerable number of the brigands were of Greek origin. On the other hand Sarandi was no longer allowed to stay at Alemdagh, in view of his background, and had to return to Istanbul, whose resident Greeks were allowed to stay on in Turkey but not to live outside the town.

Meanwhile other changes were affecting Alemdagh. Amongst these was the gradual reduction in numbers of members of foreign colonies, hitherto permanently resident in the country. This was in part due to the change in their status in the country as a result of the abolition of the Capitulations, lessening prospects for the young who, in consequence, preferred to emigrate. Also during the Allied occupation, many of the girls had married outside the community and had left. To illustrate this, of us seven brothers and sisters only one spent the rest of his life in Turkey. Another factor, particular to our family, was that with Father's progressive illness the house was used less and less, except for a few days in winter for shooting, and this became more marked after his death in 1929. The same also applied to Uncle Edwin's house, which was regularly used in the days of Sir George Clark as Ambassador, when he and Uncle used regularly to spend weekends shooting.

Alemdagh, however, maintained one important function, for every spring Mother bought three young turkeys to be reared and fattened there, with the largest to be devoted to the Christmas dinner table.

While Father was fit enough to do so, he and Mother and I used often to spend a night or so at the house, and these occasions I loved, for they were both such ideal companions out in the country. At such times, if warned of his plans, old friends such as Kara Mehmet, and Ahmet Chaoush from Samandra would drop in, and I always remember Father, characteristically sitting on a stool, with these old men squatting on their heels in a half circle around him, with Kara Mehmet as usual talking twenty to the dozen and enjoying his glass of raki. (Which reminds me that on coming to Alemdagh it was always politic to leave a bottle of this at the Karakol to avoid any potential officiousness on the part of the police.)

After Father's death in 1929 I have forgotten in which years I returned to Turkey, but I remember on one occasion spending about three days alone at Alemdagh in the company of the five dogs, who even spent their nights in my bedroom, disturbing me, it is true, with their restlessness and scratching, but leaving me at peace after dawn when they jumped out of the window. In their company I never felt lonely, and with our long walks we all became equally tired. On another occasion I organised a mixed party of ten of us to spend several days in the house. This proved a great success, despite the eyebrows raised by some of the elderly in Moda at the absence of a chaperone. Sadly this was the last occasion on which the house was filled with young and with gaiety and laughter.

My last stay at Alemdagh was in 1937, when I took my newly married Barbara to show off the place I loved so much. Sadly this proved a disaster as we had forgotten about mosquitoes and by the morning Barbara had the appearance of a spotted dick pudding, necessitating immediate return.

This was the last time I saw the house, for shortly after the house was sold, and I believe pulled down and the trees felled. I have never been back there again.

Part IV

A CHILDHOOD IN TURKEY

1906-1914

CHAPTER I

Domestic Staff

Our domestic staff in those days was quite large, with permanent members made up of two resident maids, one called Kiami and three males, Kiamil, the cook and a scullery boy. The maids were Greek – Turkish women being excluded from such work by reason of Purdah, but the men came from different origins. All ate and met together in the servants' hall but despite differences in race and religion they all got on well together without the least sign of trouble. Further employees consisted of gardeners and a stableman to look after the cows and poultry, these, if resident, sleeping over the stable.

Two women came in weekly to see to the laundry, with yet another to do the sewing and others to prepare rose and lavender water. Karabet, an Armenian came in every week to wind the clocks and Kosmar, a Greek barber, came once a month to cut all male hair. Periodically one or two sewing women would arrive on the scene as well as others who made the jam, including rose petal, quince and morello cherry. Out of this latter fruit they also made a cordial, which diluted in ice-cold water made an excellent drink for us children.

At night a watchman took up his post in the house to keep guard and to let in latecomers while yet another 'Begchi' strolled round the compound, periodically and loudly beating the ground with his heavy stick to proclaim that all was well. (Incidentally throughout the years I can only remember one attempt at burglary both before and after the Wars.)

I have casually mentioned Kiamil, and his story is interesting. Father had an old shooting friend, called Sali, who lived in a village up country and to him Father had lent some money to buy a cow. Nothing more was heard of the matter and Father had forgotten all about it when one day some time later a small boy arrived at our house in Moda and asked to see Father. He was at work so Mother saw the boy who would not tell her what he wanted, he must see the Tchelebi – the Master, (throughout her life in Turkey Mother would be infuriated by the attitude of women taking a secondary place).

Anyhow the boy was fed and made comfortable until Father returned home. To him the boy said that his name was Kiamil and that he was the son of Sali, to whom Father had lent money to buy some cows and which had not been repaid. He then went on to say that his father had died, and the family had collected what they could; here he handed over a rag containing a gold coin and some silver, and that he, Kiamil, had been sent to work for Father until the rest of the debt had been cleared. Father looked the boy up and down and remarked that he was still small and what work could he do? And to this the boy answered that he was strong and could do anything. Father then suggested that the boy return home, with his money, and forget all about the debt, to which Kiamil gave the reply that he had been sent to work for Father and this he was going to do and was not going to return home until the task had been effected. Stubbornly he would not alter his position, and eventually he was taken into the household, dressed in more suitable clothes and then packed off to school every day and set to do odd jobs of an evening such as cleaning shoes and churning the butter.

As time went on Kiamil took on more and more responsibility in the household to become a sort of butler-major-domo, with Mother relying on him more and more by reason of his scrupulous honesty and willingness to work hard and help everybody. As for us boys we just loved him. He was our friend and support in all troubles and our confidant, always prepared to listen to our woes and joys. We teased him unmercifully, while he spoilt us, although at the same time demanding a very high standard of conduct from us; a reproof from him carried far more weight than one from the governesses for we knew that he was always fair. Two things especially upset him, one being to hear us say anything even mildly disrespectful of Mother and Father and the other was to touch his fez or head – why this should have been so, I do not know, but there it was.

Later in life, when we arrived in Constantinople on our summer holidays either by ship or train Kiamil was always the first to meet us – a huge grin on his face. (He had a way with customs, allowing us to pass through without trouble).

Meanwhile Kiamil had introduced two nephews from his village into the household, one of whom became our chauffeur, and the other, Osman our cook. Mehmet left when Father died and the car was given up, but Osman stayed on to become such a cook that he was approached by both restaurants and private individuals with offers of work at far higher salaries than Mother could afford.

All in vain however, for he refused to leave her and remained an enormous help to her until she died, after which he took service with a cousin, being unwilling to leave the family. A staunch friend and a fine man.

After a time Father felt that Kiamil was too good a man to stay in domestic service, and as at the same time he wanted to get married, a job was found in town for him in a broker's office and Father bought him a house. So Kiamil left us, but ever after he turned up at the house on his return from work to find out whether he could do anything for anyone, and no doubt to keep up to date with the family's activities. On Father and Mother's return to their home after the end of the First World War, they found Kiamil already installed and the house cleaned although, as was to be expected, after five years of absence, not in the best of order.

Kiamil has remained in my memory as one of the finest characters it has been my good fortune to meet – he had all the qualities representing the best side of the Turkish villagers.

With Kiamil we always talked in Greek and with Osman in a mixture of Greek and Turkish. The Greek we spoke was never termed Hellenic but Romaic, (Roman Asia-Minor in early Turkish days was always known as Rum). Romaic Greek differed in many ways from Hellenic and so much so that when I was in Greece between the Wars my Turkish background was immediately spotted.

CHAPTER II

Domestic Economy

As children we were of course not directly involved in this aspect of life, and, in consequence, such memories as I have are in the main related to the provision of food.

Most of the food consumed in the house was bought locally either in Moda or Kadikeui, where there was a food market. Local bread, consisting of large, circular loaves of greyish texture was delivered daily, but this was not eaten upstairs, where only white bread, either bought as 'franzolles' or baked at home found favour, except on such occasions as picnics. Yet another form of bread was the 'chourek' which arrived in plaited form, and in fact more resembled a cake than bread. It was so good.

Greengrocers always displayed their wares in the most colourful fashion and down at Kadikeui the pyramids of melons and water melons just landed off boats always made a wonderful picture. Choosing one of these in good heart was a skilled art, and many that came to table were just labelled 'kabak' or pumpkins. The best strawberries came from up the Bosphorus at Stenia, while for raspberries we were lucky in enjoying two seasons a year, early summer and also in the autumn. These were brought to the house. (One great advantage was that when buying small fruit one was always allowed to eat a sample). A lot of our vegetables and fruit were brought down weekly in panniers on a donkey from our property at Chamlidja, which Father shared with Uncle Edwin. This large piece of land was never fully developed for lack of water, but nevertheless it kept us and Uncle well supplied.

Meat was available on the open market, except for any produce of the pig, the lamb being particularly good with the beef not far behind. Market meat was supplemented during the shooting season by the game Father brought home from his weekend excursions and this included partridge, quail, woodcock, pigeon, duck and hare with the occasional addition of roe-deer or wild boar. In the absence of refrigerators at that time all perishable food was stored in an ice-box, to which fresh supplies of ice were brought daily in summer. This ice was also used in the making of ice cream, this involved the use of a tub of which the handle had to be kept turning. Osman's woodcock pie was out of this world, and never likely to be equalled, also were the quail pilaffs with which we used to be served.

For eggs and poultry we were mostly self-dependent as Mother kept a well-stocked poultry yard, with supplies from home and Alemdagh, supplemented by purchase on the open market and from passing vendors, especially ducks and turkeys. The turkeys used to be driven down the streets in flocks, to the dismay of traffic. Should Mother then want any particular birds, she would stop the man, indicate her choices, pay him and he would deliver them to the house. Despite his usually being a complete stranger, Mother never lost out on the deal, such being the state of local honesty

Several fishermen were based in Moda bay and pulling up their nets early in the morning used to bring their catch to the house mixed up with seaweed in round, flat baskets carried on their heads, usually at about nine o'clock. Lobsters and crabs would still be alive, and we loved watching them crawl about the kitchen floor, half in fear of approaching them too closely and admiring the way the men handled them. Further fish could be bought in Kadikeui. In the house only the best of fish was served at table, red mullet, bass, bream, flat fish and of course lobsters and crabs. A very good fish was Black Sea turbot, kaljan, as also swordfish, while in the autumn bonitos (palamitha) and blue fish (lufer) migrated down the Bosphorus, the former in such number at times that, in the straits they could be caught in shrimp nets. These we never ate at home but the lufer were highly prized, especially as they offered good fishing, were excellent table fish and could be smoked to offer a sort of substitute for kippers. (My brother, Hugh, wrote the article on Turkish fish and fish cuisine in Alan Davidson's book on Mediterranean Seafood). Two fish products which were particularly appreciated were potagu – made from the eggs of the grey mullet and pressed black caviar, which was used in place of cod's roe, in the preparation of tarama, to go under the name of caviare salad.

In those days all milk available on the open market had to be boiled prior to consumption and this affected the taste of tea. This persuaded Mother to keep her own cows – four in Moda, to provide the house, with two 'on holiday' in the country at Alemdagh so there was always a plentiful supply of milk, cream and butter. At one time, for some unknown reason, Father kept a couple of buffalo at Alemdagh.

Buffalo milk makes the best kaymak, a Turkish form of clotted cream presented in rolls and eaten with bread and sugar. In consequence of all this we children enjoyed fresh milk and at the same time knew where it came from, just as we helped in the churning of butter, while we learnt some of the facts of life from the collection and hatching of eggs. Incidentally, it was interesting that when an old boiling fowl was served at table it was often possible to find mature eggs in its interior.

Dry goods both edible and otherwise were mostly bought from a branch in Kadikeui of the 'Economic and Cooperative Stores', a British firm of grocers. This was generally called either the Stores, or alternatively Harters after its manager. I remember it chiefly for its barley sugar sticks, which came not in spirals as in England, but in solid cylinders, half an inch in diameter, which made for wonderful and long-lasting sucking. I have heard it said that on acquiring one of these we used to proclaim to the world that we had licked it all over, to discourage piracy. Another favourite obtained there was 'shoe leather', dried apricots compressed into flat sheets, off which pieces were torn for consumption. Other edibles we appreciated were leb-lebs, small roasted peas of unknown variety, pumpkin seeds, keten halva, very thin circular sheets of crisp pastry, containing between two sheets some sweet, sticky filling.

Household stores were also available from a large English-run store in town, Bakers. I remember tins of 'Bondman Tobacco' and cubic tins of 'Melrose's Tea'. Then finally at Christmas each year a large hamper used to arrive from England containing articles not obtainable locally, such as a York ham, crackers etc.

Regarding wine and spirits in those days I knew nothing. I got my first taste of port from what was left in a discarded bottle but otherwise alcohol never entered our lives. The story runs that when we had to leave the house in 1914, Father hid away his stock of old whisky and brandy and, thinking that the war would only last a few months, kept no note as to where he had hid it. But with hostilities lasting five years, by the time he returned memory had failed him, and sadly none of it was ever found.

The close of the Moslem fast of Ramadan was marked by the feast of Shekey Bairam – sugar Bairam – when it was customary to give presents of sweets and sweetmeats to friends. On this occasion a long table was set out in the hall and all such presents laid out on it to the hopeful delight of us children, even though we were never allowed to lay hands on what was laid on the table.

CHAPTER III

Daily Routine

In general, Osies's and my lives followed conventional lines, starting the day by waking to the sound of sweeping the stairs and of Father moving about as he did his exercises and dressed.

Once dressed – and some of our clothes bore evidence of having in their day been worn by older brothers – we descended to the family breakfast at about eight, Father in the meantime having set off to the office. The meal started off with a plate of porridge and cream, followed by a boiled egg. This was all right but the crunch came when we were expected to drink a large cup of hot milk. This was not liked or appreciated, but as a general rule was dispatched without protest. But there came moments of sullen obstinacy when we refused to comply with orders as we sat still just looking at the milk set before us as though waiting for some miracle to remove it from sight which, sadly, never came to pass. So doing led to more trouble, for the longer we delayed the more likely skin was to form on the milk and milk skin was something we disliked intensely and helped further to put us off drinking it.

Meanwhile all others finished their meal and went off, but we were not allowed to leave the table until all the milk had been drunk, to leave us sitting glumly. Possibilities of relief occurred as soon as all adults had left, for there were a couple of pots of aspidistra in the window and happily we threw the milk on these – pouring it out of the window onto the bed below was not so successful. We were liable to be caught as the milk left a white mark. Despite all measures however, we had in the end to acknowledge defeat and drink up what remained in the cup.

At one time the girls were given a spoonful of a brown iron mixture, called, if I remember rightly, Ferocal, and of course there was always cod liver oil in some form. Another time Mother got it into her head that garlic would improve the health of the children and so Ossie and I were given a clove to eat every day, until aunts, cousins and all those in contact with us protested so violently that the practice was given up.

At meals we were waited on by Kiamil, in a white jacket and by one of the maids in semi-uniform. Under the eagle eye of Mother and the governesses the old adage of 'Children should be seen and not heard' applied and we were given little chance of misbehaviour. I also remember being corrected for asking "Can I have some more?" and told to say "may" and not "can".

I cannot remember details of how mornings were subsequently taken up, but in early days we had lessons at home and when older attended a school run by the clergyman. At the same time we continued with our German lessons and this entailed our learning two scripts, the customary and the German Gothic. At the same time as learning in English and German we also picked up a rudimentary knowledge of Greek, Turkish and French by ear. To our nurse and the maids we had to speak in Greek, to many men in Turkish, while French was the social language and spoken by all.

Mornings were not entirely devoted to lessons, and I have no doubt there was time for play and certainly in summer time for bathing and the like. Lunch on weekdays was an informal meal at which the adage "Children should be seen and not heard" did not apply. It invariably consisted of a main course with a sweet and fruit to follow. Saturday was also known as Boiled Beef and Carrot day, for that was the inevitable main course at lunch. During the colder months we children took tea in the schoolroom, but in summer we would join Mother in the garden, sitting under a plane tree just below the drawing room terrace, to which all the necessary paraphernalia were brought out in procession by Kiamil and one or two of the maids. Here too we were subjected to the rule no cake till after the bread and butter.

We were always put early to bed, when Mother used to come up to hear our prayers and kiss us goodnight. In summer this would be in daylight, or at earliest, dusk, and we were happy with the wooden shutters closed, but in winter a nightlight was left burning till we fell asleep.

Nights were not entirely quiet. In the summer there was the croaking of frogs, the hooting of owls and gritting of crickets, while all the year round there was the sound of the circulating night watchman breaking the ground with his heavy staff and the occasional shouting of others as fire broke out in some part of the town. Another familiar sound was that of mosquitoes buzzing outside the nets under which we slept in summer, and talking of insects, how happy we were when allowed to stay up till dark to see the numerous fireflies flitting about.

When Mother gave a dinner party, if we were not already asleep, Osie and I would sit at the top of the stairs and watch the guests arrive. Then as soon as all were ensconced in the dining room, we would scurry downstairs into the pantry with Kiamil and the maids tolerating us as we helped ourselves to the dishes as they returned from the table through the hatch at the end of each course. As soon as the meal showed signs of coming to an end we would rush back to bed.

Kiamil was always wonderful with us, thus at Christmas, if our helping of Christmas pudding did not disclose a silver token, he would take the plate, empty it and in due course take it up for a second helping to give us a further chance. He at times would also allow us to help in separating the cream and in churning the butter. In contrast to his domain, the kitchen precincts were totally out of bounds – except when lobsters and crabs arrived on the scene, and we were allowed to watch them crawling about.

Mother was a stern disciplinarian and in addition we were subject to the disapproval of the two governesses. Despite all this, and of modern theories, this period of life has remained in my mind as one of complete happiness and memories of it have only helped to strengthen the great love in which I have always held my parents, and it may be that this was because they struck the right note in the bringing up of children, affording us the prime necessities of love, fairness, security and discipline.

The sense of both love and security extended outside the home, in that outside the family and its ramifications we felt appreciated and completely at ease and in safety among all our and other servants and the local populace, cab-drivers, fishermen, tradesmen and artisans. They were all greeted with pleasure and we were regarded by them with kindliness and affection. None hesitated to express their disapproval if and when our conduct was not up to standard in their eyes. This makes me wonder whether we learnt to appreciate at an early age when we were doing wrong, and to accept the consequences with equanimity.

I cannot say that the same spirit applied to our German governess except in the case of the last one, Fraulein Muller. We greatly loved her and perhaps this was due to the fact that she was a Saxon and so not imbued with the Prussian spirit, a great contrast to Fraulein Rauter whom we all disliked. Thinking of her reminds me of how cruel children can be. On one occasion in the nursery I was playing with a bit of string which I lit, but when the flames reached my fingers I dropped it into a waste-paper basket which promptly started to blaze. I then hid it under a table as I heard footsteps approaching. At this moment Fraulein Rauter entered and saw what was happening and raised the alarm. Mother rushed in and in the subsequent excitement and to my intense joy berated Fraulein Rauter for not keeping sufficient control and forgot all about me, the original culprit. Today my feelings towards these governesses have changed and I look back on their lot with commiseration. What a life to have to lead.

Our clothing was always of the simplest nature. Over it we almost invariably wore a brown cotton, easily washable, pinafore which reached down to our knees, thanks to which we did not have to worry about getting dirty. On state occasions we were dressed in sailor suits, with, on our heads, broad-brimmed straw hats whose crown was adorned by a ribbon bearing the name of the latest British warship to visit the town.

For pocket money we were given a small silver piastre, (about 2 ½p) which did not carry us far. With this we used to buy sweets, although these were in general supplemented at times by the large stock of chocolate that Father kept and by the quantities bought for the family during the feast of Sheker Bayram. Mention has not been made of mastic gum, usually obtained from the maids, which when softened by a small quantity of candle grease, made an excellent chewing gum. This hardened on exposure to the air and we used to love drawing it out into long thin strings and then returning it to the mouth. Mother, of course, objected to this habit, and so we had to be careful she did not see us.

CHAPTER IV

Play

Conditions for play during the period of my childhood differed greatly from those of today. We had few toys and these were of the simplest variety. The girls had their dolls and dolls' houses, but in my case the only toys I remember were a castle and a number of painted lead soldiers (on Wednesday afternoons, Fraulein Muller, our German governess used to join Osie and me in great battles with these). The only other content of the nursery which I remember was a musical box, which played circular metal perforated discs, the only tune of which I remember being "The Honeysuckle and the Bee". In wet weather we were of course confined to the house, where we either played family games such as Up Jenkins or Racing Demons, or stayed quietly in the nursery. Otherwise we had to rely very much on our own initiative and imagination for our entertainments, but in this we enjoyed certain considerable advantages.

Taking all in all, the absence of toys was compensated for by the advantages of space and companionship. This was not the whole picture, for outside home territories we had the sea with opportunities of bathing, sailing and fishing, with the lovely countryside in the background offering openings for all manner of country pursuits, these being especially open to us when staying at our country house at Alemdagh. Also in the community there were numbers of children of all ages, so that it was rarely necessary to play on one's own. In general, houses were on the large size and the majority had gardens, many of them large, with us in the favourable position of being allowed to play in Granny's. Uncle Edwin's garden was even larger, but we were excluded from all but the bottom garden – by the sea.

Life started with mother singing to us at bedtimes, "Moi je dis que les bonbons valent mieux que la raisin", and at the same time teaching us the classic nursery rhymes. From this point we gradually became involved in the simple games of childhood. Mother told me that I had learnt to read by the age of four, to become immersed in a weekly paper which we received regularly called the

Children's Magazine, chiefly memorable for the school run by Mrs. Hippo, and its pupils, Tiger Tim and Joey the parrot, always up to mischief. As well as this there was a monthly magazine "Little Folks", which was of a more serious character, while later in life I remember "Chums" and the "Boys Own Paper". At the same time I learnt to read in German, to become involved in "Struwelpeter" or "Shock-headed Peter", from which Grandfather liked to hear me recite and especially "Konrad Sprach die Frau Mama, Ich Geh Aus Und Du Bleibst Da".

Following our nursery rhymes we started on simple games; hop-scotch and rolling hoops, slapping and cutting bamboos in the bottom garden to be used as hobby horses. As we grew older we were allowed to wander further and further afield in Granny's garden, which being full of trees, offered wonderful scope for games like hide and seek, while later and as our legs grew stronger we were allowed to join in a minor way in our elders' wild and more strenuous pursuit of brigands and smugglers and Red Indians.

When not playing in Granny's garden we did so in our backyard provided it was not already occupied by clothes hanging up to dry, or by carpets waiting to be beaten. A further attraction lay in the walnut tree in one corner, whose green-coated fruit used to fall to the ground in the autumn. Removing this coating and subsequently the white skin in immediate contact with the kernel used to stain our hands a dark brown, to Mother's disapproval.

Granny's garden gave no opportunity for open games and for these we made use of the field, an open grassy space on the cliff top, situated on the far side of Uncle Edwin's garden. Here we played rounders and similar games, while unlike the modern child we never played football. This field had evidently been occupied in Byzantine days, for by digging in the upper cliff face it was possible to unearth clay lamps and other artefacts of the period. To do so was forbidden under Turkish law and so care was needed.

Then we had weekly dancing lessons in Uncle Reggie's house under the care of a Miss Leather, who taught us the Highland Fling, the Lancers and Sir Roger de Coverley amongst others. In one way we boys were lucky in that we did not have to walk round the garden daily balancing a book on our heads, as did the girls in order to give them a good carriage.

Winters could be very cold with plenty of snow at times and this gave scope for tobogganing. Initially the road running downhill to the pier was used for this purpose, but this carried the risk of over shooting the mark and landing in the sea. In view of this and by reason of disturbance to passers by, this was discontinued and an inland run was chosen, a slope behind the church and near the Nowills' house. Here a fast and safer run was maintained with the aid of buckets of water but with its icy surface could only be used by us youngsters with caution. Winter in effect was a dull period.

The arrival of spring was welcomed with its possibilities for picnics, bathing, fishing, sailing but above all for the prospect of a five-week stay in our country house at Alemdagh.

Picnics involved a preliminary drive in a Victoria Carriage driven by one of our old friends, Dukoli, Yorgi or Christo. We always hankered after sitting on the box with the coachman, but were never allowed, so having to take our place in a narrow let down seat, but nevertheless, always enjoyed the drive. A favourite resort was a large garden Father and Uncle Edwin owned on Chamlidja Hill, which boasted all manner of fruit trees, a large strawberry bed in season, stone almonds yielding lots of nuts as also a tree house. With a greater supply of water this garden could have proved a fruitful paradise.

Other destinations lay up the coast either on the seashore or up country. What a joy it was to watch the meat being grilled over an open fire together with maize cobs and roasted potatoes and then to eat with one's hands and to throw all remaining bones and morsels to the pi-dogs which immediately assembled.

The sea offered us bathing initially on a sandy beach and subsequently off the club raft, anchored in deep water in mid-bay. For fishing, we either went after small fry in the bay in company of Dimitri, our boatman, or else with Father after more important prey.

Father owned a small boat, the *Viking*. On this occasionally we used to go sailing with him and this boat was also used to take the whole family to a community picnic on Buliver's Isle. On the way to and fro we would be accompanied by schools of porpoises. It is sad today that the sea is so polluted that bathing is no longer possible and fish and porpoises are rarities.

Outside the everyday run of domestic life we occasionally enjoyed entertainments of a more formal character. Every year the children of the community organised a show at the Institute, our main hall of assembly. These we always attended but all I remember of them is of Cousin Molly dancing to Grieg's music on Peer Gynt. On one occasion Aunty Gwen organised a children's show, but of this I remember little except for Esme singing a song out of the Geisha Girl: "Chin, Chin, Chinaman".

Uncle Edwin had a magic lantern which gave moving pictures, but more exciting was my first visit to the open air cinema, in which the film was based on Victor Hugo's 'Les Miserables' and I still remember poor little Cosette cowering under a table.

Christmas festivities were of course more regular. Our Christmas tree was placed in the nursery, to be hidden from view until the last moment when we rushed in to admire it in all its glory, lit by candles. We then all held hands and circled the tree singing "Stille Nacht" (Silent Night) and "O Tannenbaum", this latter sung to a tune which has been taken over by the Red International. Following this Father Christmas entered carrying a bag full of presents on his back. When these had been distributed, the sack was emptied onto the floor and we all scrambled for the nuts, fruit and chocolates rolling about. Following our tree, on Christmas Day, we attended Granny's for hers and on Boxing Day a community one at the Institute.

Easter day was more subdued and we were limited to search for birds' nests, chicks and other sweetmeats hidden in the garden.

CHAPTER V

Family Life

My earliest datable memory carries me back to Grandfather's death in 1910 on which occasion we children were all taken to lay a small posy of flowers onto his deathbed.

Throughout my life I have always connected my first hearing and subsequent love of the hymn, "Abide with Me", with the occasion of his funeral, but this was such a big occasion and our church so small that today I doubt whether I attended the service at which were present representatives of all Christian churches and the Diplomatic Corps. It is interesting that on the mile-long procession of the cortege to the cemetery, all the church bells along the route tolled, while all shops closed their shutters. These years marked the hey-day in the life of the Whittall Family.

At this time of life there were six of us children. My two elder brothers, Hugh and Vernon, were at school in England, only making short appearances during the summer holidays, so that to all intents and purposes I did not know them.

Of my sisters, Monica and Edna, both a good deal older in comparative years (8 and 10 as against 4), I have no recollection, thus leaving me to associate with Osie, two years older than me. Willy did not make an appearance till 1912 and it is interesting I have no recollection of his arrival, or of Mother's appearance prior to his arrival. In fact I have no recollection of Willie at all prior to 1914.

After the passage of so many years it is difficult to recollect details of early childhood but the fact that this has left no scars testifies to its having passed happily. True we were subject to the discipline imposed by Mother and two governesses, but I doubt whether this did us any harm, for to my mind discipline in life is an essential component to happiness. This discipline only applied in the house for once outside, we were free to move completely unsupervised and in the full enjoyment of liberty. I cannot remember ever experiencing a feeling of injustice over any punishment meted us. Naturally any such was followed by vague hopes of some form of retribution falling onto Mother, but normality was soon restored and the event forgotten.

On one occasion, I had some doubts on the justice of what befell me. In the garden we had an apricot tree whose fruit we were forbidden to touch. One day when with my cousin Denis La Fontaine, it struck me that if he picked some fruit, he would not be punished by Mother and I could not be blamed. Well she caught us and Denis escaped scot free, while I got the blame and the spanking.

On another occasion, Osie and I found the store-room door ajar and entered to root about and see what was in. Unhappily, Mother happened to pass at that moment, and in her excitement picked up a handy weapon and chased us round the room until we managed to escape through the door. Incidents like these have never left any mark on later years, except for one of amusement, and this may well be that we knew we were doing wrong.

It was the same with Granny's peaches which grew just on the far side of the low wall which separated the two gardens so that if we thought the coast clear, we would slip over, pocket a peach and be back again. On occasion we would be caught by Aleko, the gardener, who would catch us by the neck and buffet us, but never reported us to authority. He was a great friend and we never resented his punishment – it was one of the risks.

In contrast to the German governesses we had little contact with Cousin Kathleen La Fontaine, the girls' governess, especially as all three were away in Munich in 1913. On the other hand we were exposed to a large number of aunts, uncles, cousins and various other adults.

Of these, Father's sisters were generally disapproving in their rigid and rather severe attitudes, and very prone to find fault. Our uncles, on the other hand, regarded us with more fellow feeling, greeting us with smiles and teasing. Outside of these were a large number of cousins and other adult members of the community, some of whom we knew quite well and approved of, others whom we only knew by sight. Such adults, however, hardly impinged on our lives except in the way of casual greeting. All in all we felt much more at ease with servants and what our aunts would have described as the lower orders.

In 1913 the girls were sent to Munich for a few months to further their education, while either in this year or the next Mother took Osie and me to Smyrna to stay with Grandfather who was almost the first man in Turkey to run a motor car. Riding in this, a Napier, was a great thrill. He had a huge garden of which I chiefly remember a tall date palm, a mandarin tree in full fruit which we were allowed to enjoy and a platform up a tall tree to which Grandfather was reputed to betake himself periodically and to sleep at night. I also remember falling out of a high bed in the middle of the night and being made to play with our female cousin Ailsa, which we boys thought somewhat degrading.

All this brings me back to Father and Mother who, in all probability and in the manner of most children, we took for granted. Father had his peculiarities but when with us he was a grand companion – and this especially so when in the country or on the sea, but by and large I have few memories of him in these early days.

Mother falls into very much the same category. I remember some small details such as her love of Roger et Gallet's Vera Viletta Soap. She used to play bezique with father and on one occasion was reputed to have thrown the pack of cards at his head, which is quite possible as she was known to be impatient.

After the passage of so many years, it is difficult to recall the exact state of my feelings for Father and Mother during these years of childhood. No doubt I experienced moments of aggravation and had to contend with certain parental peculiarities, but all goes to suggest a very happy childhood, which, despite the exercise of punishment and discipline, has, contrary to modern ideas, left no scars, and in their stead a love of parents and appreciation of their activities which has endured throughout my life.

CHAPTER VI

Sunday Pre 1914

Mother strictly adhered to the principle that Sundays were not as other days, and we children were made aware of this at an early hour, being dressed in our best clothes on the strict injunction not to dirty them. Breakfast followed normally, but once finished there was no running about in the garden. We had to sit quietly until it was time for church. For this the entire family gathered in the hall, the men in suits and girls and ladies all wearing hats, each one holding prayer or hymn book in hand.

The walk to church took less than ten minutes and once arrived we settled in our pew, which overflowed when all seven of us children were present. With the church full, all awaited the arrival of Grandmother, accompanied by Great-Aunt Maria, who, once settled in their pew, gave signal to the clergyman that the service could start. When very young we were let out before the sermon, but later in life had patiently to sit still, in hot weather, procuring some diversion in watching the reception given to flies as they settled on bald heads. After the service everyone gathered outside for a few words and following this all went home.

Luncheon on Sunday was a formal affair in that it was always attended by the Parson and his wife, and by Janey, Father's old childhood nurse, a Yorkshire woman; she had come abroad for a short spell to stay with the family for sixty years. We children all loved her and this perhaps because she always spoke her mind. We never sat down at table fewer than twelve in number, with Mother at the helm, carving the almost inevitable joint of beef. On these occasions we had to keep quiet, while the governess tried to get us to sit with the tips of our fingers resting on the edge of the table. A sweet would follow and then fruit, with Kiamil sweeping away all crumbs before serving the former. For the fruit course we were always handed pretty porcelain plates, laying them on a lace mat with knife and fork placed on either side and a glass water bowl. Lunch was followed by a period of rest and a walk and then by tea in the school room, or in summer in the garden with Mother, after which we had to remain quiet, with no card playing or boisterous games allowed and only selected books to read, and so the day ended.

Part V

THE FIRST WORLD WAR

CHAPTER I

England 1914 – 1915

In August 1914, in the absence of any hope of peace, all British women and children were embarked on the *SS Malatian*, a semi-cargo ship, for the long sea trip to England, not to return for five years. On the way we had to pass through the heavily mined Dardanelles, to reach Malta without mishap. On leaving however, we encountered a heavy storm, which laid all low except for sister Monica. I later heard that the Captain was worried about the security of the ship but what I do remember is that when sitting on deck one day, an exhausted quail landed on the deck just by me.

The Bay of Biscay was calm and here we saw whales spouting in the distance. On the voyage we children had to drink condensed milk which we loathed. On landing at Holyhead, we took a train to London where we stayed at the Ivanhoe Hotel in Bloomsbury. Here I ate my first kipper and also found sixpence in the street.

I attended a local school, while the girls were looked after by their governess, cousin Kathleen La Fontaine (CK), while Marina, the Greek nurse, who had accompanied us, was in charge of Willy. After a short time, Mother rented a house in Esher named Lammas Cottage, a house with a large garden and a resident dog, Caesar. Here in Esher lived Barker relatives – Uncle Bertie and Aunt Lella, Great Uncle Alfred and Aunt Eveline. We settled down comfortably with Christmas 1914 marking the last occasion on which all members of the family sat down to a meal together. Shortly after, Father returned to Greece, while Hugh joined the army, with Vernon at Rugby and Osie at Eagle House.

A narrow lane connecting two aspects of the village ran along one side of our house, down this of a late evening drunkards used to walk home noisily, frightening me and giving me a wrong impression of the country. Kingston-upon-Thames was our main shopping centre and here we were taken to the theatre to see a play called "The Flag Lieutenant" a tale of British heroism. In those days we were brought up to be proud of the British Empire and its achievements with a large part of the world coloured red on maps to indicate the British Empire.

After a stay of about six months in Esher we moved into London, to settle into a tall Victorian house at number 1 Prince's Square in Bayswater, under the care of the Misses Evans.

The London of those days was very different to that of today, with horse drawn vehicles mainly filling the streets, although buses were petrol driven, all open topped but fitted with waterproof coverings in case of need. The streets were much more cheerful what with bands, barrel organs and boys and men whistling the current popular songs – 'Tipperary', 'There's a little Grey Home in the West' and the like of

"Won't you join the Army?
Won't you come with me?
Won't you come with me boys?
To Berlin on the spree?"

There were also open carts collecting old clothes, old iron, with hand carts selling muffins and the like. Marina used to take Willy and me into Kensington Gardens each day. Here all the parks were bordered by low railings, while flocks of sheep grazed the grass. In warmer weather model yachts were sailed on the Round Pond and race meetings held. Another feature of the day was the custom of laying straw on the road outside a house in which someone lay ill to reduce the noise of passing traffic – horses' hooves not being silent.

On occasion we suffered air raids from Zeppelins – giant gas filled air ships but these stopped after a couple had been shot down. When these occurred all assembled in the basement of the house.

Naturally, we attended the local church regularly, one in which Sunday services tended to be prolonged as the Vicar had a liking for the Litany and also tended to read out the names of parishioners serving in the forces in his prayers.

As for shopping, the huge emporium of Whiteley's was close at hand, while in Westbourne Grove there was Bradley's, London's most elegant fur dealers. I cannot remember attending school when in Bayswater, but may have been taught by CK.

CHAPTER II

Athens 1915 – 1916

After a year in England, Father sent for Mother, Willy and myself to join him in Greece, leaving Osie at school, the girls with CK at the Misses Evans, and Hugh and Vernon in the Army. So we set off to arrive in Naples – although how we got there I cannot recollect. Of Naples I only remember a visit to the Aquarium, my surprise at seeing children openly performing their natural functions in the streets and a trip to the Solfatara to see the bubbling lava springs.

We carried on by sea through the Corinth Canal to reach Piraeus and so on to Athens. (Piraeus was, in those days, separated from Athens by green fields). After a few days in the town we moved into a small house which Father had rented in the village of Kiphissia on the Northern outskirts of the town. Here we settled to find a number of families from Turkey in residence mostly with children of about our age.

Here I enjoyed considerable freedom in the company of a number of other English children who went to school in Athens every day on a small train, the school being run by the Anglican clergyman, Alan Gardner, who had married Uncle Edwin's daughter Audrey. Mr Gardner also took services in one of the large houses in Kiphissia, and on one very hot summer's day I fainted in the middle of the service, to be carried out, regaled with cold lemonade and told to remain outdoors which suited me admirably.

There were no motor cars so that we could wander about safely to play in one another's gardens. Mother was in her element with the open country close at hand, covered in the springtime by sheets of flowers of which I particularly remember the anemones. Many of the pine trees were also scored, with cups to catch the exuding resin, used in the local retsina wine.

Father often took me out for walks, and I especially remember climbing Mount Pentelicon from which the marble used in the construction of the Parthenon was quarried. From the summit of the mountain there was a clear view of the Bay of Marathon and on its slope we found an abandoned section of a marble column, which may well have been intended for the Acropolis. After a time we moved to another house on the outer edge of the village and here we witnessed the burning of the Tatoi forest surrounding the King's Summer Palace. A frightening sight even at some distance as we heard the roar of the fire which eventually extended to a mile from our house.

Otherwise our life was uneventful but I will close with a story. Father used to buy fruit at the same greengrocer's shop in town, but one day this job fell to Mother's lot on her way home from town. On his way home Father called in at the shop to enquire whether mother had called in and then, on hearing her description, the shop keeper handed Father some money explaining that not knowing the lady to be Father's wife he had overcharged her.

After a time political trouble blew up from King Constantine's wife being sister to the Kaiser, and Father thought it best for us to leave. So, without Marina who had decided to return home to the Island of Chios, we boarded a ship, inappropriately named *Arcadia*, to enjoy a most uncomfortable trip to Brindisi and so on to Rome.

CHAPTER III

Rome 1916 – 1918

Once in Rome, after a move or two we eventually settled in a third floor flat at number 66 Via Sialia, a road running off the Via Veneto and close to the Borghese Gardens. Here we were joined by Monica and Edna and CK. We were soon joined by other expatriates, Daisy la Fontaine with Donald and Daphne and Janet la Fontaine with Denis, Dorothea and Helen. Also in this town were a number of Pengellys.

In our block the flats were built round a courtyard, each kitchen boasting a small balcony, from which a basket could be lowered to pick up small deliveries. This courtyard was a great source of amusement as women used it to talk and quarrel with neighbours. From these we got to know the vulgar tongue.

My daily routine ran as follows. First thing of a morning, I went to the dairy situated in the Villa Borghese grounds to buy our milk and butter, these having to be picked up early as they soon ran out. Later after breakfast, I walked to the flat of Professor Bullock for my private lessons. We children met every day in the Villa Borghese to run about and play energetic games, watched by the Italian children, who had no conception of such pursuits. I also had to take Willy to the Park every afternoon to play.

Meanwhile, Mother found scope for her natural instincts in the way of sightseeing, and we were regularly taken all over the town and the surrounding countryside, to learn all about Roman and early Christian history. Her enthusiasm was wonderful and was readily imparted to us. She loved walking, especially in search of flowers, and also picnics. The Alban hills were a favourite resort and here the "Turkish refugees" such as the Pengellys and the La Fontaines held an annual picnic in spring. More distant excursions such as to Tivoli or Frascati always provided an excuse for picnics. On these occasions in spring or autumn Mother was in her element organizing, directing and laying down the law, with her friends teasing and protesting and Mother popping up unconcerned just like a celluloid duck in a bath. Father paid us occasional visits, and on walks with him I enjoyed my first taste of well diluted wine.

Of an evening, Mother and the girls went regularly to the opera at the Constanzi theatre and concerts at the Augusteo. We also went to the cinema to see the early D.W.Griffiths classics – "The Birth of a Nation", "Intolerance" and others, as also the early Chaplin and Max Linder films.

In summer 1917 the whole family moved up to the town of Torre Pellice, a stronghold of the Waldensians, in the Alps near Turin for a month. On the way up by train Edna distinguished herself, for on being asked the name of the station at which we had halted, she came out with a loud "Latrina". Here we learnt all about Catholic persecutions.

"Avenge, O Lord, thy slaughtered Saints of old,
Whose bones lie scattered on the mountains cold."

Mother got very interested and we visited all the shrines within reach and the story of these poor wretches aroused strong feelings in her mind. Religion always played a large part in Mother's life so in Rome regular church-going was the order, with Sunday school for me. (The church we attended has now been closed.) These religious observances included fish on Fridays. Generally this was only obtainable in the form of dried cod and with our Ernesta being no chef, the form in which this tended to be presented for lunch was usually pretty horrible. She had not learnt the eighty Portuguese ways of cooking this fish. Monica and I also spent another holiday on the coast, staying with friends from Turkey, to have a wonderful time especially as our hostess was a superb cook.

Looking back on these two years spent in Rome makes me realise how much I owe to the experience gained then at an age when the majority of boys were confined to their prep school. Much of this was due to Mother, who on the one hand led us into the countryside on walks, picnics and in the search for wild flowers, while on the other, she was intensely interested in the history of the town and such artistic achievements as were open to the public.

Wartime circumstances led to our going about almost everywhere en famille and in this way I missed out on very little. As a result of this I listened to adult conversations. My interest was aroused and I acquired knowledge of both early Christian history and medieval Rome together with an acquaintance and appreciation of pictures and sculpture. Of paintings, I cannot say that I remember many but of sculptures I have never forgotten Bernini's Apollo and Daphne and

Canova's Pauline Bonaparte in the Borghese Gallery. I also had my heroes, one being Cola di Rienzi, a tribune of the 12th or 13th century and the other Beatrice Cenci, a murderess, but whose portrait in the Barberini Gallery enchanted me.

Mention of Cola di Rienzi reminds me that Willy and I used to go off for walks in the town together, unbeknown to Mother, but I do not think she worried for the Rome of those days was safe, with only trams and horse-drawn carriages for transport. Thus we walked down to the Tiber to see the house of Cola di Rienzi, accidentally stumbling on the remains of the Theatre of Marcellus tucked away in the old Ghetto, before Mother had seen it.

To add to the joys of life, I was given private schooling by Professor Bullock, who, as I look back, was the ideal teacher for me. Firstly, I enjoyed my lessons, he being an excellent teacher and having the capacity to make even Greek and Latin interesting, so that there was no question of Shakespeare's "dallying schoolboy". In addition he was a man of wide culture and vast and wide interests, and often brought them into play. In this way, for example, I became acquainted with the names of Schopenhauer and Nietzsche as philosophers, with only a slight, very slight, understanding of their theories. Other subjects such as Mendelism and Grimm were brought up, memories of these to remain in my mind. In consequence my education covered a wide field, to arouse my sense of curiosity and led me to recognise wide fields of diversity and knowledge, even Latin finding its use in enabling me to decipher inscriptions. I also learnt the rudiments of the Italian language. I owe an enormous debt to Mr Bullock – who led a sad domestic life, poor man.

Life in Rome offered us all an excellent education and as a result of all this I, at an early age, learnt unconsciously that the arts played a normal part in everyday life, enabling me both to keep in mind such works as the Apollo Belvedere and the Laocoon, as also the names of artists from Raphael and Michaelangelo downwards.

In the summer of 1918, with the end of the war approaching, it was decided to send me to school in England. Mother and the girls, however, stayed on until conditions allowed them to return home, leaving CK behind, as in the meantime, she had got married.

Part VI

ENGLAND

CHAPTER I

School 1918 – 1924

After a regretful parting from Mr Bullock, Donald La Fontaine and I set off for England in company of an elderly English photographer lady, crossing France by train. Having arrived at Eagle House School, I soon settled down to the new life, especially as I was soon joined by a number of cousins.

Life at school was spartan. The winter was cold, heating kept at a minimum with our school uniform not of the warmest, as a result of which almost all the boys suffered from painful chilblains on hands and feet. Of an evening the only heating for the boys came from an open fire in the big school room. We were given plenty to eat, although I loathed the frequent ground rice puddings. Sugar was rationed, and we were each given the option of having our share given us in the form of sugar or jam. I opted for the latter, and in consequence have never drunk sweetened tea.

School work was in general uninspiring except for the private German lessons which were given to me by a Mr Forgas, a Spaniard who was generally known as "Fungi" who introduced me to German poetry. Beyond this I was introduced to the pleasures of Thackeray with Sam Housely's interpretation of the role of Captain Costigan in Pendennis. That winter the school acted Moliere's "Le Bourgeois Gentilhomme" and also performed the "Gondoliers". Outside of these Rupert Lockhart gave song recitals. Only one song "I Did But See Her Passing By" remains in my memory. On the more practical side I learnt to play and enjoy Rugby football, auction bridge and chess, so all in all, in the course of my stay, I did not do too badly, but went on to Rugby without regret.

School at Rugby was of course a different proposition and here I was reduced to the lowest ranks of society, though, fortunately, fagging was no longer practised in our house. Here, I joined my brother Osmond and cousin Edward, with whom I went for walks on Sunday afternoons.

Life was more comfortable, for although we still slept in dormitories the house was properly heated and we all shared studies to give us a modicum of independence which we enjoyed in a variety of ways. Outside the set games of rugby, football and cricket we had fives, squash and rackets courts to occupy any spare time. There was an excellent school library and a swimming pool at our disposal – not that I used this last – the River Avon was preferable.

In the way of learning I had to associate with those who were much cleverer and more advanced than myself and this acted as a stimulus. My last year was one of intellectual freedom for at this point I had passed my Preliminary Medical exam, as well as all others. In consequence I had a lot of free time on my hands and mainly spent this reading or in summer searching for wild flowers. So I ended my career at Rugby as Head of House and wearing my school 2nd XV colours, and won the school German prize.

We were allowed to keep pets and a friend kept a pair of ferrets with which we used to go rabbitting on Sunday afternoons. One day we were late for Chapel, through which my friend sat with a pair of live ferrets in one coat pocket and a dead rabbit in another. The school owned a white cockatoo, which had been well educated in the way of bad language by generations of school boys.

CHAPTER II

Cambridge 1924 – 1927

I spent the summer holiday of 1924 in Switzerland where Father was undergoing treatment for tuberculosis, from which he was suffering, never to recover. It was very sad to see a man of such former vitality reduced to lying on a couch all day long with only slender prospects of improvement. Illness, however, did not prevent Father from encouraging me to go mountain climbing, under the care of a local guide who led me up a number of peaks, some offering somewhat searing experiences. The most enjoyable climb was that of the Wildhorn, some 10,000 feet high, which necessitated an all night climb to reach the snow covered summit at dawn to enable us to watch the sun rising over the Valaisian Alps, Matterhorn, Monte Rosa and others. On my return from each such excursion, I gave Father a full description, and I think he derived satisfaction from one of his sons enjoying what he would have loved to be able to do himself.

On my return to England, I went straight to Cambridge, to Gonville and Caius College, where I was allotted rooms on the first floor in Tree Court. Here I enjoyed a sitting room and a bedroom, the latter, if I remember rightly, with furnished wash-stand and jug and basin. The bathrooms however, lay on the opposite side of the court. To reach these it was necessary to cross the court in snow and all weathers exposed to the open sky.

For meals, I had a hot breakfast dish delivered to my rooms from the kitchen every day which left me to provide the rest of the meal myself. This service was available at lunchtime but I did not make use of it, as it was too expensive. Luncheon usually consisted of sandwiches or the like and this was made up for by the fact that dinner was served in Hall, which we had to attend on at least five nights a week. This meal was always very substantial and served with the college silver cutlery.

Beers, wines and spirits were available from the Buttery. These included strong, college-brewed ale known as Audit Ale – one pint proving enough for most people. Of an evening, College gates remained open till 10.00pm and were then closed till midnight to be then locked for the night, after which there was no admission possible except by climbing over the wall. This I never had to do, but I was told that there was a well tried route. After one year in College I had to find rooms in the outer world and I was lucky to find a very pleasant landlady.

My working day started at 9.00am and in general carried on till about 5.00 pm. In the main it consisted of attending lectures and laboratories. Initially, it came as a shock to be presented with a human arm or leg (strongly smelling of formaline) and told to dissect this, but after a day or two I lost all feelings, and settled down to the work comfortably, without any thoughts for the human being on whose remains I was working.

Anatomy as a subject was interesting, but involved memorising a lot of detail, a process which was helped by learning a number of rhymes, many of them bawdy. The other subjects under review were pharmacology – "bugs and drugs". The Professor of Physiology was of worldwide repute, having started his career as a lab boy. His counter-part in the field of pharmacology, blessed with a ruddy complexion, regularly impressed us with the dangers attending the drinking of tea.

I found learning how the human body worked was fascinating and all in all I enjoyed the work. At the end of the course I had to pass an exam known as the Second MB, but prior to taking this I attended a special revision course in which we were given a number of questions which we were advised to swot up in detail, being likely to be presented at the examination. The help and advice given proved sound, and I passed with flying colours. To enable me to be granted a BA degree, I had to offer a further subject and the one I chose was French. So after all this I was ready to move on to St Thomas' Hospital.

Life at Cambridge was not all work, and much of my free time was spent in reading and playing bridge. One of my friends was an excellent pianist and many an evening was spent listening to him playing and expounding on the music. In this way I became involved in the music of Wagner, which led to my listening to the complete "Ring", sitting on hard wooden backless benches in the gallery of Covent Garden. Apart from all this, Cambridge offered all manner of opportunities for endless discussions on religion, the state of the world and all manner of subjects. In the college, there was a group who considered themselves to be superior but otherwise all others mixed freely whatever their background. My great friend was a Brazilian and together we wove great plans for our future, one being to set up a joint nursing home in Rio. Sadly, on his return to Brazil "Du" did not have long to live, dying I think of TB.

One feature of the time was well organised "Rags" taking off some political or other event. I remember one connected with the discovery of the tomb of Tutankhamen, in which one of the underground public lavatories in Market Place was taken over as the tomb. These rags were immensely cheerful and boisterous affairs giving rise to no unpleasantness.

CHAPTER III

St Thomas' Hospital 1927 – 1930

My next move took me to St Thomas' Hospital for a further three years study. I was not sorry to leave Cambridge for apart from the work I did not find life at the University fully satisfying. So in due course I descended on Philbeach Gardens, where for three guineas a week, I became entitled to bedroom and breakfast and an evening meal every day.

Once at St Thomas', after a preliminary introduction, I was set to work in Casualty to be instructed how to deal with most of the minor ailments and accidents of life. In due course I learnt how to dress and bandage cuts and wounds, to insert stitches, set minor fractures, take out teeth and the handling and use of local anaesthetics and the scalpel, all under a strict regard to sterility.

In those days, before the days of penicillin, local infections, especially those of the fingers and boils and carbuncles were common and often very painful and long lasting, many requiring surgical intervention. All in all the work was interesting and I enjoyed it (at other people's expense). We did not work under conditions of pressure, except on one occasion when the pavements were covered with ice causing many to fall and suffer fractures of the wrist.

On the opposite side of the Lambeth Palace Road there was a Students' Hostel offering bedrooms and all facilities. I could have lived there, but preferred not to be in constant contact with the Hospital. At the same time social life there was very pleasant, with acquaintances from Cambridge and new ones from all over the country. After a period in Casualty we moved to a medical ward, under the care of Physicians. The ward was under the domination of an all powerful Sister whom we students soon learnt to hold in the deepest respect and some nervousness, St Thomas' Sisters being decidedly authoritarian. On arrival in the ward, Sister introduced us to the practical everyday side of ward life – how to make beds, arrange pillows, under the strictest injunction never to sit on a patient's bed.

The Matron of the day, Miss Still, was a martinet, but Thomas' nurses had an unrivalled reputation. Our first job was to learn how to take and record case histories, how to fully examine patients and to record findings and after this to keep daily notes on progress or otherwise. Each of us was allotted a certain number of patients and was expected to know all about them. This was interesting for it allowed us to come into close contact with men and women from totally different walks of life.

Outside of all this we attended ward rounds taken by the Physicians in which we were quizzed over matters of diagnosis in new patients as well as all other aspects of the patient's illness and treatment with no mercy being shown. In addition to learning how to examine a patient properly, we were taught how to take blood pressures, to give injections, and to take blood and other samples, all jobs today in the hands of nurses, but not in those days.

Treatment with drugs was still in a very primitive state and a lot of time was lost in deciding on the proper drug to be prescribed, and its correct dosage, all often to no great advantage. I remember discussions on the best hypnotic to use in a case of pneumonia – chloral might affect the heart, the barbiturates were too depressive, paraldehyde had a foul odour, the final choice falling on whisky.

Physicians in general were mild mannered, quiet and modest but not so some of the surgeons whom we met in the next lap of learning, many of these resembling actors in regard to their liking for the limelight. In the surgical as in the medical wards we had to take histories and keep records of all patients under our care, but in addition we also had to change dressings and take out stitches all under strict condition of sterility and to perform a number of minor procedures.

Outside the wards we attended operations in the theatre, to watch the surgeon at work, to admire his skills and the close co-operation between surgeon and all in the theatre. During this period, we each had to spend a week living in the hospital, during the course of which we were called upon to attend to all acute surgical admissions and to follow them to the theatres if necessary. This week was one of hard and continuous work covering all hours, night and day – on one occasion spending ten hours in the theatre.

But it was all very worth while for we were able to get first sight of acute abdominal and other emergencies – early recognition of which is of vital importance. During these months, we also had to attend Orthopaedic clinics. The Chief Surgeon here was a great character and a man of wide reputation but he, when in doubt, always sought advice from his junior. Of the surgeons in our team, one deplored the lack of surgical skill shown by gynaecological surgeons. One day, a woman somehow got into his out-patient clinic to be diagnosed as suffering from a mass of fibroids and the surgeon decided to operate on her to show how this should be properly carried out. So, in the theatre she was opened up, to expose to the surgeon's dismay, and to our amusement, a pregnant uterus. She was hastily returned to the ward, where to her delight she aborted.

One other story about a surgeon who one day in the theatre told a nurse to go to the devil. She complained to Matron who asked the surgeon for an explanation; to get the following reply: "It's strange Matron, I told the nurse to go the Devil and she came straight to you."

Another surgeon complained to his anaesthetist "If you can't get the patient to sleep you might at least keep awake yourself."

Following on medicine and surgery, we next turned to gynaecology and obstetrics. Glandular treatment had not yet come into prominence, so gynaecology was mainly a matter of surgery in a new field of action.

Obstetrics were different and offered us new and interesting experiences. It was fascinating to watch the birth of a child and await with anxiety the sound of the first breaths. We learnt how to diagnose possible complications, but in general not how to deal with them, being seldom able to be present at the critical moment. On the other hand, it was exciting when we went on the "District" periods of a week or so when we had to attend and to supervise deliveries in patients' homes.

For this purpose we had to find lodgings within call of the hospital porters, and I found mine in a house, reputedly one of ill repute, across the road from the hospital. It was very ill fitted, to have a bath I had to cross the main road in pyjamas and dressing gown to make use of the hospital baths and facilities.

Work carried on normally, but we were open to being summoned to attend a woman in labour in her home, and this meant collecting any necessary equipment and setting off on foot. This was easy in daylight, but at night it was no joke wandering through badly lit streets with which one was not familiar in some of the worst slums of London, with the added complication that few houses bore numbers and no-one was about to help me find my way in the dark. On the first occasion or so I felt extremely nervous wandering about in the dark, but then got used to things. Although it was always with relief that I finally reached my destination. (In actual fact, I do not think that anyone on this duty had ever been molested).

The majority of houses were small with ill-lit rooms, and in one I would find the good lady lying on the bed under the care of the local Mrs Gamp, an unqualified, usually elderly lady, who greatly took after the Dickens original.

The first task was to persuade the baby to appear, and in this the Gamp was expert at stimulating the mother to activity, while I added a periodic encouraging word. Once arrived and found to be breathing, the baby was washed and put aside, and tea arrived to be accompanied by gossip. This I enjoyed as most Gamps had a good fund of stories – not always Drawing Room.

So back to the Hospital, this time happy in that events had proved successful. Hitherto, in Hospital I had met men and women of all types, but midwifery gave me the first opportunity to see how people lived in their own homes, and to come into contact with real poverty.

During all this time I had been attending courses in the other Hospital departments to learn all about eyes and ear, nose and throat, to give anaesthetics and other aspects of necessary knowledge. Then came the final exams. I took two lots, firstly the "conjoint", which allowed me to qualify in medicine with the letters MRCS, LRCP (Member of the Royal College of Surgeons) and Licentiate of that of Physicians. At the same time I passed the Cambridge exams in Surgery and Midwifery and subsequently in medicine (MB, B.CH, Cantab). Thus, thankfully I was now able to give up studying for exams.

CHAPTER IV

Life in London

I settled down to life in London very comfortably, delighted to be now completely free to do as I wanted. It is true I had to work hard at Hospital, with no chance of an extended holiday, but, on the other hand, had every opportunity to develop my tasks.

I eventually settled in a room situated some 200 yards from the Queen's Hall, in those days the principal concert hall of the day. Its proximity to my room proved ideal for it allowed me to drop in as and when I liked, making up for the cost with a very cheap supper. Here, I was able to hear all the great soloists of the moment and listen to conductors such as Toscannini and Beecham, while the Promenade concerts were still in the hands of Sir Henry Woods.

Attendances at the opera were few – too expensive – but I did sit through the Ring, Tristan, the Mastersingers and Parsifal. Wagner I could not resist. I also loved the music hall and attended a number of these in Central London and the Metropolitan, the Canterbury and Collins in Islington. This love brought me one enormous benefit. In those early days the Diaghileff Ballet used to appear as a turn on the stage at the Alhambra and this led to a great love for the art. I cannot remember whether I saw Nijinsky, but I certainly have happy memories of Lopokova in the Boutique Fantasque. Otherwise, in my lunch hour I often attended lunchtime lectures at the National Gallery and supplemented these with visits to any current exhibition of note.

In Istanbul, Mother had acquired some pottery dishes which were locally listed as Marseilles ware. Seeing an example in the window of an antiques shop near the British Museum I asked about this ware, to be told it wasn't Marseilles but Italian. I became very friendly with Mr Fenouil the dealer, and he set me on the way to collecting French faience and in general to be interested in "antiques". A great and most loveable man. At the same time there were books and London was in those days a haven for second-hand book shops. So in one way or another I was kept busy, spending weekends with friends and relations outside London whenever possible.

Alone, as I was, meeting people in London was also very good for me, allowing me to spend a pleasant social life. During this period, I fell in with an Armenian family, the Gulbenkians, who became great friends. In this period London was a much quieter city. With far less traffic on the road walking was a great pleasure and so I covered areas of the town on foot. I loved London and in it found a huge variety of interests, which have persisted.

CHAPTER V

Holidays

From the date of my arrival in England in 1918 until I settled in practice in 1934, I never had a fixed home, and in the intervals of working or studying I had a peripatetic existence, always in doubt as to where or how to spend my holidays.

Early on, Mother's brother Uncle Jim had invited me to stay with him and his family. From the first moment no-one could have shown me more kindness than he and Aunt Ethel. At the time of my first visit, Uncle was working in Hull, living in the small village of Elloughton, some seven miles out of town and some one or two miles from the nearest railway station, from which on my first visit, on a wet night I was driven to the house in a horse-drawn cab.

The house at the moment of my arrival was in a state of turmoil as one of the boys had dropped a number of shoes into the rainwater butt standing outside the front door. This state of affairs did not interfere with my welcome from all the family – Uncle, Aunty and children, Yole, Dick, Donald and Wendy.

The house, which stood in a large garden, was lit by oil lamps and candles and heated by open fires, with a long passage leading to an 'earth closet' liable to be invaded by chickens. Every evening an array of candles stood on a chest in the hall to light us all to bed. I soon felt at home with both Aunty and Uncle proving kindness itself, giving me a whiff of home life. Uncle was a most attractive character and I soon fell under his spell, while Aunty, typically English, showed her feelings less openly, being reserved.

In the past, Uncle, as a young man who had not yet made his mark in life, had fallen in love with Ethel, the daughter of a very wealthy family. In view of this disparity in circumstances he kept quiet until one day he was summoned by the father to explain his attitude. Uncle confessed to being in love but that in view of his financial circumstances, he felt he had no right to propose. To this the father replied that Uncle was exactly the sort of young man he would like his daughter to marry, and told him to get on with things.

We youngsters amused ourselves in a variety of ways, I learning how to ride a bicycle. Of an evening Aunty would sing to us – she had a lovely voice, while on other occasions we would play family bridge. On occasion Uncle would invite two of his men friends to a game with me as his partner. Such evenings were enjoyable but also frightening for I was still unskilled. Stakes were high and with Uncle taking over my financial obligations I was nervous of making mistakes. But on one occasion I triumphed. I had made a doubtful high call, which was doubled, with high side stakes also involved, so it was with relief that I made my contract.

Uncle Jim's taste in reading was confined to the wild west, but one day he returned from the office delighted over having found a rather funny book, this being "Piccadilly Jim" by one PG Wodehouse – and so to him I am indebted for one of the joys of life.

Here I met a Mr le Bailly, an old friend from Smyrna who periodically arrived to escape the disciplines imposed on him by the nurse he subsequently married and to enjoy his whisky and bridge. Uncle Donald was another visitor and on one occasion he took to his bed, acting as though he were dying and creating an awful fuss. One morning breakfast was served to him in bed when suddenly there was the most appalling clamour, not at all in keeping with a dying man, for on uncovering the dish he found the plate to be full of earthworms wriggling about.

In after years the family moved to Berkhamsted and here Aunty fell desperately ill, to be bedridden for close on six months. Uncle nursed her devotedly but on her recovery he died and she survived him for years.

During Aunty's illness I naturally never stayed at the house and as I grew older my visits became fewer and fewer, until the family moved to the Sussex coast after which I only saw them occasionally. During these years in Hull a fifth member of the family, Ian, was born. In these early years, Uncle and Aunty took the place of parents, in the knowledge that I could rely on them for help should I ever need such. This reassurance greatly helped me. A strange family who were always delighted to see me in person, but otherwise totally forgot me. Thus when Aunty died, no-one let me know, and it was only as a result of seeing a death notice in the newspaper that I was able to attend her funeral.

Another favourite holiday resort was the village of Blakeney in Gloucestershire, where the vicar's wife (Louisa Allen) had been born a Whittall to be generally known as 'Aunt Lou'. The vicarage was large and during school holidays, Aunt Lou used to take in expatriate children from Turkey, up to 10 or

12 in number, all of them relations in one way or another. Osie and I, however, took rooms in the village, in a house in which the loo lay at the bottom of the garden while we took our baths in a tub in front of the sitting room fire – a most admirable arrangement. Aunt Lou made all inmates work, the boys in the garden, the girls in the house, never hesitating to upbraid if necessary, but at the same time, she was kindness personified, and we all loved her.

By and large, so long as Uncle Reggie was left in peace, all could do as they wanted, and with the Severn River on one side and the forest of Dean on the other there was plenty of scope. The nearest cinema was three miles away and to attend entailed a three mile walk each way.

My cousin Winnie Whittall spent one holiday there, very proud of her legs, always encased in the best of silk stockings to annoy all. So one day, on a paper chase she was enticed onto a lovely looking green patch to sink up to her knees in mud. Everyone was delighted as she returned home with her legs and silk stockings covered in mud. Winnie was no country girl.

Osie and I both loved these stays in Blakeney and this was largely because of Aunt Lou, whom we all loved. She and Uncle Reggie had had a hard life in that their youngest son had died at the age of 14, while their daughter, Enid was in the process of going blind, to have only one normal son in Roland, who was in the Navy.

Aunt Lou made a most unlikely clergyman's wife, being lively and outspoken with somewhat brusque and loud manners, in contrast to Uncle Reggie's quiet and retiring disposition. She got on well in the parish largely on account of her great kindness and spirit of help. She was wise enough when really angry with any of us to berate us in Greek, which enabled her to be as outspoken as she liked. On one occasion she accused us of not doing anything for the Church, and this induced us to write and act a play which was presented to the villagers with great success.

Christmas holidays were always spent with my sister Edna and her husband Charles Strafford who always made us welcome and could not have been kinder. Staying with them was always a joy, but such holidays in England were not to be compared with those spent at home in Turkey in the summer.

We always travelled out in parties of seven to ten in number in the early days by sea from Marseilles or Trieste, the journey taking up to a week but with the wonderful sight as we approached Constantinople by sea. Later the Orient

Express took over, the journey only taking three days. It was wonderful to be at home again with Father and Mother and in the midst of all our relatives, and to enjoy the bathing, sailing, fishing, shooting and tennis. It was hard only to see parents for six or seven weeks a year, but this led to independence and to learning how to care for oneself.

Once Osie had left England I had to arrange my own holidays, the first of which I spent my time in Provence. On another occasion, on my way to Turkey, I took a trip by boat up the Rhine and then found my way to Constanza on the Black Sea in Romania, where I was so broke that I had to travel steerage and sleep on the deck of the boat to Constantinople. At some time I had picked up a book called "The Happy Traveller", in which the author described walking holidays in various parts of Europe. This inspired me, and in the company of a friend or friends, we in turn covered the Auvergne, Brittany, Savoy, Provence, the Ardennes and the Rhine.

On such occasions I carried my necessities on my back and we generally covered some 15 to 20 miles a day, spending nights in small village inns – a fortnight at a time on these occasions. I was the linguist, except in Brittany where Welsh speaking Dave was at home with the Breton language. We mostly stuck to country roads which in those days were car free. Sadly, after leaving Cambridge such trips had to be abandoned – in the interest of work.

Part VII

MEDICAL LIFE

CHAPTER I

Hospital Intern 1930 – 1931

To my great relief I finally passed all my exams to become qualified for medicine in January 1930, but my joy was tinged with sorrow over not being able to pass the good news to Father, who had sadly died a couple of months previously. In ignorance of Mother's financial future, I was glad to be potentially independent of the family and this led me to reconsider my future. Hitherto I had always wanted to specialise in the diseases of children, but to do so would have required several more years of study and exams and also some financial assistance.

On the other hand I had begun to doubt my abilities in this direction and the prospect of more study and exams over several years was not pleasing. In the end I decided to enter General Practice, a decision which offered me immediate freedom. After qualification, the normal custom was to gain experience by working in a hospital as a junior and this was the course I took up.

In those days the majority of hospitals were "voluntary", independent of state control, but with strong local connections and with most of their income arising from voluntary donations. Medically these were staffed by a number of consultants who received no pay for their work and by a number of resident junior doctors, who were given free board and lodging and free laundry in the hospital as well as a salary of about £150 a year. Each post lasted six months, with no provision for annual paid leave. I worked in three hospitals, in posts dealing with the diseases of women, medicine and with surgery.

We junior doctors – or Housemen as we were called – lived in the hospital building in separate bedrooms, with a common mess, supervised in general by a friendly and helpful lady. In my experience food was good and plentiful, enlivened at Reading by the free supply of beer donated by a kindly brewery. Each of us Housemen was officially entitled to a weekly half day and alternate Sundays off duty, but otherwise was expected to be available for 24 hours a day – absences were condoned provided we left a colleague on duty in our stead. In this way it was always possible to get away of an evening.

My first hospital was the Grosvenor Hospital for Women, situated in Vincent Square in Westminster. Here I was the sole resident, but the work was light and enabled me comfortably to settle down to my new life, which mainly consisted of ward rounds in the morning during which all patients were seen and assisting in the operating theatre in the afternoon. Each surgeon had his own way of doing things and to each of these I had to grow accustomed. At the same time I was often called upon to give anaesthetics, which enabled me to become up to date with modern methods.

While at the Grosvenor Hospital, one of the surgeons used to take me out to give anaesthetics at home confinements and operations. I never knew the character of these at the time but now, with more experience, I realise that they involved illegal abortions. But I was ignorant and paid five guineas a time – a real fortune. Through this surgeon I came into contact with several members of the Meyrick family, whose mother ran the most notorious night club in London at 43 Gerrard Street. On one occasion I assisted at an operation on the youngest of her four daughters. A lovely girl, whose insides were in a tragic state as a result of previous interventions.

My stay at the Grosvenor Hospital was intellectually not very educational, but it put me into the right way of hospital requirements.

My next move took me to the Miller General Hospital in Greenwich as House Physician (HP), and here I came properly under fire as I was kept fully occupied, serving under four consultants, two purely medical, one in charge of psychological and one of venereal diseases. These two latter had beds, but I had to attend their out-patients clinics. One of the medical consultants was an elderly gentleman of great repute and of vast knowledge, though what I chiefly remember about him was the firm but inevitably courteous manner in which he handled his patients, setting me an example which I tried to follow in later life. His colleague was younger and ambitious to make a name for himself, but, more importantly from my point of view, he was an excellent teacher, a man to whom I owe a great deal. All in all I was kept fully occupied, for which I was glad as I was busy learning.

I also received great help in the preparation of the thesis required for my Cambridge degree and with this accepted I was able to put the following string of letters after my name, BA, MRCS, LRCP, MB, Bch.

Medical techniques were still primitive and to illustrate this point, blood for transfusions did not come in sealed bottles, but was directly drawn from a matched donor, lying on one bed, to be immediately injected by me into the vein of the recipient on an adjacent bed. Disposable syringes and needles were unheard of. The training of nurses was also restricted, many of the tasks which fall to their lot today, such as the taking of blood pressure and blood samples, fell to the lot of the House Doctors.

My great friend was the Sister of the women's ward, with whom I took to having coffee of a morning whenever possible. She was an Irish girl – as were so many of the nurses in those days. Lily Miller by name, she was great fun, and an excellent ward Sister. I have often wondered how the world treated her in later life – she deserved the best.

One of my patients was a girl suffering from tuberculosis and she slept each night on an iron framed balcony. From time to time she shot a high temperature of a morning. At one time I had under my care both the manager of the local Music Hall and the licensee of the pub across the road – so I was thereafter catered for.

I thoroughly enjoyed my stay at the Miller, in part because I was fully occupied and learning. Life in the mess was friendly and lively and the whole atmosphere of the hospital was warm, friendly and highly efficient, this latter because Matron had been trained at St Thomas' under Miss Lloyd Still. The nursing was excellent and relations between House staff and nurses were friendly and co-operative. On my night rounds, the night staff and I often joined in a chat.

On one occasion, when on casualty duty, I was woken up to see a man suffering from a dental abscess. A huge man to whom I explained that this was really a dentist's job, that I was not a skilled hand and that there was no question of an anaesthetic, but that if he liked I would have a go at extracting the tooth. I set about things feeling highly nervous, for one sweep of the man's arm would have swept me sideways. But luck was on my side, the tooth came out easily, and with all pain gone, the man shook my hand, and putting some money in the box, left.

Circumstances were different in those days and to illustrate this, one of the surgeons always insisted on being served with chicken on his Wednesday attendance, and how we enjoyed this, for chicken in those days was a luxury.

One day on arrival at breakfast we found an ex-Houseman, one O'Toole sitting at table clad in full morning dress. In explanation he told us that he had been to a wedding in Dublin on the preceding day and had woken up to find himself in London remembering nothing as to how he got here.

Life in my next hospital, the Royal Berkshire at Reading, was not so agreeable, as, though the work was well up to standard and life in the mess most enjoyable, my Chief was unsympathetic, made no attempt at teaching and even never paid me the customary guinea for assisting at operations on paying patients. But the work was first class, by reason of the number of acute emergencies admitted, giving me a good experience in the diagnosis and treatment of acute abdominal and other conditions. True, I did not take to surgery as a career, but my hands were kept beautifully clean as a result of the intensive washing required in the theatre.

One other practical lesson I learnt was never to do a service for a lawyer without being paid in advance – for those who took up accident work were all unreliable. While here, the renowned aeronaut Douglas Bader was admitted after his crash.

I also learnt how to drive a motor car and enjoyed long walks on the Downs, as well the five shilling cheap evening return trips to London. But our main evening entertainment when on duty was to cross the road to the Royal Berkshire Arms to play shove-half-penny under the eye of Horace, the landlord. And so I ended my life in hospitals and now was considered capable of facing up to life in earnest.

CHAPTER II

Locums 1932 – 1934

After 18 months I felt that I had had enough of hospital life, and had learnt enough to enable me to embark on an independent career. But with only a few savings in my pocket I had to face up to the immediate need of keeping alive. Two alternatives presented themselves; one being to act as assistant to a doctor or doctors, which involved being tied down, or alternatively, to earn my living by doing locums, i.e. acting as substitute to doctors, ill or on holiday. I decided on this latter, as it offered freedom after years of being tied down by studies.

In consequence I applied to the Bovril Medical Agency for a job and there met Miss Thew, the lady in charge, who was to become a very good friend. I was almost immediately offered a post in the wilds of Essex, to be met on a very wet night by the doctor at the station, to be driven into remote country. Here, as we got out of the car, the doctor asked me if I liked pigeons, to which I, cold, wet and hungry and scenting pigeon pie, replied "yes". However, instead of being led into the house, I was taken into the garden to view a large number of carrier pigeons and to discourse on their respective virtues. I politely showed every interest but was glad to be led indoors. Later at midnight I was woken when every one of the Doctor's collection of clocks struck the hour of midnight.

The practice was set in flat, low-lying and featureless country, bordering on the sea. It was old-fashioned, as was the Doctor in his ways and methods, but, for the first time in my medical life, I was called on to accept full responsibility in my work. I was amused when visiting an elderly couple, I saw to the wife's needs but on asking about the old man was told that there was no point in seeing to the old man as he was "in decay". Pay was at the rate of eight guineas a week, with board and lodging and car either provided or expenses paid, profitable when, as in this type of country, there was nothing to spend money on. A good report on my work must have been sent, for on my return to London I was immediately offered further work.

My next job took me to Lowestoft where the bachelor doctor was lying in bed puzzling over which abdominal disease he was suffering from. He was looked after by his aged mother, a missionary's widow, who anathematised the theatre and the cinema but who proved to be a superb cook, especially of Indian food. Here a lot of my work took me among fishermen, which was interesting and I stayed on until the doctor "recovered", an occasion marked by a superb and highly indigestible feast, not at all compatible with his recent illness.

And so my work carried me to all parts of the country and led me to meet men and women of all conditions and from all walks of life. In addition I also worked in mental hospitals, a prison, a workhouse and a municipal hospital over the next two years – an invaluable experience. In this way life was interesting as with every new job I never knew what to expect. Thus in one practice I had to ask for clean bed linen as that offered me was very dirty and had clearly been in use for some time, while on other occasions I lived in comparative luxury. The worst practice I came across was in Wimbledon. In this there was no provision for full examination – patients standing on one side of a counter with the doctor on the other. In addition there was a totally inadequate supply of medicines for the dispensary, the most important being a bottle of dark brown burnt sugar, which made the medicine dispersed darker in colour, rendering it stronger. In addition I was instructed never to let go of a bottle of medicine until I had received payment. How patients survived astonished me.

In some other practices facilities for full examination were missing and I remember one in which the consultation room was too small to hold a couch, while in another the couch was covered by a mass of unopened copies of the British Medical Journal. But these were the exceptions.

The amount of work and the hours of work on any particular job varied with the locality and other factors. In Dagenham, for example, it was not uncommon to find patients standing in the street as the waiting room was already full. Under such circumstances it was necessary to work fast and this could result in the danger of allowing a more serious case to slip through one's hands.

On the other hand there were more amusing aspects. On one occasion, on arrival, I was shown a largish cupboard full of bottles, with the Doctor telling me to help myself and if I ran out of liquor to order more. I told him that it would take two years for me get through that lot, at which point he apologised and said that he preferred his locums to get drunk on the premises rather than in the pub.

In the meantime I had bought a car, a second-hand two seater for £40, this allowing me greater freedom. It ran well and allowed me to get about at an average speed of 25mph.

I spent some months in Huddersfield in place of a doctor who was slowly dying. The town had very little to offer except for a superb railway station and the surrounding moors. It afforded me my first experience of Yorkshire outspokenness, which startled me at first, but to which I soon became accustomed and to respond in kind. The practice was beautifully run and I was driven about in the doctor's car by a chauffeur, who most usefully advised me about the patient I was going to see. But the Great Depression of the thirties was raging and poverty and hardship were extreme – so much so that a man was employed to go round and collect sixpence a week off patients' bills. In one very distressed flat, I came across a man with a very badly set leg. On asking him about this he told me that he had had an accident when working in Smyrna. On discharge from hospital he found himself destitute and so unable to return to England. But at this point a kindly English gentleman had stepped in and in addition to relieving his distress, had paid for his return home by ship. I was not surprised to hear that this man was my grandfather, but in a way this family connection made me more sensitive to the local conditions.

I was called one day to see a lady suffering from a digestive complaint, one which she experienced whenever she ate a certain food. I gave the necessary treatment, and advised her not to take any more of that food. A few days later I was summoned again, to hear the same story and this time told her not to be a fool but to follow my advice – to this she flared up telling me that I was a damned bad doctor and that she did not want to see any more of me. Nevertheless, some days later I was summoned again, but this time after midnight, after a heavy snowfall. Had she been my patient I would have refused to go out, but I was employed by the doctor so was obliged to do so. She lived up a hill and with the snow a car was out of the question and so I embarked on the 20 minute walk to arrive and hear the same story. I said nothing except for "Last time I was here you said I was a damned bad doctor, so why did you send for me?" The reply came, "You see doctor, I know that you are damned bad doctor, but you are better than the others in the neighbourhood." In response all I could do was to burst out laughing and demand a cup of tea, over which we held a happy conversation.

Another encounter ended not so well. Talking at one house, I was asked if I liked eating tripe and thinking of tripes a la mode de Caen or Turkish tripe soup, I inadvertently said "yes". Following this, on my next visit I was proudly presented with a plate, on which lay a large piece of cold, boiled tripe – and also with a bottle of vinegar – and this I had to eat to my disgust, but to everyone else's satisfaction.

A practice in the Sussex countryside offered me very comfortable conditions of work and in the early summer was very enjoyable. One night however, I was woken by the sound of bump – bump – bump – followed by a wail. Getting up I found that the domestic bulldog had fallen down the back stairs, at the bottom of which he was lying. He had never approved of me and so I approached him with caution, but he allowed me to examine him for a possible broken bone. Once having done so, I did my best to console him by making a fuss of him. He appreciated this and eventually I got him to his bed and from then on we were the best of friends. One of my charges in this practice was a convent, but fortunately I only had to attend once and that was to the kitchen which smelt strongly of onions, also one of the nuns was quite a tyrant.

During this period of life I had no fixed home and nowhere to house my belongings. Here K.P. Gulbenkian came to my aid, for he had a spare room in his flat which was put at my disposal. We had great times together, and I remember going to Portobello Market on Saturday evenings to buy our Sunday lunch at greatly reduced prices, eg. half a crown – thirty pence – for a leg of lamb – refrigeration not being fully developed.

CHAPTER III

Life in General Practice

The experience I had gained in the course of doing locums had clarified my mind as to the type of practice which would best suit me. So when the moment came in 1933 that I felt it was time I settled down, I approached my old friend Miss Thew at the Bovril Agency and told her of my requirements. These were simple, for I had no ambition to make much money and was only desirous of earning a comfortable living which would in due course allow me to support a future family in reasonable ease. As to the practice I wanted this to be mixed, covering patients of all classes and of all degrees of wealth and to be situated within easy reach of friends and family in London as well as open country.

Miss Thew brought forward details of a prospective partnership in North London. This I proceeded to visit and finding both Doctor and conditions to my liking, I agreed to enter on a three months trial assistantship, at the end of which we decided to enter into partnership.

Dr. Gleed had set up his plate (squatted as it was known then) in this area a good number of years previously and was now finding the practice too large for him to manage on his own. He turned out to be a hard-working, straightforward and conscientious person, whose ideas largely coincided with mine and whom I personally liked, all of which made my decision easy.

He was offering me a third share with an option to buy a further twelfth in 3 year's time, at a purchase price of two years income, which meant that I had to find £2,400 to pay for my gross income of £1,200. In addition to this payment I would also have to buy a house. The money for the practice I borrowed from an Insurance Company, on the security of a 20 year endowment policy and for the house I had recourse to a Building Society. Fortunately I had made some savings and with these and the aid of a loan from my family I was able to pay the necessary deposits, leaving enough in hand to set me up in a house, fully furnished and equipped with all medical necessities. I settled on a three up two down small semi-detached house, with a garage and garden in a quiet area, No. 243 Nether

Street. The two rooms downstairs were fitted up as a surgery and dining-waiting room, while upstairs I had bedroom and sitting room with a second room for a proposed male servant. Furnishing the house was a pleasure, with my tastes running to the antique. Luckily I found a dealer who understood my position and found what I needed at a price which satisfied both my tastes and my pocket. (It would have cost just as much to furnish in modern style). Fortunately I already owned a car.

How to find a servant was likely to prove a problem, but I was lucky, for sitting in KP's office one day, a young Anglo-Canadian on his beam-ends came in. He had no domestic experience and no references to offer, but I liked the look of him and offered him the job, at which he jumped. He proved a great success and was honest and satisfactory in his relations with patients. We got on well together and remained in contact until he died in Australia.

So I moved into my house, and how delighted I was for the first time since the age of 12 to have somewhere I could call home and to be able to live among all my books and belongings. Over all the preceding years, with my parents living abroad, I had had to live out of my suitcases. George King turned out to be quite a good cook, so that side of life was all right. There had always to be someone in the house to take messages when both King and I were out and I was lucky in finding two girls willing to sit in for this purpose.

The practice comprised three main groups of patients whom for brevity's sake we referred to as Private, Panel and Parish, with the main bulk attending surgery at my partner's house on the main road. The Panel consisted of all those insured under the National Health Act of 1911 (the Lloyd George as some people still called it) and these received treatment free of charge with medicine on prescription, with us being paid for their care on a capitation basis. Private patients paid for their treatment and these included the families of those insured. Our fees for seeing them started at a minimum of 5 shillings for a visit and three and sixpence for a consultation inclusive of medicine, which we dispensed. Parish patients comprised all those who were too poor to pay for medical attention and were not insured, these came under the care of National Assistance and we took charge of all such in the area in return for a small salary, dispensing any necessary medicine.

Other sources of income arose from charges for certificates, vaccinations, insurance examinations, dental gases and from anaesthetics or attendance on operations on private patients.

The main surgeries at Dr. Gleed's house were held for an hour each morning and evening every weekday. It fell to my lot to take those on Monday, Wednesday and Friday mornings and Tuesday, Thursday and Saturday evenings, which blighted all hopes of a weekend off. But in return on Wednesday I was free after having done any necessary visits and Monday and Friday I was likewise free from about five o'clock onwards. We took alternate Sundays off and four weeks holiday every year. Hitherto in my working life I had never enjoyed having weekends off, and I cannot say that this matter worried me in any way and in fact very few Doctors of that era were able to indulge in such luxuries.

I enjoyed the work and got on well with patients, this in particular because many of them had survived from the days when Finchley was still a country village. In addition, as the junior partner I tended to look after those in the locality who were too poor to pay for treatment. In this way a considerable number of old people came under my care. I liked them and it came as a privilege to be able to help people reduced to this pattern of life in their old age.

In due course patients came to see me at my house to form a small local clientele, most of whom were new to the practice. With everything running smoothly I added to the household with the purchase of a black cocker spaniel puppy, a scion of the great Whoopee of Ware, and he, whom I called Dan, took me out for daily walks in the nearby fields.

The house had a small garden which I found to be in a mess. My mother was an expert gardener, but I was totally ignorant of the art and so on my rounds I sought advice of all who showed evidence of knowledge. This, in the manner of the great majority of gardeners, was freely given together with presents of plants and cuttings. In this way I became initiated into a lifelong hobby and pleasure.

So with a steady and interesting job, and a home of my own and a dog and garden, I was fully satisfied with life. Then two years later I married, to my great happiness and to my family's satisfaction, but not to that of Dan and King, the former jealous of anyone sharing my affection and the latter not desirous of working under a woman.

So Barbara and I underwent changes in our lives, changes which were easier for me to bear, as I was nothing but a gainer, whereas Barbara found difficulty in settling down to be a Doctor's wife with constant interruptions from telephone and door, restrictions on her freedom of movement and the irregularities of my engagements. I had warned her that in my life the requirements of patients took precedence of all else. This she found particularly hard to bear, especially when some much looked forward to date had to be scrapped. On the other hand she had a husband who was not away at the office all day, but one who tended to drop into the house at any odd moment and was always home for meals. She did not take long to accept the situation to become an invaluable helpmate whom the patients greatly liked.

The next phase covered her pregnancy, Maya being born in 1937. Her arrival was greeted with delight, although attended by complications, as we had to find room both for her and all the necessary paraphernalia in our already cramped quarters. But we managed successfully until some months after Maya's arrival, Barbara announced she was pregnant once more. This necessitated finding a larger house, which led to a move to 1 Finchley Way, a detached house with four bedrooms and ample rooms downstairs for private and professional purposes.

Then followed the so-called phoney war with its attendant anxieties and it was by way of a relief when war actually did start and we knew where we stood. This first winter of the war was one of the coldest winters on record in the course of which the snow, ice, blackouts and the reduced visibility from masked headlights made car driving in the dark very difficult and potentially dangerous. Fortunately patients realised our difficulties and calls for visits after dark were reduced to a very great degree. One further advantage was that in their anxiety over the war, many people lost their own personal anxieties. One lady who had been a regular customer volunteered as an Air Raid Warden and did extremely well.

All went well until my partner suffered a slight stroke and I was left to carry on alone. While so doing I received my Army call up papers. I was given a month's grace in view of Dr. Gleed's condition, at the end of which he was able to return to work and I set off to a new career, having decided with Dr. Gleed that the best solution to the financial problem would be for me to have my pay paid into the practice account.

The next five years were spent in comfort by me in the army, enjoying plenty of good food, but Barbara experienced a hard time. She decided to stay on in our house for a variety of reasons, of which the main one was that she did not wish to be separated from friends and relations, the other that, wherever I might be posted, when on leave she would be much more accessible in London than in the provinces. And so I set off on a preliminary training course after which I was posted to Cardiff. Then, after several months I was posted abroad and returned home for a fortnight's leave. I had remained anxious over how my partner was coping on his own and was relieved to hear that he was managing satisfactorily. (In retrospect I feel that those Doctors who 'stayed behind' probably led a far harder life than those of us in the Services). As for Barbara she was coping satisfactorily with the aid of food parcels from America and the kind help of local shop-keepers who were very good to her as a mother with two small children.

So I set off for Africa in 1942, to hear, soon after my arrival, that Barbara was pregnant once more. What with worrying over her safety and over how she was managing, it was an immense relief to hear that Michael had arrived on the scene. It was only later that I heard that to her great joy and relief her Doctor had somehow managed to escape from his Army duties to deliver him. But, although I was sent photos, I was not to see Michael until he was three and a half years old.

On my return home after four years absence I found everyone in the best of form, with the only note of sadness arising from the death of my dog Dan. During my time abroad I had only enjoyed a fortnight's leave, and so it was blissful to be allowed to settle down to the family again.

I found my partner suffering from wear and tear after his years of running the practice on his own and so, after a short refresher course, necessary after having only looked after fit men for the past four years, I was glad to settle down back to work, pulling my weight and relieving Dr. Gleed of some of his load.

My only anxiety was over finance. During the war what with movements of patients, Dr. Gleed's ill-health and other factors, practice takings had fallen very considerably, while against this family expenses had increased. I found myself without sufficient money to buy a car, an absolute necessity in view of the scattered nature of the practice. I worried and worried as to how I was going to manage, when suddenly, out of the blue, a cheque arrived from my ever-generous Mother to solve the problem. Slowly things began to improve as patients returned to the practice and its numbers increased, but nevertheless I had to sell my beloved French porcelain collection in order to ease family finances. (This had been deposited for safety's sake with an Aunt of mine living in the country to escape damage, however, a bomb fell on her front lawn.)

Life carried on quietly and uneventfully, with me working harder and harder, until our Doctor advised that John, in view of a nervous state, probably resulting from the war, had better be sent to boarding school in the country. This of course proved a considerable financial set-back, but fortunately, at this moment, a friend offered me the opportunity of doing German-English translations for a large pharmaceutical firm. This I immediately accepted to my great interest, the advantage of my pocket and my knowledge of German.

Troubles only proved temporary and with a steady increase in the practice I found myself able to cope with the increasing cost of the children's education. Then Dr. Gleed's health began to give concern again and this set me to think of the future, for my present premises were too small to allow any adaptation. So, after much consideration I decided that my best solution would lie in buying a larger house and this I set about trying to find. As luck would have it, at this moment a friend decided to sell his house. I bought it with an eye to the future, being large enough to serve a large practice.

Meanwhile much discussion was going on over the question of a National Health Service, to which many of my colleagues were opposed. For my part I was in favour of it for a variety of reasons. On the practical side there would be no more dispensing and sending out of bills, many of which were never paid. More importantly, however, such a Service would do away with all financial considerations between Doctor and Patient. This would allow me fuller freedom in that I would be free to visit and treat in whatever way I felt necessary without any worries over whether the patient could afford to pay or not; this also applied to the prescription of drugs. I felt that such a Service would allow me far more liberty in the handling of patients, but of course while this might apply in my practice, it might not in others.

My feelings on the subject were strengthened when, at a meeting which both Barbara and I attended, we had the opportunity to talk to both Aneurin Bevan and to Charles Hill, the then Chairman of the B.M.A.. From these short conversations we came away greatly impressed by the former and distrustful of the latter.

With the introduction of the N.H.S. now a certainty, Dr. Gleed suggested introducing his daughter into the practice, a newly qualified girl, of very short stature, who, to my mind, would not be able to stand up to really hard work. In view of this factor and of Dr. Gleed's ill-health, I said I would only agree to the proposition on consideration of a half share in the takings. To this Dr. Gleed would not agree and so we decided to break up the partnership as from the start of the N.H.S. I was upset over things having come to this pass, for the two of us had always got on well, but I was not prepared to sacrifice the family.

In due course, everyone in the country was given the option of signing up with the Doctor of his or her choice, while I sat back anxiously wondering how things would turn out for me in the way of sufficient numbers opting for me to give me a reasonable living. As it turned out my fears proved groundless and on the appointed day I started on my own with enough on my hands to keep me busy. From this point on I had no further financial worries – in fact I was even able to start saving. Numbers on my list soon reached the maximum allowed of 3,000 and from now on I had to refuse further applicants. This led to my financial position at last coming under control, enabling me to spend more on the children's education. I was further helped by the Government repaying me the original cost of the practice when I joined it in the thirties.

I was now in a position to run things according to my own lights. The first of these was to engage a proper firm of accountants, being fed up with the man Dr. Gleed employed, whom I found generally unsatisfactory. With all records cards now in my possession, I became able to keep proper records of all visits and consultations, to take pertinent cards with me on my visits and make full entries at the moment of seeing the patient. I also introduced cards for private patients, something the practice had never indulged in.

The number of patients opting to remain private was small and I cannot say that this worried me. Some came to me for advice on what to do, with these all I could do was to point out advantages and disadvantages and leave the final decision to them. In the case of those, such as diabetics, suffering from long-term conditions requiring expensive therapy and in others in which I knew the family conditions well, I was able to stress the advantages of the N.H.S. more strongly. In retrospect I hope that my advice was unbiased. Some annoyed me in wanting to enjoy all the benefits of the N.H.S. while at the same time have those accruing to private patients. "If we join, Doctor, I know you will appreciate that I and my wife could not be expected to attend surgery." These were disappointed.

Seeing private patients carried the advantage of keeping me in mind of standards of care and approach to which, in my heart of hearts, all patients, whatever their backgrounds, were entitled.

Barbara had now to face up to the full impact of patients phoning and arriving at the door at all times of the day. When I was in the house this did not affect her too much. During surgeries the front door was left open for patients to walk in and out, and at such times I always answered the phone, for, in spite of this at times proving tiresome, I preferred to keep in direct touch with people either to give advice (which might avoid the need for a visit) or to determine how urgent it was for me to attend. Later I engaged a retired nurse to help out and to relieve Barbara of a morning. I cannot claim that she was overworked but her presence proved a great help both to me and to Barbara. (Incidentally surgeries were held from 9-10 of a morning and 6-7 on all evenings except Wednesday.)

Domestically our Irish Nanny was still with us but for further staff we employed Swiss and German girls, who all proved eminently satisfactory; learnt to speak English well, all staying with us for two years and, flatteringly, still keep in touch. For holidays I employed a locum. On other occasions I tried to keep on the phone, while otherwise Dr. Gleed, with whom I remained on excellent terms, was always ready to help out.

And so the years passed with me working too hard, becoming difficult about the house and probably also in the practice, without, as is so often the case under similar circumstances, my realising the position and pooh-poohing any suggestion to that effect. And then one day I heard our daughter asking her Mother: "Is Daddy in a good temper because I want to ask him something?" and this made me realise that something was wrong when the children regarded me in this light. So, I talked things over with Barbara, who did not mince her words, telling me that I was becoming impossible to live with. In consequence of this I decided to take on a partner.

And so Donald entered into our lives. I could not but compare the ease with which he entered into General Practice compared to the difficulties I had experienced, although there was a difference in his having private means which enabled him to buy a large house straight away. As to experience, he had dabbled in psychiatry but had had none of General Practice. His arrival on the scene immediately eased my life by taking over half the surgeries and enabling me to enjoy my time off without concern for the patients, although in some ways I worked just as hard in consequence of now having more time to devote to individual patients. But of far greater importance Donald proved to be reliable and knowledgeable in his work, and, though of necessity, my income had fallen greatly, I was initially too happy to worry about this. However, in compensation for this I had expected him to attract more patients to the Practice. This, however, did not occur and I found myself signing on far more new ones than he.

Despite his presence I continued to work very hard and the time came when I had to consider the future. The character of the area in which we were living and working slowly began to change as more and more houses were split into flats and large gardens built over, while at the same time our local friends were tending to move elsewhere. Many of my old patients, who had long lived in the area, were beginning to die off, to be replaced by newcomers with whom I had little sympathy. In consequence Barbara and I were faced with the prospect of living isolated lives, without the usual relay of friends dropping in to the house at all hours, while in my work, I would be occupied with comparative strangers. Apart from this I was beginning to feel tired. This was no doubt largely because I was not too happy about the partnership and such feelings were not helped by a couple of local Doctors falling to coronaries. But I continued to love my work and to get a lot of fun out of my patients.

At the same time a more important problem was being imposed by the children. These were now growing up and, with their local friends disappearing, their social lives were more and more involved in central London, from which they were already finding difficulty in returning at night. At the same time, due to the distance involved, they could not easily entertain their acquaintances at home. This state of affairs led Barbara and me to further consider our future, for it was quite clear to us that the children would leave Finchley to live in London as soon as this became feasible and this would leave the pair of us even more isolated if we stayed where we were. In view of her refugee life Barbara had never enjoyed a permanent and stable home, while I, at the same time, since arriving in England at the age of twelve, had led a hand to mouth existence, either staying with relatives or in rooms and so never able to lay down roots until I settled in practice at the age of 28. In consequence we both felt strongly that we ought to offer our children a stable home and the only way do this would be to settle in inner London.

There was yet one other and equally important consideration, in that I felt that my Barbara deserved a break. She had supported me wholeheartedly in the practice and without complaint ever since our marriage. In this respect her life had not been easy and I now felt she deserved a break.

And so we discussed the situation and decided that a change of life would prove of advantage both to us and especially to the children. Then, as luck would have it, in the midst of our deliberations I heard of a job going at the Ministry of Health and to this I was successful in being appointed. This involved leaving the

Practice to Donald and selling him Cornwall House and also involved a considerable drop in income, but this worried neither of us as we would have a far more congenial life with free weekends and evenings and no night calls. I cannot claim to have been entirely happy over the change in life. My new job, though not without interest, was much more impersonal, but in it I felt somewhat isolated and no longer in the midst of life and its enormously varied pattern.

Today in retrospect it is interesting to look back on the differences in the attitudes of two Doctors separated by experiences in the War and by quite a number of years in age.

With the abolition of the former system of buying one's way into General Practice, D. escaped many of the difficulties which had attended my entry and possessing private means was able to settle straightaway into a comfortable home.

Hitherto he had spent most of his time coping with Service personnel and enjoying regular hours on and off duty. In consequence neither D. nor his wife seemed to be prepared to accept and face up to the rough and tumble of life in the General Practice of those days. They did not take kindly to inconveniences such as uncertain and irregular hours of work. Any interruption in the routine of life they had laid down for themselves, such as a late evening call to visit, was regarded as something closer to a calamity than a mere annoyance or misfortune. Following any such experience, we, at coffee next morning, were exposed to a sad tale of hardship and woe over the brief separation from wife and children that had resulted. This in the face of one who had been separated from his family for four years during the War. Barbara and I felt it to be more politic on such occasions to listen in silence, but, as time went on, we both became more and more irritated.

As time went on he became more reconciled to the state of affairs, but despite previous involvement in psychiatry, he never showed any signs of interest in the persons or circumstances of life of his patients, limiting his attentions to their ailments alone. In consequence he never became acquainted with the backgrounds or motivations of his patients. This indirectly increased his exposure to fatigue and frustration in that a closer knowledge of human beings facilitates intercourse and leads to greater tolerance of their behaviour and misbehaviour.

Whereas in the handling of patients I felt I had the advantage of D., the position was reversed in the sphere of modern therapy in which my innate caution and scepticism held me back. D., however, displayed enormous faith in the curative value of drugs and showed no hesitation or fears over the prescription of modern introductions even in large dosage, proving my fears to be out of place when none of his patients came to any harm. But what horrified me was that he even dosed his small children with phenobarbitone to keep them quiet at night.

Outside these matters D. showed a great interest in current ideas on the modernisation of General Practice, some of which he suggested we apply. To some of these I would not have been averse, but all would have cost more money than our small practice could afford. In those days there was no State assistance. But I did set up an examination room, to find it invaluable, whereas he seldom made use of it.

By and large D. and I got on well together. Despite his presence, however, I had to continue working hard, but what a relief it was to have no anxieties at the back of my mind when enjoying time off. But there was no question of his wife participating in the running of the practice.

In retrospect so many years later, it is interesting how even at the onset of his work in General Practice, D.'s mind was veering in the direction of changes which were to be implemented later. Although the concept of the Family Doctor may have lain dormant in his mind, his basic desire lay along more practical lines and more in the direction of a job, entailing fixed hours of work with a minimum of domestic harassment, ensuring the patient received the best possible treatment, but without the need for any display of human interest in the individual concerned.

Post Script

GWW's new job with the Ministry of Health, whilst not giving him the wide contact with people in all walks of life which General Practice had given him, involved interviewing doctors throughout Southern England and discussing their problems with them. These tended to be prescribing ones but he still dealt with people, albeit mainly doctors. He was offered promotion during the latter part of his career but refused it as it would have entailed being totally office bound. Subsequent to this he was transferred to Reading for the last three years of his career. He was able to arrange that he could continue working after his official retirement on a reducing number of days per week until he reached the age of 75.

JWW 2011

CHAPTER IV

Doctor and Patient

Despite the passage of many years since I left General Practice I often look back on those days with happiness, especially so when my thoughts turn to the many friends I made in the course of work. I was indeed very lucky when I decided on my future career.

Prior to entering General Practice I had led a very privileged life both in the way of family and of education. This left me with no knowledge of those outside my immediate social circle and in total ignorance of the ways and manner of life of the vast majority of people in England. It was not until I started working in hospital that I came into contact with men and women from everyday life. But, even here, such contacts were mainly medically orientated, with those I met outside their normal environment and it was perhaps only in the Casualty Department that I came across life in the raw.

Having spent two years working in hospitals and having neither the desire nor the means to become a specialist, I had to earn my living whilst looking for a General Practice in which to settle. As a temporary measure I took to doing "locums", i.e. standing in for doctors who were either ill or on holiday. This work brought me into contact with all manner of practices, from the best to the worst, and with all types of mankind, from farm workers and country dwellers to fishermen, industrial workers living in depressed areas and to the bulk of what might be classed middle-class Britain.

To begin with I felt very nervous about entering strange houses and having to cope with patients of whose medical background I knew next to nothing and for whom I and I alone, was now totally responsible as well as having to cope with their relations and friends. Gradually, however, matters improved as I found that I liked meeting people and that I was able to get on well with them whatever their background. Of the greatest help were some six weeks which I had to spend in Huddersfield, in Yorkshire, where people are very different from those in the

South. Here manners were very rough and ready and speech very outspoken, quite different from anything I had been hitherto been accustomed to. I soon got used to such ways as I learnt to retort in kind and finally felt flattered when people expressed the hope that I would take over the practice, the doctor having meanwhile died.

In addition I was for short periods attached to a prison, a workhouse and a couple of mental hospitals, all of which enlarged my horizon. Eventually I settled down into a niche in General Practice in 1934 in which, as Junior Partner, I was allotted the more ordinary work, mostly looking after insured patients and their families. Outside of these I cared for those whom we termed as being on the Parish, these being made up of those who were not insured and were too poor to pay for medical attention. These, on registering with the authorities, were allotted to one doctor in each area who had the duty of looking after them in return for a small annual salary. As Junior Partner it fell to my lot to undertake the duties involved.

In my youth with high ambitions I did not relish the prospect of caring for a collection of old and possibly infirm men and women with poor prospects of any being of any medical interest. As time went on my feelings began to change, as slowly I felt more and more at home with these mainly old people and also to like them, so that whereas at the start, I had looked on the task of seeing to their requirements as somewhat of a burden, this slowly came to change into a pleasure. Just as they seemed to enjoy my company I began to enjoy theirs, especially as, apart from any warmth of feeling they might show me, I found it fascinating to hear about their past lives and experiences. And of course it was flattering on most occasions to be given a warm welcome.

As time went on I began to take a proprietary interest in these 'parish' patients and to feel that they were my people, so that whatever their state in life might be, I was responsible for them and it was up to me to pay them the best and fullest attention that lay within my power. Then, as I got to know each individual better there was increased scope for fun and laughter (though not with all). Getting them to talk about their families and past experiences helped to brighten their lives and feel that someone was interested in them, so that they did not feel entirely neglected, whatever the state of life to which they had been reduced.

With some, of course it was impossible to relieve their habitual gloom of mind, but when I was with them they at least had an opportunity to come out with their complaints and grumbles. As we got to know each other better it did become easier to make fun of them and possibly raise a laugh or at least a smile. From all this one might get the impression that such visits were burdensome and a waste of time from a medical point of view, but I enjoyed seeing these old people and felt (as I still do) that periodic visits of this kind did them more good than any bottle of medicine, and, morally, proved of considerable value. Apart from all this, both patients and I enjoyed these contacts, and, in the middle of a day seeing nothing but sick people, contacts of this nature offered me a welcome relief to what, at times, could border on monotony.

Before I felt fully established the war intervened to break the sequence of relationship with my patients and kept me away for five years. During this period a few stalwarts kept in touch with me and one of these was Mrs Fotheringham, one of my regular surgery visitors. She was a short, fattish, voluble and determined lady, of whose illnesses, if any, I remember nothing. She would regularly complain about her husband, a most pleasant and hard-working man, whom I personally admired for putting up with her, although I believe they were very happy together. While abroad Mrs Fotheringham kept me supplied with the most beautifully knitted woollen socks, which I appreciated to the full being so much more sympathetic to my feet than army issues.

A rival in kindness was Mrs. Hutchinson, who lived with her husband, a retired naval petty officer and their adored and only son John who when young took in a juvenile weekly magazine called the "Magnet". Mrs Hutchinson had kept all these, and proceeded to send me periodic batches when I was abroad. I had never come across this paper before and would have turned up my nose at it under peacetime conditions, but here in the army I loved it and thoroughly enjoyed the exploits of characters like Keyhole Kate and Dennis the Menace. But above all there was fat boy Billy Bunter, who, in the company of his friends at Greyfriars School, spent his time trying by fair means or foul (and almost invariably by the latter), to lay his hands on more food and to avoid being involved in any sort of work. Poor Billy, he always came to grief, but reading about him while being shelled or bombed took me away from reality while things were unpleasant. These papers found their way to everyone in the unit and in no way was it possible to express our full gratitude for their arrival.

Sadly on my return home I found that John had been killed, leaving the old couple devastated. During the actual fighting one tended to regard death as an almost everyday affair and it was only on return home that one realised what havoc it played in people's lives.

The War came to an end and I soon picked up the threads of normal life again. Soon after, the National Health Service was introduced and with all my old people now insured against illness the former stigmata of poverty and indigence resting on them were removed. So once again I resumed my former friendships and started to make more and to some of these I will now turn.

One of these, Miss Lenman, was in a way typical. Short, bespectacled and shabbily dressed she lived alone in a squalid room, surrounded by all her belongings in a state of utter disorder. I felt bad with her as she always greeted me with the offer of a cup of tea, but such being the surrounding dirt, I never had the courage to accept this. She was a delightful old soul, but with no conversation and, like so many elderly people, she was adept at 'losing' things and accusing others of theft. On one occasion her landlady was the culprit in the matter of two knitting needles, which she was incapable of using and which she had bought for two or three pence some thirty years ago. In all the surrounding mess, what suddenly put these things into her mind remains a mystery, but eventually her landlady got so fed up with being accused of stealing that she threw Miss Lenman out and, not for the first time, she had to change her place of abode. I grew quite attached to the old lady and visits were often enlivened by the latest drama. So it was a sad day when I had to send her to hospital, never to be seen again.

Another elderly lady also lived in one room but with what a difference, hers being spotlessly clean and tidy. She had spent all her life in this district and related to me how she had got married. At that time she was working as a housemaid in a very large house and in due course became engaged to one of the gardeners. She told this to her mistress who immediately offered to let her have her house for the reception and provide everything for it herself. On the wedding day, all friends and relations attended the reception and following this Mrs Cripps moved into her husband's cottage, which had been equipped with all the necessary linen as a wedding present from her mistress. She then continued to work in the house until babies started to arrive. This lady wrote to me on several occasions while I was abroad and I still have one of her letters.

On my return I found that quite a number of families who had been bombed out of their homes in Dockland had been settled in empty properties in the neighbourhood, with quite a number in a block of flats across the road from my house. Here it was hoped they would live in safety. My wife was not so sure about this, a bomb having fallen not far from our house and having broken all the windows on that side. These people, coming from a poor and industrialised area, had the reputation of being uncouth and very tough and I was somewhat nervous as to how I would get on with them. I need not have worried. I found them blunt and outspoken, but things clicked and I soon found myself quite at home with them, provided I spoke simply and to the point.

The children were grand and mostly tough little hooligans. One day as I was working in the garden a boy came up to me and said: "Please, Doctor, it's Mum's birthday tomorrow and I would like to give her some flowers, so could you please give me some from your garden?" I immediately picked a bunch for him and, following this, I soon got to know the dates of many Mums' birthdays. My reward came later, for in the autumn these same boys raided all the local apple trees but never touched mine.

Nearby a large house was occupied by other East-enders, comprising two families, the Briggs and the Kents with their children. Mrs. Briggs and Mrs. Kent were sisters and they were joined by a third, Mrs. Grantham, after the death of her cantankerous old husband. There was also another sister, Mrs. White, who lived close by.

I cannot remember anything about my first contact with these families, but Mrs. Kent stood by the following story. I had been called in to see Mrs. Briggs, who, feeling in a contradictory mood, did nothing but raise difficulties over what I suggested and especially over what medicines she could take, until, in exasperation I handed her my prescription pad and a pen saying: "As you know so much better than me, write your own blasted prescription and I will sign it." There followed a moment of shocked silence and then all but Mrs. Briggs burst out laughing. From that moment I was accepted as one of them, for clearly I spoke the same language and my only dispute over the story is that she makes me out to have used the word "bloody" and not "blasted" as I am sure I did.

We became the best of friends, with me always enjoying my visits to the household. I never got to know Mrs Briggs well and she died soon after I met her, following which her children continued to live in the household. Mrs. Grantham was quite different from her sisters considering the rough conditions

Father

Father and Mother

Mother

Mother in her garden

Granny (Smyrna) on her 100th birthday

Kiamil

House in Moda

House in Moda

House at Alemdagh

House at Alemdagh

Father out shooting

Geoffrey and Karamehmet shooting at Samandra

Geoffrey and Barbara on their wedding day 1936

Geoffrey and Barbara at their granddaughter's wedding 1995

Captain G W Whittall RAMC

Alexandra Pouschine in her American Red Cross uniform

John, Michael and Maya 1946

Michael, Maya and John 2006

Geoffrey, Barbara and Maya in front of Cornwall House

Cornwall House

Pevers Cottage, Weston Underwood

Villa Ribeaupierre

under which she was brought up and had to live, especially in view of the nature of that old curmudgeon, her husband. She was quiet, gentle and kind, never speaking ill of anyone; these qualities were reflected in the expression on her face which was always one of peaceful serenity and goodness.

Her sister, Mrs. Kent stood in complete contrast, tall, gaunt, loud-mouthed and outspoken, one whom I would not like to come across when angry. Nevertheless she was kind-hearted and a devoted mother and aunt and was greatly immersed in the family. Visiting this household formed one of my greatest pleasures, with me always receiving a hearty and genuine welcome. What I particularly liked was the open frankness in our relationship, there never being any need to regard a spade as other than a spade. I never sorted the children out satisfactorily, but I had a favourite in Kitty. But how things change. The last I heard of her was that after having had three children she now weighed eighteen stone. There was an open-hearted quality about this family which greatly appealed to me, as did the way they enjoyed life and had faced up to their wartime experiences and hardships without a word of complaint.

After retiring from practice I visited them regularly. Sadly Mrs. Grantham died when I was on holiday one year, to be followed by Mrs. Kent some years later. I was upset at not being able to attend her funeral, but sadly was in bed with 'flu at the time.

Also on my visiting list were the Misses Dewhurst, a queer old couple living in one room, in a state of total disarray, in company of two white Pekingese dogs and two cages of canaries. One of the sisters was said to be a poetess, but I never had occasion to come across any of her work. How they fended for themselves I never found out, but every day they were brought a hot midday meal (at very low cost) by an organisation called "Meals on Wheels", which served the poor and the disabled. On one occasion I arrived to find both the ladies sitting on their beds, eating their lunch, when one of the Pekingese snatched a potato off one of the plates. Before he could run off, a hand shot out to seize the dog, rescue the potato from his mouth and pop it straight back into his mistress's mouth.

These two old ladies always asked after the children and one Christmas Eve I took them round together with a cold roast chicken for their Xmas lunch. (In those days chickens were birds of some repute and not the dross they are to-day). The old ladies were delighted and as we were leaving, pressed a white ball of fluff into Maya's hands ... a Pekingese puppy. Now if there was one type of dog I loathed it was the Pekingese, but to refuse the gift would have upset the ladies and so we returned home.

Well, on Christmas day we sat down twenty-six at table and no one enjoyed the occasion more than Chang, for so the pup was now called, as he weaved his small way in between the legs of the guests and was made a fuss of by all. Subsequently it turned out that the pup was very highly bred, of a nervous disposition and had to be treated carefully. Advice which was ignored.

Despite my original attitude, as time went on I became fonder and fonder of the dog which became a really lively and fearless little animal. On one occasion, prior to going on holiday, I tried to get him into a dogs' home for a couple of weeks. The owners were most unwilling to take in a Peke, as they did not like the breed, but eventually consented to do so. When I went to collect him, he appeared in magnificent form, with the owners of the home asking whether I would not like to leave him permanently with them.

On another occasion, also just before Christmas, I happened to visit a blind couple, who asked me to read them a letter which had just arrived. This was from the General of the Salvation Army to wish them a happy Christmas and this left me greatly impressed that the Head of such an organisation should think of sending such a letter to those who had occupied such a minor role. And so from now on I took to dropping in at this time of the year to make certain that their letters were read to them.

People can be astonishingly brave and from the likes of these I never heard a word of complaint, and this reminds me of a man I saw later on in life. He had suffered from poliomyelitis as a child and had been chair-bound ever since and now in his early thirties was going blind. Having finished with the work side, we were chatting when he came out with the statement: "You know Doctor I have been very lucky in my life." This remark left me almost speechless, but I managed to ask him in what way this was so, to which he replied: "You see so many people have never been able to see, whereas I have had good vision for thirty years." I left him feeling thoroughly ashamed of myself and my petty grumbles and try to think of him whenever in trouble.

We had a domestic help in Mrs. Crowley who helped to clean and man the telephone. Her husband was a retired and highly skilled carpenter. She was large, bluff and hearty and one who always made her presence felt when she was about. The time came when Maya was doing the Season and going out to dances and parties more or less every night. From this moment on Mrs. Crowley took her in hand to become her lady's maid and slave and the house was neglected. Having become such an institution, nobody minded, in any case I doubt whether she would have taken any notice of complaints, with Maya's activities so engrossing her. But heaven alone knows what gossip she spread in the neighbourhood that is if any, for none came to our ears. But all of us loved her, while our visitors were all intrigued with her outspoken ways. She, for her part, delighted in our household and when not engaged with Maya, worked really hard. She was a grand person and I only hope the likes of her still exist.

Another old friend was Miss Violet Mitchell. I first got in touch with her when on a visit in connection with her severe chronic bronchitis. She asked my advice over how to deal with one of her lodgers who was creating disturbances in the house since he had taken to drink. I suggested her consulting a lawyer and eventually I had to give evidence in her favour in Court, where I stressed that she was a sick woman with a reduced expectation of life and tactlessly referred to her as elderly. She won her case and the lodger had to leave the house. Meanwhile I had found out that Miss Mitchell gave typing lessons and asked her to teach me. To this we agreed and she told me her fee would be two shillings and sixpence a lesson. I protested over this fee, saying it was absurd and that I would prefer to pay her a proper fee, but she was not having any of this and from her I learnt the rudiments of typing in a class of teenage girls.

Later she left the area but I kept in touch on the telephone and with an annual Christmas visit. She was a strict vegetarian, a Vegan, as also a confirmed atheist, so in her annual December letter she always wished me a Happy Winter Solstice and not Happy Christmas. She also used to write to me every year on my birthday. All her letters enclosed vegetarian recipes, including one for a vegetarian Christmas lunch. I used to tease her over recommending vegetarianism for human beings but not for her dog, who was allowed his bones and meat. In her last letter to me she wrote: "You are a better doctor than prophet. Thirty years ago you said that I had a poor chance of survival, and here am I still going strong." Soon after she disappeared from view … no answer to my phone calls and none to my letters.

One day I was called to see an elderly Jewish lady, who, on arrival I found lying in bed. She held a catalogue of complaints, although on examination I found nothing peculiar. Anyhow; I listened to them, gave her some medicine and said I would return in a week's time to hear exactly the same tale of woe. On my third visit, while leaning on the bed rails, my patience gave up, and I muttered under my breath as I thought. "Malchi staraya karova" .....the Russian for "Shut up you old cow." She immediately sat up straight in bed and said: "Doctor, you speak Russian, how wonderful." I felt horrified at my lapse in manners and told her that my wife was Russian and that I only knew a few words. "Oh, please Doctor, bring her round to see me, I haven't spoken Russian for ages." So I took Barbara round to see her one day and the two had a long chat. From that moment Mrs. Shaw, as she was called, became a changed woman and, forgetting all about her ailments, talked to me about her past life in Russia. Like so many Jews she had arrived in London penniless to get married and bring up her ten children. I became very fond of her, and of her husband for whom she had hardly a good word to say. Amongst other things she accused the poor old man of running a brothel in a neighbouring house and whenever he went out alone he was taunted over his going to see his girls!

Meanwhile, I became involved in all the family. Eventually she left the area and when I heard that she was very ill in a nursing home, I went over to see her. She was in bed and looking ghastly, but in reply to my query as to how she felt, she retained her old spirit and sense of humour by answering "the staraya karova is not at all well." She died a few days later. I still keep in touch with one daughter and from her hear all the family news. Strangely, time and again it happened that patients whom at first sight I thoroughly disliked ended among my favourites. Was it because they showed more character?

A younger patient who cheered my life was my beloved Sarah, a girl who normally looked like nothing on earth, who, if properly dressed and made up, could have looked lovely. I first met her with her mother, an amusing but rather dreadful old woman, whose chief joy in life lay in a bottle of Guinness, whom I visited on occasion, each time seeing Sarah also. One day, before Christmas, I asked what she was going to do for Christmas and to this she replied that she would be going to prison – to Holloway gaol. I stared at her in amazement and said "You can't be serious." She replied that she certainly was as Christmas in prison was far more enjoyable than that at home. Sure enough, I later read in the local paper that she had been caught stealing and had been sent to gaol.

As time went on she picked up a husband who was sent to gaol for some petty crime. Some time later I learnt that he was about to be released and meeting

Sarah mentioned that she must be feeling happy about this. Not she however, for how was she to explain away the boy-friend with whom she was living at the moment? Sadly I never heard the outcome. I was very fond of Sarah. There was an engaging frankness and simplicity about her which I found appealing, despite a complete lack of any moral sense. And what a waste of a potentially lovely face.

Another one involved in crime was one of the Taylor boys coming from a very respectable family. He had got mixed up with a gang and had taken to thieving. His mother implored me to talk to him, but prior to my seeing him he had already served two short periods in prison, having on the last occasion been caught fast asleep in the shop he was burgling. So when he turned up one day in surgery I raised the matter. As I felt it would be quite useless moralising I attacked the question from a more practical point of view and said: "You must face the facts of life, Robert. Were you a successful burglar I would have nothing to say, for after all a successful burglar can make a good living, outside the risk of spending an occasional spell in prison. But you are so damned inefficient at the game you always get caught and if you continue you will be spending more time in prison than out. In other words I think you would be an idiot if you did not change your way of life." Whether this sound advice was taken or not, I never heard. He was such a nice young man and I was very fond of his parents.

Another old friend bore the name of Dunton. His father had been a game-keeper, and he had started life as the official Rat-catcher to the West End of London, and was furious when the County Council suddenly became genteel and labelled him as 'Vermin Operator'! He despised rats as being the only animals he knew of which in times of danger would abandon their young to their fate. He also kept me amused by telling me which of the fancy restaurants in the West End had dirty kitchens. He had four children, the last of whom was called after me, and with his small salary had difficulty in feeding the family properly. To remedy this problem he laid elaborate traps for pigeon on the small terrace which lay outside his kitchen window, and was so successful that his wife told me that all the family were fed up with eating pigeon. So he set his eyes on another way of getting free food. He knew the director of a local cemetery who was very keen on growing vegetables but suffered from the ravages of pigeons. So he gave Dunton permission to shoot in the cemetery and keep the pigeon population down. Dunton had other ideas, and these were helped by the presence of a large pond. Here Dunton would hide with his gun, while his children were dispatched to a neighbouring park on which many duck used to spend their time on a pond. Here the boys were instructed to create such a disturbance that the birds took to wing and flew off in hopes that they would settle on the pond in the cemetery, where they would be dispatched to supply a good meal. I never found out how successful this manoeuvre was.

He and I used to go off shooting together either to the salt marshes on the Essex coast or to Canvey Island, the law being that land lying between high and low-water tidemarks offered free shooting. Ostensibly we were after duck, but seldom returned with anything in our bag. On the other hand we enjoyed a wonderful day out in the open, had a good lunch and did a good deal of walking, and on these deserted marshes escaped from humanity. When John was old enough he accompanied us, when Dunton taught him shooting and I taught him how to handle a gun safely. Dunton was always interesting, a confirmed poacher and up to all the tricks of the trade.

Sadly he died young from cancer, after which his family moved out into a small house. Here his son John was one day idling by the garden gate when a car mounted the pavement and killed him. Later his widowed sister, Margaret, whose husband had died of cancer, followed in his footsteps and died of the same disease, leaving three small children. Mrs Dunton, more or less confined to the house with heart trouble, was at her wits end as to how to look after them, when Peter, another son in Australia, phoned her and said, "Send Margaret's children out to us and we will look after them." So off they went to Australia and when last I heard of them they had settled down well. It was as well, for in the meantime Mrs. Dunton died.

At the same time I was looking after an old man of the name of Briggs, living by himself. I never found out what work he had been involved in, but now in his old age he claimed a relationship with Lord Nelson. How this worked out I was never able to make out, but a grandfather whose mother was called Nell was involved, in consequence of which he was Nell's son and so on. Anyhow he gave me some bits of jet and some cloth which he claimed to have belonged to Lord Nelson. So in return I invited him to lunch one day and asked my brother Vernon to help me out. Neither stopped talking throughout a very good lunch washed down with plenty of beer, and then the two, reminiscing, began to sing old music hall songs in their cracked voices, with Barbara and me hardly able to contain our laughter. Eventually I had to break up the proceedings to get back to work, with satisfaction at having given the old man an enjoyable break in his otherwise dull life. It always struck me as so sad that so many old people, after the end of a lifetime's work have to settle down to solitary lives on the slenderest of means.

In contrast was Miss Marshall, an elderly spinster of means, living on her own in a good flat. She had taken to the bottle in a big way, and although in attendance as a doctor, there was nothing I could do for her. She would ring me up at all hours, demanding visits, which usually lasted a half hour or so but enabled me to settle her down for the night. One night I continued to have calls from her every hour until mercifully they ceased at 1 a.m. Next morning the telephone operator rang me up to say that the same lady had continued to try and get through to me at regular intervals all through the night, and that she had taken it on herself not to put any through to me, and was now worried as to whether she had done right, to which I replied that far from finding fault I blessed her. Poor Miss Marshal, alone and unhappy she committed suicide shortly after.

Another elderly lady on her visits to me always asked whether taking an occasional tea-spoon of brandy whenever she felt faint would do her harm, to which I replied that if she limited herself to a teaspoon and not too frequently there was nothing to worry about. Some time later her husband came to see me in distress, for on opening a cupboard a cascade of bottles had fallen out.

Coming closer to home I had three patients who like me originated from Turkey. One of these, of whom I was very fond was old Mr. Machray. He had spent his working life in Constantinople involved in shipping and was now retired to England where his daughter, a very great friend of ours, asked me to look after him. This I was glad to do, and especially so as he always talked to me of Father in the most glowing of terms. Evidently Mr. Machray's business methods were not always of the whitest, and on several occasions he was landed in difficulties, and on each such consulted Father, who gladly helped him out, and was the only man in the town willing to do so, whence the great admiration in which he was held. (Father was very secretive about those he helped and these were numerous, and it was not until his death that Mother heard of many cases.)

There was very little to be done for Mr. Machray, and on one occasion he apologised for summoning me, saying that he had suffered from exactly the same trouble on a previous occasion in Salonica, but on that occasion he had cured himself with a bottle of gin, which sadly he could not do to-day as he could not afford to buy a bottle. Later on he was dying and asked me whether this was the case, and when I told him it was so he lay back and said: "Well I can't complain, for you know Geoffrey, I have led a wonderful life and have enjoyed every minute of it. In its course I think I have broken everyone of the Ten Commandments, except perhaps the one about murder, and I am not quite certain about that."

One day a sort of cousin whom I had never met before arrived on the scene. She was Murielle Barker, married to a Colonel Saunders of the Gordon Highlanders, and she had brought her son to see about some symptoms the nature of which I have forgotten. She had heard of a wonderful Ear, Nose and Throat surgeon and asked me to fix things up. So I took her to see the man. He examined the boy and said that he ought to have his tonsils removed. I both distrusted and disliked him, and told Murielle that if she had anything further to do with him, I would retire from the scene, and meanwhile strongly advised her to take the boy to see my specialist. This I persuaded her to do and he, after a very full examination, gave as his opinion that there was nothing wrong with the tonsils, but that he was suffering from a chronic inflammation of the mastoid. Mireille was unwilling to accept this opinion and so we saw a third specialist and he confirmed the mastoid diagnosis. So the boy was operated on and never looked back.

I also had trouble with Winnie, a genuine cousin. She had suffered from quite a lot of illness in the past, and had always been treated in nursing homes. Ill again, I suggested she enter hospital, but in a public ward. She flew at me and said that this was impossible, she could not descend to this form of treatment etc. etc. So I told her not to be an idiot, as first she could not afford nursing home fees, and secondly I had already made all arrangements, and an ambulance would be calling for her within the next hour or so. She was absolutely furious, but off she went. I visited her a couple of days later, to find her full of cheer, as she told me what a fool she had been always to go into nursing homes, for here in the ward there was always something going on, the other patients were a delight, and. she was thoroughly enjoying herself talking to them, and so, instead of hearing a catalogue of woes she was full of the joy of life. And the next time she needed in-patient treatment it was she who insisted on being admitted to a public ward.

But the most glamorous and also the most amusing patient I ever had was the Sheikh. My brother-in-law, Charles, had been in command of the Royal Air Force in Iraq, and one day phoned me that an old friend of his, staying in the prestigious Savoy Hotel, was ill and would I go and see to him. So off I went to find him suffering from the 'flu. So I kept him in bed and got day and night nurses for him. There followed a series of daily visits, which took up a lot of time as I had to travel some distance, but eventually he had recovered sufficiently for me to suggest leaving off the nurses. However he wanted the Night nurse, a young and attractive girl to stay on, but was happy to see the elderly and rather staid day nurse quit.

After recovery his secretary phoned me and asked me to send in a bill, but before doing so I phoned Charles to ask him whether I should in view of the fact that the Sheikh had been a very good friend to him in Iraq. To this Charles replied, that if I could manage it, he would be much happier if I did not send one in, the Sheikh having been so good to him in Baghdad. So when the matter came up again, I told the Sheikh that he had been so thoughtful where my brother-in-law was concerned that I could not see my way to sending him a bill especially as, at the same time, I had so enjoyed meeting him.

So I left things at that and thought no more of the question. Then one morning a Rolls-Royce appeared at the house, and out of it came two men carrying large packages, which, they told me, were sent by the Sheikh. These were placed in the hall, and then one man, as he was leaving, handed me a small parcel, which I slipped into my pocket and forgot about in the excitement of seeing what lay in the large parcels, out of which came some marvellous Eastern delicacies, including some manna, which I had never come across before. Then I suddenly remembered the packet in my pocket, and this contained two gold watches, one for Barbara and one for me.

The foods and sweets were all familiar except for a slab of dried meat which I took to be Turkish pastirma. Barbara and I then had a discussion on how to cook this and she tried her hand at it without success, so I took over, not a bit surprised that an ignorant Russian had no idea of how to cook Turkish food. So I tried frying thin slices with eggs in the approved style, but this provided such an all-powerful smell, that I ran out of the kitchen, while in one minute, the children's nurse, Mary, whose bedroom lay above the kitchen scuttled out of it, like an alarmed rabbit out of its hole, wondering what on earth had happened. We made no further trials with this meat, and buried it in the garden. Since then we have often wondered what animal it came from, and finally decided on the camel.

On the occasion of his next visit I was in hospital, where the Sheikh visited me bringing with him a bouquet of flowers, all wrapped up in a parcel about five feet high, and with this an enormous box of chocolates, these of course causing somewhat of a sensation in hospital circles. The flowers stayed with me but Barbara took the chocolates home, to find that the family had eaten them all by the time I got home. Needless to say I was furious and not comforted by Barbara telling me how good they were.

We dined with the Sheikh on two occasions, but meals with him were somewhat of a trial, for firstly he spoke no English, and so all conversation had to go through an interpreter, in spite of which we found him very knowledgeable on world affairs. Outside this, according to Arab ways, one first sits and talks for quite a time prior to eating, with the guests expected to leave immediately the meal was over. This would have been all right except for the fact that the Sheikh liked his whisky, and knowing only one word of English, namely 'Cheerio', glasses were raised far too often. And so after an excellent dinner and superb wine we were glad to return home.

The Sheikh gave us each a further gold watch, and it is typical of human nature, that having for years longed to have one, possessing two after a time meant nothing to me, and I gave them to the boys and returned contentedly to an ordinary steel one.

Whereas the Sheikh never made mention of his wife or wives or daughters he talked about his sons and left me with the problem of keeping an eye on one who was a schizophrenic and whom he placed in a special home for those suffering from mental disorders. Here I visited him once a month, feeling intensely sorry for the boy, as, speaking no English he was completely cut off from the world and all those who knew him. It struck me that the Sheikh just wanted to put him away as far as possible from his neighbourhood. What happened to the boy later on after the revolution I was not told.

Another instance of the Sheikh's hardness was in the sacking of his interpreter, for what reason I never knew, abandoning him in London apparently without any money or means of returning home to Iraq, The man turned to me as the only person he knew in London, and eventually I managed to fix up his return with the help of someone I knew in the Embassy.

A similar sort of story relates to another son. He had been given a Chrysler motor car with instructions never to drive it. Well, one day he persuaded the chauffeur to let him drive it and piled it up against a rock. I asked the Sheikh what he did next and he blandly said: "I punished the chauffeur and bought my son a Mercedes".

The Sheikh had suffered an accident to one eye, which had left him blind on that side. Hoping for something to be done about this he asked me to arrange a consultation with the three best eye specialists in London. So this I did and as I expected their verdict was unanimous – there was nothing to be done. On hearing this Sheikh turned to me and asked: "Doctor Whittall do you think these Gentlemen are talking sense?" to put me in a most awkward position in front of three such experts in their field.

Poor old Sheikh. He was closely involved with the King and one of the great men in his country, and I fear the worst happened to him after the King was expelled. I never heard of him again.

I will end this section with two stories which have just come to mind. One concerns an elderly lady who lived in a top floor room into which water poured through a defective roof whenever it rained, leaving me with memories of her having to lie in bed with a basin between her legs. The house in which she lived belonged to a prominent member of the local Council who despite requests did nothing at all about the matter. Then one day on a visit I found her room absolutely dry and asked the good lady how she had managed to get the roof seen to, and the answer came: "I wrote to the Queen about the state of affairs, and within a week workmen came and put things right." Since then I have often wondered whether things really happened in this way.

To end up with an amusing incident. On a visit to a very personable young actress suffering from a chest infection, and anxious to get back to work, I told her that the best way out of the problem was for me to give her some injections. To this she agreed but laid down the condition that these must be given into a part of her body which was not exposed to public view when she was on the stage, for fear of the injection leaving a permanent mark. This raised a problem, for in so far as I could make out, her costume on such occasions amounted to no more than a few strings. Finally we found an area of about a quarter of a square centimetre which met with her requirements and thereafter all went well.

Part VIII

MARRIED LIFE

CHAPTER I

Marriage

It was not long after I had first settled into my recently acquired practice in 1934 that I received a phone call from my cousin, Joan Langston Day, to join a party she was getting up to attend the Aldershot Tattoo. As this was on one of my evenings off duty I readily accepted an invitation, following which Joan asked me to pick up a girl in Hampstead and to bring her along, to this I readily agreed.

I duly picked up Joan's friend at Golders Green Underground Station and off we set for Aldershot. Conversation at first was desultory and polite and continued so until I discovered that my companion was Russian. This intrigued me for I had shortly returned from a holiday in Istanbul and here I had met a very attractive Russian girl. She had introduced me into her family and the Russian colony, greatly to enjoy and feel sympathetic to their attitudes and ways of life.

My interest in the girl was aroused and after the end of the party I drove her home. I found her to be very much to my liking and also fond of ballet. I had fallen in love with ballet, starting with Diaghileff. At this time the De Basil Company was performing in London, to which I went regularly alone as none of my friends had similar tastes. So I immediately invited Barbara (such being her name) to join me and off we went once a week, always sitting in my preferred seats in the stalls circle at Covent Garden. In return Barbara took me behind the scenes, where she knew several of the dancers, to meet Baronova, Danilova, Massine and others. This of course I found fascinating, although it surprised me to see how small in size most of them were.

So we met regularly and we saw a lot of each other and our friendship progressed. Then Barbara accepted a post as a sort of governess to a French boy in Paris.

This came as sad news for me and for several months I heard nothing of her. Then, to my delight, a letter suddenly arrived. Barbara had met a lady who had acted as hostess to one Wendy Whittall and was she a relation? I promptly replied that Wendy was a cousin of mine and this episode allowed us to keep in touch until Barbara returned to London in December when she invited me to attend a party she was giving at her mother's flat in Abbey Road. This I accepted with delight and turned up to make my first close acquaintance with exiled Russian nobility.

The party proved quite an experience. The Russians I had hitherto met had all been of the middle class, but here I was plunged into high society, an environment of which I had had no previous experience. I felt very shy and somewhat out of my depth, but at the same time enormously impressed by the bearing of these people, who, in their time, had had everything and were now leading precarious lives in varying degrees of poverty. Here they all were, laughing and chatting, in these somewhat dingy surroundings, just as happily as though they were still in their former grand houses or palaces. Amongst these were Prince Youssupoff and his daughter Irina, formerly one of the wealthiest men in the world, and now cheerfully content to share in the very simple fare, presented on cheap crockery, just as though this was the most natural thing in the world. But it was fascinating to meet and talk to such people and I survived the evening without discredit. It proved a lesson in how adversity should be faced. Further acquaintance with Barbara's mother and other members of the Community drove that lesson home very strongly, making me wonder whether under similar circumstances I would be able to display the same spirit.

From this moment Barbara and I saw more and more of each other and at the same time I became very fond of her mother who, with her lovely sweet smile, I found enchanting.

The ballet had meanwhile departed, and our evening entertainment depended on the state of my pocket. When money was tight we had supper at a Lyons Corner House or at Demoes, a Greek restaurant run by one Demosthenes Kehayoglu, who came from the South of Turkey, and to whom I had been introduced by an Armenian friend. Here we often found my brother Vernon and I felt at home talking Greek and Turkish while Barbara talked Russian to Madame, who also spoke German, French, Italian, Spanish and of course Turkish and Greek, but no English, despite 20 years in this country, her excuse being that the language was too difficult. To add to the atmosphere an old Turk, of the name of Hajji, hung around, doing the odd job from time to time, with whom I talked about life in former days. Besides all this the food was excellent and cheap.

In consequence meals were multi-lingual in character, with an atmosphere reminiscent of Turkey.

When in money our preferred restaurant was the Hungaria in Lower Regent Street, which offered the best in the way of food with a superb Hungarian band, good dancing and a Maitre d' Hotel who had served many years in Russia. (He, Vecchi, was sadly drowned when he was sent to Canada during the war). Here we spent wonderful evenings, not to be repeated in later years, for sadly, with the war the place closed. Despite the restaurant's chic, we used to meet a rather dishevelled old Russian there, one Makaroff who had a dog which did amazing tricks, in return for which his master would get free drinks and food as the two wandered round the pubs. Why he was allowed into the very smart Hungaria, apart from sentiment, I could not make out.

When the weather was fair we often drove out into the country, to take dinner in some small inn. On one such occasion Barbara remarked on the beauty of a group of trees outlined against the setting sun, leaving it to me to gently point out that her group of trees was in reality a gasometer. At the same time I slowly began to meet more and more Russians at Barbara's home, to find myself conversationally at a disadvantage and like a tennis player unable to compete with the rapidity of their delivery. But it was interesting to participate in a new level of society.

Then one fine evening we drove into the country and dined in the Two Brewers Inn on Chipperfield Common, after which we walked in the lovely woods to emerge – happily and delightedly engaged, to leave me unable to account for my good fortune.

My next move was to call on Barbara's mother, to ask her approval of our engagement. The only trouble lay in the fact that she knew nothing of my background, but as soon as the announcement had been placed in the Times, a childhood friend of hers, a Prince Troubetskoy phoned her to say that he had known all the family in Turkey and that they were fully "comme il faut".

So now the next question was for us to meet each other's friends and relations. On my side Barbara had already met my brother Vernon and one day I took her off to meet my sister Edna who was living in the country. So we set off one Sunday to call on her. On arrival, as the front door opened, we were greeted with a terrific cacophony of shouts and shrieks as her children Monica and John settled down to one of their periodic fights, in which no holds seemed to be barred. Peace was soon restored and lasted for the remainder of our stay, after which I left feeling happy that Edna approved of my choice.

My next task was to take Barbara to meet my elderly cousin, May Barker, who with her mother had always been very good to me, in that I had an open invitation to spend the weekend with them whenever I wanted. May had sounded most disapproving, when, on the phone, I had announced that I was engaged to a Russian girl. In consequence I was somewhat hesitant over the reception Barbara would receive. To my surprise on seeing each other the two fell into each other's arms as old acquaintances, having met at the Galitzines who were renting her brother's house at Chessington, at which Barbara used to stay. In consequence of all this, my choice was fully approved of, for in May's eyes Barbara was linked with Royalty, and so beyond all suspicion.

At the same time I was taken to visit a number of Russian houses, in which, in view of my conversational abilities I was generally known as the "Silent Englishman", but after these meetings I always enjoyed hearing what Barbara had to say about those we met. Often too, I was forcibly kept silent, as when I was the only foreigner present and conversation slipped into Russian. In due course I began to feel more at home in the atmosphere of this society, in part because of its foreign nature, but also on account of its warmth and friendliness.

From now on I spent most of my spare time in Barbara's company. I either used to meet her at the shop where she was working or in the flat. In this latter her mother, whom I had taken to calling Mum, was very tactful, going out for a walk to leave us together. As I got to know her better I would tease her, accusing her of making use of the opportunity to take a glass of her beloved port in the Ladies' Room of the pub across the road.

I also got to know Barbara's sisters and at the same time was taken round the Russian colony to meet old and young and at the same time to be left in a state of confusion as to who was who. The visit which caused me most anxiety was that to the Grand Duchess Xenia, sister of the Czar, at Hampton Court – but she was charming and easily put me at my ease. One point in my favour came from my having been brought up in the midst of a number of rather peculiar old aunts, this allowing me to feel at home in the company of several formidable old ladies, likely to be severely critical of anyone taking over their greatly cherished Barbara.

Meanwhile Barbara did not want a long engagement – and eventually we decided on getting married in early October. We had to be married first at the Registry office, and for this purpose set off with my Armenian friend, Krikor Gulbenkian and Barbara's loony sister-in-law, Helen Nebolsine, as witnesses. En route Barbara asked me whether I had brought the ring to which I said no, it not being necessary, to arouse a heated argument on this point – our first and one in which I was proved wrong. Fortunately when it came to the point I had the presence of mind to turn my signet ring round and put that on her finger, with Krikor and Helen hardly able to suppress their laughter. However, we were well and truly married. This did not prevent Mum from later asking Barbara whether she still wanted to get married.

All preparations had been made for our wedding on October 5th 1936, at St Phillip's Church, near Victoria. As the hour approached I nervously stood at the West door of the Church, in company of Alexander Zvegintzoff, our ikon bearer. Eventually the car carrying Barbara and Prince Galitzine drew up, Barbara having suffered the almost inevitable last minute hitch over her dress. She looked lovely and I took her by the arm to walk together up the nave to the Altar. In an Orthodox wedding, bride and bridegroom walk from the Church door to the altar together preceded by a boy, traditionally dressed in a sailor suit, carrying an Ikon. Half way up there is a small mat on which, tradition has it, whoever steps first will be master in the house. I always accuse Barbara of pushing me away at the critical moment, while she claims to have pulled me on to the mat, but as things have turned out it is more likely that we stepped on the mat together.

The service was lovely but to me a bit of an ordeal as I did not understand a word and had to carry a candle in the proximity of the flimsy wedding dress including circling the Altar three times, It was not until at the end when we two moved to the Ikonostasis to kiss the ikons and then each other in full view of the congregation that I really felt that Barbara was now mine.

I remember little about the reception, but following this we went to the wrong station, and caught a slow train to Dover which brought us to the Hotel after its restaurant had closed, so that we started life together on sandwiches and a bottle of wine.

Next morning, we picked up my car which had previously been driven to Dover by a friend and boarded the boat for Ostend on our way to Baden-Baden. The sea was miraculously calm, so that Barbara was able to enjoy lunch. We spent that night at Bruges in a hotel recommended for its food. This proved to be excellent but the helpings served us during the meal were so small that after the meal was over we had to go out to the Grande Place and fill ourselves on chips.

The journey to Baden-Baden was uneventful, except for our lunch at Bastogne, where we ordered the plat du jour. This arrived, but as the cover was taken off there stood revealed a number of small birds' heads, with open beaks, staring up at us. Barbara could not face eating these and so I delightedly finished them off. Baden-Baden was eventually reached and in our hotel we had a large room offering a wonderful view. Here we settled down to get to know each other. I heard of Barbara's former days in Baden-Baden, when Mum was in a sanatorium and she spent a school holiday there. It had been a great resort for refugee Russians after the Revolution and here she had been able to make the acquaintance of many people, including her Grandfather and Grandmother who had broken off all relations with Mum after she had eloped with Lawrence Pouschine. But this was all in the past and here we were on our own.

I had hitherto pictured my Barbara as a sweet innocent, to receive a nasty shock when she suggested it would be fun to visit the Casino of whose presence I had been unaware, to see, as she said, what was going on. This we did and to my astonishment I was offered a different aspect of my beloved wife for, in the hall, she immediately took some money off me and sat down to roulette – to leave me no opportunity to find fault as she won enough to buy me a pair of gold cufflinks as a wedding present. By the Casino there stood a tea room carrying the name of Rumpelmayer, which brought back memories of lovely chestnut cakes in an establishment of that name in St James' Street. But I was to suffer a great disappointment – both cakes and tea proving wishy-washy.

Our hotel was most comfortable and the food in it, so far as it was allowed by the Nazi regime, good – except for the fact that we were served a surfeit of venison. On certain days we were only allowed one dish at mealtime, but I made up for this by drinking a superb and suitably named wine called Bernkasteler Doktor. We suffered one misadventure. Barbara remembered once staying at a small hotel in the Wolfschlucht and wanted to repeat the experience, so off we went. Our evening meal proved a disaster and our bed so uncomfortable that we returned to Baden-Baden delightedly and laughingly.

Eventually and far too speedily the hour of return came. En route we spent one night in Treves, where I was interested in the Roman remains, but more so in an evening spent in an open air beer hall with music. That night I was woken up by the ominous sound of troops marching. We had not heard or seen much of Nazidom, but what we did was disquieting.

Arriving at Ostend there was a gale in the channel and so on boarding the ship Barbara withdrew to a cabin, while I in the meantime enjoyed an excellent meal.

By the time we had disembarked and the car was unloaded it was late and Barbara was hungry. In view of the hour we did not want to stop at a restaurant, but otherwise it was early closing day and all shops were shut so that Barbara was delighted when we eventually stopped at Mum's flat to spend the night and recount our adventures – and to sleep on a mattress reduced to a corrugated iron state. It was lovely to be back home again and next day we loaded the car with Barbara's earthly possessions, one suitcase full of clothes, and one of books, postcards and odds and ends, to set off for home. We both felt happy at the prospect of a settled home.

Since arrival in England, Mum, for one reason or another, had never stayed for long in one abode, so that Barbara had led a peripatetic existence. At the same time I, since coming to England had led a hand to mouth existence, so that we were both delighted to be firmly settled in one spot. From this point on we now slowly got to know each other's backgrounds and friends and relations. Fortunately this was accomplished without difficulty and with appreciation and no disagreement with me delighting in the Russian atmosphere.

On paying a visit to Paris we called on a much married aunt of Barbara's with her latest husband, both of whom disliked the English, and were upset over their favourite niece marrying one. At first the atmosphere was somewhat strained, but then the vodka appeared and Uncle was heard to say "at least he learnt to down his vodka in proper style", as I swallowed the potion at one gulp.

Which reminds me that while still engaged, we attended a party in celebration, and according to Russian custom I was given a glass to empty while all sang a certain song. This I did and told Barbara that we must immediately return home, by mistake I had been given a large dollop of neat gin.

Initially we did not have long together for after four years I was in the army, to spend four years abroad without sight of each other. But on my return, I met a patient in the street who greeted me with "what a wonderful wife you have Doctor, I never meet and talk to her when in the street, without my leaving feeling happier and more cheerful."

CHAPTER II

1936 – 1938

Our return home from our honeymoon was uneventful, and the next excitement in life came with Barbara announcing that she was pregnant, and this started a hard period of life for her, for instead of finding it to be the happiest period in life she found it a torture. On hearing the news King decided to leave, to be replaced by one Mary Weber from Gateshead, who proved a jewel and to my delight taught Barbara how to cook a proper Yorkshire pudding. Dr Scott arranged for Barbara to be confined in a maternity hospital by the Brompton Cemetery and here in due course, and to everyone's relief, Maya was born, Dr Scott complaining that in the process Barbara had given him a hard kick. After leaving Hospital after ten days or so, Barbara spent two weeks at a convalescent home in the country prior to returning home.

Soon after Maya's arrival Barbara announced she was pregnant once more. This necessitated finding a larger house, which led to a move to 1 Finchley Way, with four bedrooms and ample room for my surgery. For her confinement Barbara was booked to enter the same hospital as that in which Maya had been born, but, as her full term approached the Munich crisis erupted, and in view of the possibility of war and bombing her Doctor thought that it would be safer for her to have the child at home, rather than in central London. And so John arrived in due course in 1938, a very welcome other male to give me support in a house full of women.

The move to No.1 Finchley Way made life far more pleasant for Barbara, as she was now able to entertain in comfort, while the spare bedroom made it possible for guests to stay in the house. This was especially helpful in the case of friends coming from abroad, and, as a result, when dropping in for meals I seldom knew whom I would find ensconced. And of course, one of the most frequent visitors was my beloved Mother-in-Law, anxious to see that the baby was being properly treated. This house also gave far greater scope for holding large family parties such as at Christmas.

On moving into 1 Finchley Way, the Russian Priest came to bless the house. I arrived home as he was still upstairs and on asking Maya what the Priest was doing I received the answer "making puddles in the bedrooms", i.e. by sprinkling Holy Water. He also came to baptise each child into the Orthodox faith by total immersion, a proceeding which filled me with alarm, but was so skilfully carried out as to leave the children unmoved. The arrival of the Priest led to some outsiders thinking that he was a Rabbi and that we must be Jewish.

CHAPTER III

1938 – 1942

John's safe arrival came as a great relief. At the same time political tension and anxiety were for a short space of time relieved by the Munich Agreement. This state of affairs did not last long, as doubts over Hitler's intentions grew to become more acute until dispelled by the Declaration of War in 1939 to be followed by a large number of new governmental measures and restrictions, aimed at ensuring public safety.

Large numbers of children were evacuated from London to the countryside. In the cities air-raid shelters above and below ground were constructed. In London the tube was adapted to receive thousands of those seeking safety, some of whom spent night after night in these shelters. At the same time equipment was also freely supplied to those who preferred to build their own shelters in their gardens.

After dark a total blackout of lights was imposed, with no naked lights allowed to show, while street lighting was reduced to a minimum. All car headlights had to be fitted with special masks which so reduced lighting that driving in the dark under bad weather conditions became hazardous. The number of cars on the roads was, however, greatly reduced by petrol rationing.

To conform, all the windows in our house were fitted with lightproof curtains and a specially provided adhesive transparent plastic was applied to them to prevent glass splintering. We decided not to build an outdoor shelter, preferring to stay indoors during raids, but had the hall roof shored up with vast timbers in anticipation of the raids which started as soon as days became longer and nights lighter.

We wondered whether to evacuate the children and with some friends, the elderly Gibbs, offering to take them in, we packed the two of them with Nanny off to their vicarage in Aldenham, not too far from London. Visiting them proved a problem, as with petrol rationing my use of the car was limited and this necessitated Barbara taking to a bicycle, at which she was no expert, in order to see them more frequently. This terrified her as she had to follow main roads. On one occasion she had to circle a roundabout several times before the traffic allowed her to escape.

Meanwhile our children's hosts were becoming somewhat restive over the presence of the children in their home. A further source of trouble arose from our also having evacuated our dog Dan, for he and the household animal spent a lot of time quarrelling, much to everyone's disturbance, so in the absence of any air activity we decided to bring them back home again.

Incidentally in the meantime I had received an offer from a Doctor in America to look after the family over there until the war came to an end. In contrast, a Jewish patient had sent his wife to the States to escape from the bombing, only to find her back at home again, soon after this started in earnest, saying that she could not allow her husband to face up to danger on his own.

Naturally, our mode of life became restricted, but we carried on quietly until my partner fell ill, doubling my work, and delaying my call-up, which eventually came through. I was sent to Aldershot to learn how to be a soldier but was allowed home each weekend. Prior to all this all members of the public had been issued with gas masks, which they were supposed to carry at all times. At the same time all those who in the course of duty or work had to be out of doors during air raids were given steel helmets to protect their heads from falling shrapnel. (For some reason or other our friend Betty Frederici, a nurse, had not been issued with a helmet, so she used a saucepan instead).

One evening after dark when I was at home for the weekend, the front door bell rang and on opening it, Charles Strafford (my sister Edna's husband), in uniform, literally fell into the house, obviously completely exhausted. We saw to his immediate needs and helped him to bed, noting that he placed a small bag he carried under his pillow. His arrival gave us our first warning that France had fallen and in the morning he told us how he had spent three days escaping from France, during which period he had had no sleep and that he had just caught the last transport home. He did not stay long for a car came to collect him and the important papers he carried in his bag.

From Aldershot I was sent to Cardiff and shortly afterwards Barbara and the family came to spend a month in a rented house. Soon after her return to London I was posted to Leeds, where I was told I was due for service abroad and sent home on a fortnight's leave. Before we left Barbara came up to spend a weekend to give me the last sight of her for four years.

CHAPTER IV

Barbara in Wartime London

On my departure overseas Barbara was left to face up to financial and domestic responsibilities, of many of which she had had no previous experience. It stands greatly to her credit that she managed as well as she did without ever uttering a word of complaint.

Once on her own, it did not take her long to realise that she was pregnant whereupon Dr Scott, who at this moment was serving in the army in Scotland, took things in hand and placed Barbara into the hands of Dr Douglas McLeod, the senior gynaecologist at St Mary's Hospital. She was eventually delivered of Michael, during her absence from home Maya and John were sent to a children's home which they happily survived.

Michael was born with long black hair and the jaundice, which delighted Tamara Gough-Rodzianko, for not only did he resemble Jenghis Khan, but had acted after his manner by hitting her in the eye with his fist as she leant over him, to show his contempt for women and how they should be treated.

With the arrival of a third child Barbara, under wartime legislation was entitled to engage a full time help but as such were impossible to find in England at that time, she sought the help of a friend in Dublin who found a girl willing to undertake the job. She set off to arrive in London in the middle of an air-raid, to feel utterly lost and confused and anxious to return immediately to Dublin. Fortunately a very kind man, noticing her predicament, took things in hand and escorted her safe and sound to Finchley. She soon recovered to be henceforward known as Nanny by all and to prove an invaluable friend to Barbara. She was liked by everyone with the exception of Mum, who never ceased to find fault over her handling of the children, much to Barbara's great annoyance as such accusations were totally unjustified.

At one point in time Barbara's sister Masha was teaching at a school in Nantwich in Cheshire and the children were sent there under the care of Nanny and Mum – away from the bombing. When Liverpool, some 20 miles away was subjected to an air raid, Mum became nervous and in this state of mind returned with the children to London. From Nantwich Masha returned to London to work in Reuters, while Mum joined the American Red Cross, to look superb in the uniform provided her.

With the return of the children, life in Finchley proceeded quietly, except for the almost nightly bombing. This did not directly affect our surroundings except for one stray bomb which demolished a house and its inhabitants some hundred yards away. On this occasion Barbara, hearing the bomb falling, threw the children into an armchair and fell on top of them as a protection. Friends rushed in to help and brother Vernon, who at that moment was in a pub, paid Barbara the supreme compliment by leaving an untouched pint of beer on the counter to rush to the house and make certain all was well. Fortunately little damage was done except for some broken window panes.

As the bombing of London became worse and more intense, those living in the country were asked by the Government to take a further lot of women and children into the safety of their homes. In response to this appeal, Mr and Mrs Hingston, the parents of my brother Bill's wife, Elfrida, invited Barbara and the children to seek shelter in their house, situated on the outskirts of Nottingham. This invitation was gratefully accepted and in due course Barbara, in company of three children and Nanny, moved north to be very kindly welcomed on arrival. The Hingstons lived in a large house, set in a large garden, with an adjacent orchard. In it the children were lodged in separate quarters and all soon settled down happily.

Maya and John attended the village school, in which Maya, being a good reader and better than the other children, was set to supervise the younger children's reading. Whether the two started to acquire a Nottinghamshire accent is however not known. Otherwise they played happily in the garden although on one occasion they were put to flight when approaching a flock of geese too closely. The orchard housed apple trees of many varieties. Mrs Hingston knew the history, origins and qualities of each one. Pickings of each variety were kept separate and Barbara and Mr Hingston were set the task of sorting them out in respect of size and quality in preparation for package and despatch to the market, a task which kept them both busy, especially as that year's crop was abundant. There were peach trees against the walls of the orchard and here again the crop was excellent, so much so that the children implored their mother not to serve any more at meals.

Barbara got on very well with Mrs Hingston but periodically used to go to London for a couple of days to check the house. On one of these trips she heard widespread talk about a new kind of bomb which had fallen near Nottingham in recent days. This came up in conversation with Mr Hingston who was horrified. He said, "This bomb is a total secret, known only to me as Lord Lieutenant and to one other," going on to express horror at the way Londoners talked and carried on without any sense of responsibility.

This bomb was fitted with its own engine and on its release from the aeroplane could fly off in any direction and was also capable of changing route, giving no indication as to where it was going to fall. The ordinary type of bomb, once having passed overhead, could be accepted as not likely to cause any trouble but with this new type there was no such sense of safety, for having passed overhead there was always the possibility of its return and this fact kept feelings of tension at a high level over prolonged periods. On her return to London Barbara had to put up with these, to find them frightening and very stressful – far more so than the former bombing.

After her return from Nottingham Barbara never left London until I returned home in 1946. During all these years the war was never discussed in the presence of the children with the result that they emerged comparatively unaffected. I remember that on one occasion when at home before leaving the country a loud crash awoke John, who in some alarm called for me, to be completely reassured when told "it was only a bomb".

CHAPTER V

Finchley in Wartime

Finchley was an out-lying suburb of London and under wartime conditions, I always felt that Barbara would be left to lead a rather monotonous existence. This in fact turned out not to be the case, she maintaining that, on the contrary, she led a very interesting wartime existence. She had a number of local friends with whom she was able to consort daily, to discuss events in the home and in the world at large.

As Finchley was out of the way of bombing, friends in London who had suffered material or nervous damage found that Barbara in her house offered peace and quiet and an ever welcome relief, some homeless actually staying for some nights. Among the latter, though not immediately affected, were Mum and Masha, Mum of course regarding Finchley Way as her home.

Interestingly, Barbara who in her early days had undergone Red Cross training in nursing, offered her services, to be refused on account of being alien born. In the same way Count Armfeld, a Finn, was removed from his job as Air Raid Warden for the same reason, only to be sent to camouflage a most secret new factory under construction. The arrival of the Free French brought Barbara in touch with a number of Russians from France and Belgium, including Natasha Pototski and others. Barbara kept open house for them, to allow them a break of civilian life, but she kept no record of names for security reasons.

At the same time Barbara came into contact with Edna McRae, whom I knew out in Constantinople. As well as being a most interesting and intelligent lady, she also gave hilarious parties, mainly at the Belgian club, along with her old friend Lily Pototski who was editing a French Forces' newspaper and Andrew Apraxine from Belgium.

Through these and the like Barbara was kept well up in such news as was available. Through such friends she also met a whole bevy of men and women about to be parachuted into occupied France – the bravest of the brave. Lily Dunderdale had married my cousin Arthur Whittall and Lily's brother "Biffy" was very high up in the Secret Service, his name only being uttered in whispers.

Edna was one of those people who are always full of news and she enjoyed the hush-hush terms under which every reference to Biffy was made, without ever knowing anything about what he was up to. What with this and her natural gaiety and sense of the dramatic she made a very welcome friend and contributed much to Barbara's otherwise hard life.

I do not know how Barbara got into touch with Tony Barcroft, a distant cousin of mine, a very odd man, of half Italian extraction, who was regularly in trouble and haunted us for some years. His Italian fiancée's name was Maria, but this being too common it was changed to Georgette and when he bought a house in Parsons Green he said he lived in 'Chelsea'.

Masha was one day having a drink with him at the Ritz, when Tony suddenly excused himself and left her for a few minutes to return highly agitated. Shortly after two men entered the bar and escorted an officer standing by out of the room. Tony was by now so agitated that he and Masha left, Tony telling Masha that he had had his suspicions about the officer involved as he was wearing the wrong tie with his uniform. In fact he turned out to be an escaped German prisoner of war.

As Christmas approached one year, Barbara got in touch with the local barracks to enquire whether there were any men with nowhere to go to that day. She was told that all the 'men' were catered for, but some officers had nowhere to go and an unknown number of these were invited to Finchley Way.

She was always ready to open her house to those in trouble and at the same time opening it as a centre in which all those speaking foreign languages were welcome and could meet their compatriots. These circumstances meant that she met a fascinating number of people, had some surprising encounters and a most interesting life. It is difficult to write about Barbara's activities during the war, as I can only do so from hearsay, but life during the war was not dull.

CHAPTER VI

Rationing

Food rationing was introduced after the outbreak of war and covered the sale of meat, sugar, butter, fats and eggs. The system was simple, with each individual having a monthly book of coupons, each dated and each entitling the holder to a week's supply of the specified food, the shopkeeper retaining the coupon after the issue of the client's requirements.

Barbara incurred no difficulties except on her return from staying in Wales. She found that the butcher there had cut out all her meat coupons, in consequence of which the family lost their entitlement to meat for two weeks. Fortunately our butcher was sympathetic and helped her out as best he could, especially by supplying offal, livers, kidneys and sausages which were off ration. In a war the coupon system made life easier in that less thought had to be paid to shopping; except in the case of what remained unrationed. Thus, being off ration, Mum was occasionally able to buy goose and duck eggs in Selfridges.

One December day a soldier arrived at the house carrying a large turkey, in all its feathers, a present from Scott, then stationed in Scotland. No-one knew how to cope with the bird and so Barbara placed it in a pram and wheeled it to Mr Semple, our butcher, who very kindly had the bird prepared for the table. But the main source of extra food came from the parcels sent regularly by relatives in the USA, these containing foods which were unobtainable or in short supply in England. These were a real godsend and it is difficult to see how Barbara could have managed without them, although, of course 90% of the population had to do so.

One other possible source of extra meat was a butcher in Golder's Green who sold horse meat, which Barbara, used to French ways, would unhesitatingly have bought had not the shop been so far away. An alternative was offered in the shape of whale meat, which looked exactly like beef steak but tasted fishy and horrible. Barbara, being uninterested in bacon, cannot remember whether it was on ration or even available, but there was a form of pressed pork called

Spam on the market, I forget whether it was freely available or on meat coupons.

Clothing was also only available on surrender of coupons, so many being required for the purchase of each type of garment, but without reference to cost. Thus purchase of a simple cotton dress necessitated the surrender of the same number of coupons as purchase of a silk one. But a range of cheap, well-made and durable clothing was available under the heading of "utility" and this went down well.

Barbara found other means of solving the clothing problem. The milkman had six children and no means of using up all his coupons. So by a mutual arrangement, Barbara gave him all the children's outgrown clothes and he in return gave her coupons, to leave both parties satisfied, Barbara with her coupons and he with clothes for his children at no cost to his pocket.

Once the War was over and at the earliest possible opportunity, Barbara went to Paris to find out how an aunt had fared. She turned out to be in good form, but in the course of the conversation the aunt said that she had received some packets of extraordinary food from America which, appearing to be uneatable, she was proposing to throw away. Barbara pointed out that these were packets of dried eggs, but this led to no change in the aunt's attitude. So Barbara took charge and brought them back with her – six packets of dried eggs, a real windfall in those days.

Food and clothing rationing persisted for some years after the War, but by this time people felt fewer qualms of conscience over breaking the law. When our good friend Edna McCrae (now Woodman) suggested we drive to Cambridge to buy eggs off farmers whom she knew, we readily concurred and off we went one Sunday, to visit half a dozen farms and to return with about 200 eggs as our share.

Outside the satisfaction derived from acquiring the eggs, we enjoyed meeting the farmers and their wives, some of them very amusing characters. From one lady, a vicar's sister, we bought fruit and vegetables, but with her we soon found that we had to take care that we got the full weight – she had tricks up her sleeve. Apart from all else it was wonderful to spend a day in the country and I particularly remember a sight, almost unknown today, of a field covered in cowslips in full bloom.

At one point we entertained a French sailor, introduced by Masha. On his second visit he brought us a leg of lamb and on his next appearance he promised me another and asked me for a certificate to say he was unfit for active service. This I refused and we never saw him again.

A final story. We were entertaining some Americans to lunch with the main course a leg of lamb. On seeing this an American lady started to run down the British for complaining about the shortage of meat. "I have seen no sign of shortage and look at this lovely joint served at table." At this point I intervened to point out that this joint represented the whole household's allotment of meat for the week. She had no answer.

CHAPTER VII

Return to Normal Life

With the end of the war I returned home after four years of absence, with some anxiety in mind as to how the children would receive me. As it happened, I need not have worried, for we all settled down immediately. I enjoyed two or three weeks leave, but the army did not let go of me and I was put in charge of a small hospital in Wendover. Then after a few weeks I was demobilised, and issued with a complete outfit of utility clothes which fitted and served me well. So back to a civilian and a normal family life.

Having got my finances settled, all looked well until Dr Scott advised sending John to a school in the country as a boarder. I immediately got in touch with my old Prep School who were delighted to take him in for the following term. This caused further financial worries – but we survived.

My partner's health did not improve, which brought on the necessity of buying a larger house, from which it would be possible for me to run the practice on my own, should he have to retire. Then as luck would have it, just at this moment our old friend Bill Webb decided to sell Cornwall House and we bought it, to satisfy both Barbara and myself. It was an L shaped Regency house set on two floors, dating from about 1800 and lay in a walled garden, not far from the main road, but far enough off to be quiet. Upstairs, there were six bedrooms, while downstairs my proposed professional quarters lay at one end of the L and totally cut off from our living rooms. A curious feature lay in the presence of three staircases which the children appreciated in their games of hide and seek. On the ground floor we had a fine dining/waiting room, my consulting room and beyond this a very large sitting room and the kitchen quarters formed the branch of the L. The kitchen was stone flagged, with an adjacent larder having hooks on the ceiling to carry hams and bacon. With out-houses consisting of a coal and a work shed in which to store all tools etc. and to do any carpentry it proved ideal both from a family and a work point of view. We all had ample space and with it all went a large cellar.

We moved in and were blissfully happy, for the house had something to offer to everybody. In my case I had excellent professional accommodation and, with the practice now well on its feet, I also had plenty to occupy me in my spare time, for, odd jobs about the house and work in the garden, which needed complete replanting, gave me plenty of occupation together with the laying of stone paths and the building of a terrace on which we could take our meals in summer. This involved the laying of some tons of stone paving.

Decorating the house, both in and out, some of which I did with Barbara's unfailing assistance, took some time, but gave us the occasion to make friends with Ibbetson the builder and his workmen. These raised an outcry when we decided to offset its general white wash with bright blue woodwork, brown being considered much more conventional, but the end result was superb. Later I noticed several other houses painted in blue. Cornwall House had at one time been known as Selina Cottage and in former times when surrounded by fields had acted as a farmhouse – one of my elderly patients remembering coming to the back door as a girl to collect the family milk. To us Cornwall House became a real home.

The family were equally pleased, the children having more space both in and out of the house, while for Barbara the shops were closer by and it was easy for friends to drop in for elevenses or at any odd moment when out shopping. Life in consequence proceeded quietly but very pleasantly and, although we were never able to get away for weekends this did not disturb us, as with the three children it would have been difficult to get away. With our month's leave we were able to spend excellent holidays, either with Barbara's Aunt in Switzerland, or with my Mother in Turkey.

On holiday in Switzerland we stayed with Mima Cantacuzene in Glion. Here at teatime, Kolya, a son of the house, announced that he intended coming to England to stay with us. Barbara, having noticed how much sugar he put in his tea, said that we would be delighted to see him, but that he must bring his own sugar. A month later a large parcel of sugar arrived followed a week later by Kolya.

The children had never tasted rich cakes, so as a treat we took them to Zurcher's, famous for its cakes, where to our surprise the children turned up their noses at the rich cakes and preferred the plain buns – to which wartime conditions had left them accustomed.

Here in Switzerland, in the absence of rationing, we bought the children excellent winter clothes and in hopes of avoiding custom dues on arrival in

England, the children, despite the warm weather, were dressed in these in preparation for landing. The custom official looked surprised at the sight, but kindly understood the position and let us through.

Then came the N.H.S. and once on my own I was faced with hard work but at the same time was offered the opportunity of putting my finances into order, for Michael was at Eagle House, while Maya had decided to become a boarder at her school, the Channings. As for John he was due to leave Eagle House, but flatly refused to continue schooling as a boarder. So he was fixed up as a day-boy at Highgate School, where he won an entry scholarship. He had threatened to run away if sent to boarding school.

With all this I was working too hard and after discussions with Barbara I decided on taking on a partner, at a consequent considerable loss of income. The selection was made, but my choice was not totally successful and I found myself working as hard as ever.

I thereupon applied for a job in the Ministry of Health offering fixed hours of work, excellent holidays, and free weekends. The latter was a luxury I had hitherto never enjoyed – but all this at a greatly reduced income. My move to the Ministry of Health also involved moving to Central London. This latter task was difficult as money was very tight. Eventually we found a suitable, but somewhat dilapidated, dirty and tattered old house in Park Road in St John's Wood, facing Regents Park, which had once been elegantly got up. It had no garden and backed onto the tube behind and the main road in front – disadvantages which were overlooked and ignored. Into this we moved in 1956. The lady who sold it to us made all sorts of promises, and these were never kept.

I had loved my work, which had brought me into close relation with men and women of all types, and had also, in many cases, involved me in their family lives and I missed the close contacts I enjoyed with human beings and being asked for and giving advice.

I also missed Cornwall House and the garden which had cost me so much thought and time and energy. Without a garden life lost a lot of its glamour. One further disadvantage, though one which did not cause much worry was a considerable fall in income.

All this is not to say that I did not benefit. For the first time in my working life I was able to enjoy free week-ends, to make plans without fear of interruption, to return home after work and feel that the evening was my own and to go to bed and to sleep without fear of disturbance. In addition I was able to leave the telephone entirely in Barbara's hands and to sit back when it rang without thoughts of work entering my mind.

The brighter sides of life proved however to be of far greater importance. Chief of these was that Barbara could now lead a normal life, able to indulge in personal activities and see and entertain her friends as and when she wished, free from the shackles imposed on her by the Practice. The same applied to the children who were now in the midst of 'life' and able to entertain friends at the house and in fact lead normal family roles.

I never entirely lost touch with old patients, keeping in contact with many and doing a sort of milk round before Christmas. On these occasions it was a joy to recapture the old spirit and to hear all the family news and gossip. I particularly enjoyed returning into the fold of the Kent-Briggs-Bentham-White families of wartime dockyard evacuees, with whom I had such fun and from whom I received such genuine welcome.

At the same time I had no doubts about having done the right thing for my family and never regretted the change in life. Here we spent 12 years and following these three years in Reading. Following my retirement, I undertook part time work until I reached the age of 75 to stop all work.

Postscript.

The house in London was a great success and they both led a very active social life. He retired on leaving Reading and they settled in London in a flat in Phillimore Gardens, off High Street Kensington, in 1971, eventually moving to Troy Court at the end of the road when the stairs began to become a problem for our mother. Later on his eyesight deteriorated to the extent that he was partially blind. Having finally stopped working, he and my mother travelled a lot, to the USA and Canada, China (twice) to stay with Michael, Zimbabwe to stay with his brother Willie, the Shetland Islands, and Portugal several times. During his retirement he wrote extensively on a variety of subjects, including these reminiscences and, despite his deteriorating sight, he continued writing up to his death in 2003. He died peacefully during the night in his own bed in the flat and all the family were there on his last evening. Barbara carried on living in Troy Court until she had to go into a home, where she died in 2006.

JWW 2011

CHAPTER VIII

Weston Underwood 1961 -1984

Following on my Mother's death in the 1960's, I received a small legacy which Barbara and I decided to devote to buying a small cottage in the country, a course of action of which Mother would have greatly approved.

Living in St John's Wood our thoughts turned to the North and we started our search in the Home Counties. We saw all manner of houses, large and small, with one in particular attracting our fancy, situated on an island in the River Ouse connected by a bridge, with no nearby shops. Sadly, however, this was not suitable by reason of its isolation and impossibility of access in wet weather across a muddy field, so we left it to its fate. Eventually we found what we wanted, a small and cheap cottage in the village of Weston Underwood, one mile from the small township of Olney, famous for its annual pancake race on Shrove Tuesday. So after some negotiations I paid up to become its owner.

The cottage was situated in Pevers Lane giving off the main road and had in times past housed the gardener to the adjacent large house. The cottage was detached, with one long side facing the lane and the opposite number looking across a field to the church on its far side. It was entered from the garden which was stone walled, and which had attracted me by reason of its good well-worked soil which had been mainly devoted to the growing of vegetables. Round about stood a number of similar cottages, most of them with thatched roofs. However, Pevers Cottage, as we named it, was two storied stone-built with a slate roof.

By way of accommodation there were two bedrooms upstairs and a reasonably sized living room with a small kitchen and a small offshoot used as a washroom. Mains water, drainage and electricity were laid on, but there was no bathroom and the toilet lay at the end of the garden. We were delighted with the purchase but not so Kapa Nebolsine (Barbara's brother-in-law) who thought we were mad.

Plans for conversion were drawn up to include a porch to the front door and to these the Planning Officer agreed, commenting that nothing we did to the cottage could make it look uglier. So the builders got to work and in the end we had two bedrooms, one fitted with a large cupboard, a living room fitted with electric night storage heating, a small kitchen, a washroom and toilet combined and a bathroom. This was achieved by cutting off that part of the living room in which had stood the old cooking range and fitting the bath under the chimney. The next step lay in finding suitable furniture and what was available from our London home was supplemented by purchases from local antique dealers.

The end result delighted us and we were also lucky in finding suitable domestic help; the former owner of the house suggesting we employ his daughter Joyce, who lived some 100 yards away, to clean the place and look after things in our absence. She proved a treasure and a good friend. Then for laundry we found Kathleen who, though unmarried had two daughters whose names were such that she was reputed to have been the consort of some noble Lord. She had a spare room which we could always rent.

Weston Underwood was a small village of some 200 inhabitants. All houses, except for those in a small council development, were built of grey limestone. On entering the village from Olney the road passed between two stone ornamental pillars, to run straight through past a small green, with one or two side-shoots, such as Pevers Lane. It was a village of great beauty, at one time home to William Cowper the poet, and frequently winner of the competition for the best kept village in the county. The village boasted of a pub, a post-office and a shop run by a Mrs Janko, the wife of a Hungarian émigré.

Full shopping facilities were available in neighbouring Olney, with its large central square, in which stands the Cowper museum in a house in which the poet once lived before moving to Weston. The vicar at that time was John Newton, a converted slave-trader, the writer of "Amazing Grace" who in collaboration with the poet published the "Olney Hymnal". The town lay on the bank of the river Ouse, which regularly flooded in the winter months.

Once settled in the cottage I set about getting to know our neighbours, most of whom occupied similar small cottages to ours, one of whom, Jack Clark, suffered from a gastric ulcer over which I was frequently consulted. He also had the reputation of having been a great ladies man and also a water diviner, in which capacity he once directed the Police to a body in the Ouse, though how and why is not revealed. The cottage next door to that of Jack Clark was occupied by a delightful old couple, Mr and Mrs Perkins. He had worked on the roads but now at the age of 80 was acting as jobbing gardener.

The third cottage in the road, next door to the Perkins, housed two huge Great Dane dogs – very friendly and good tempered. On the occasion of our second weekend, when things were still in a state of partial discovery, a knock at the door heralded the arrival of an elderly lady who presented a visiting card. We ushered her in and gave her a cup of tea and soon fell to chatting. She was a Miss Constance Stewart formerly in charge of some women's educational establishment and the sister of Bill Stewart who ran a local large farm. We got on famously and our friendship lasted till she died in her 100th year.

A short time later we were invited to drinks by a Colonel Leon Jones who lived in one of the large houses. We accepted and after a short time found that we had friends in common and so passed muster. (I had had occasion to talk to the Colonel's chauffeur and he had evidently given a good report on us). Next followed a further invitation and on this occasion we met all the gentry in the village and were accepted by all and sundry. In this way we settled down to a very pleasant social life, in the course of which we met men and women of a very wide variety of interests, extending well beyond farming and country pursuits.

Amongst others I here met Sacheverell Sitwell, who immediately enquired after Granny, while in another case my comments on some Persian tiles led to his showing us a fine collection of Chinese ware, to become the only people in the area to know of its existence, so well was it guarded.

Our butcher was a fellow of the Linnean Society and an expert naturalist. Another friend edited a Catholic journal; another had a collection of raptor birds, while another had helped design the Great War planes and so on. Plenty of variety.

One day when talking to our butcher he happened to mention that three Russian Orthodox nuns had settled in the vicinity. We called on them to find a trio made up of one Swiss, one English and one Anglo-Russian in deep distress as their water system was out of order and gave no hot water. We offered them the use of our cottage on weekdays for washing and bathing. They did not use it for long and thereafter became great friends, with me subsequently offering practical advice as required. One of them, Mother Theckla, subsequently wrote words set to music by John Taverner.

My daily routine consisted of an early breakfast followed by an hour or two's walk, followed by gardening – this involved starting from scratch. Firstly I had to find sufficient flat limestones with which to lay both paths and a small terrace on which to take meals. This having been done, the next step was to define flowerbeds and then lay the rest of the garden to lawn. Then to accede to Barbara's wishes I planted a Silver Birch which I dug up from a railway bank and a Nevada rose, which grew to a height of five feet and a diameter of six, to be totally covered in white flowers in the summer – a superb sight.

The terrace was equipped with a table and chairs and we took our meals in summer, often in company of a robin, which helped itself. The flower beds were filled with a variety of plants, many introduced from abroad. I also planted an apple tree which did us proud.

In the course of my walks I kept my eyes open for wild flowers and so found quite a considerable variety and was particularly pleased to find a stand of cowslips, today a rarity in some areas. On them I always talked to anyone I met and amongst such a gang of woodcutters, who included in their number one Pete, a very dumb youth, but in the pub he was always ready for the pint of beer I stood him. Meeting and chatting to country folk as opposed to town folk gave me much pleasure.

In London, in the main our family and social lives were private affairs, but in a small country village like Weston everyone's life came under scrutiny and Barbara soon learned that it was much wiser to be quite open about our affairs, which at least ensured that there was no gossip and tittle-tattle. Mrs Covington the post-mistress was a great help in this respect, for any information given her was soon known to all. She was also a great help to me in that being in possession of a large vegetable plot, I would give her the seeds of any unusual vegetable I wanted to try out, buying the resultant produce off her when mature.

Apart from vegetables we enjoyed a limited source of game, for Bill Stewart had given John permission to shoot on his land. This led to the occasional arrival of a rabbit or pigeons which we had to clean, a process usually left to me.

On one occasion, when Natasha (Barbara's sister) was staying with us she asked a farmer for a real fresh farmyard chicken, but was rendered speechless when after a short absence he returned carrying a dead bird, feathers and all, only to be calmed when he returned a few minutes later with a plucked bird.

On another occasion the daughter of an American niece, Katiousha, was staying with us and one morning she decided to play her violin in the garden, the sound of which, to our astonishment, set all the cows in the neighbourhood loudly mooing, as though in harmony.

Shortly after our arrival Constance Stewart made a second appearance to ask whether we wanted to join the Parish Register. I said that I would like to but that Barbara could not as she was Orthodox, to receive an immediate reply of "Of course she can, do you think anyone in the village has even heard of the Orthodox Church?" Barbara's name was added to the Register, only to be removed at a later date. We attended church services regularly, these proving much to my liking in being simple and straightforward, with no choir to take over the singing. In addition we knew everyone present which made the services somewhat of a family affair.

Meanwhile, a new, young and somewhat inexperienced Vicar, of the name of David, was appointed to our four small Parishes. One day he called on us in a state of great distress. Members of one Parish had collected enough money to set up an East window in their Church, in memory of a former much loved Pastor. Work on this project had not started, but in the meantime, their Church roof had sprung a leak. Whereupon David immediately and somewhat forcibly gave out that the money collected for the window must be diverted to mending the roof. This suggestion was met with immediate opposition, leaving David totally unable to understand how people could place more emphasis on an East window than on their church structure. The position had so degenerated that there was a possibility of open hostility. We sympathetically listened to David's tale of woe and then suggested that he was setting about things in entirely the wrong way, in that he was making no allowance for the feelings of his flock. Why not let them set up their window and then, when this was in place, ask for money to mend the roof. Others gave the same advice and this being followed, within two years the window was in place and the roof mended.

Every year, Weston held a church fête to raise money and in this everyone helped, whatsoever their creed. The fete was held on a Saturday on the village green and proved a great social gathering, with music displays, games, competitions, stalls selling all manner of goods, the whole usually ending in a dance in the evening. The prize in one competition was invariably a piglet, which thankfully I never won. We also attended such fetes held in other villages – all of the same pattern.

On the occasion of the Queen's Silver Jubilee we celebrated with a church service followed by a luncheon on the village green, set out at a long table decorated with red, white and blue cloths and napkins. The excellent lunch was followed by all manner of games, including a tug of war competition and a baby pram race – the baby being an adult male.

There was no hall or room in which to hold meetings, whist or social events, but the villagers were offered the use of the disused school at a peppercorn rent. It was decided that a committee be set up under the Chairmanship of the Parish Clerk. To convert the school required £12,000 to which the local District Council offered a handsome contribution. To make up the rest it was decided to hold a "Steam Rally", an open air show in which lovers of old fashioned engines of all kinds showed off their choices cleaned, repaired and in working order, such engines being of all sizes, from almost a toy to an actual steam roller. A site for the occasion was lent by the Woburn Estate and Barbara and I were given the task of collecting the entrance fees. By the time we arrived all the engines were in place, each attended by the owner and all in immaculate condition. At the same time there were stalls selling food and the like and amusements and competitions. The event went off well with visitors from all over the neighbourhood and owners bringing their exhibits from considerable distances.

I personally found the exhibits most interesting and instructive and everything went well. The financial result was so good that it was decided to hold a repeat performance the following year, this leading to the accumulation of sufficient money to convert the old school. The work was soon completed and when we attended an old age pensioners' lunch we ate in a largish hall, complete with fully organised kitchen and bathroom facilities.

With my retirement from work, with reduced income, the need for a new car, road congestion and increasing age, we sold the cottage. Since then all our former friends have either left the village or died, and the newcomers are not of the same categories. It was sad to leave and for me especially sad to leave the garden, on which I had worked so hard and which the new owners wrecked.

CHAPTER IX

Visitors

Up to the moment of settling in Finchley I had had no fixed abode of my own and hence was unused to the ways of social life. Marriage, however, changed all this, although Barbara was initially restricted in her activities by the small size of our house, and the arrival of babies.

The first indication of what the future was to hold for me came with the arrival one morning of Tatiana Vassilchikov (now Metternich) one morning for elevenses. I left her and Barbara talking, to return to lunch to find them still talking, back again at tea time and still talking to find her gone when I returned for supper. Tatiana visited us in Nether Street, but the full impact of visitors was not fully felt until we moved to Cornwall House with its greater facilities. Prior to this move Mum and Masha had been regular visitors, but after Masha's marriage we saw little of her.

A regular visitor was my brother Vernon, not always welcome after having lingered too long in a pub on the way to us. He was my brother and I had to look after him, but this was not the case with Barbara and I remain eternally grateful to her for having to put up with him for so long. Yet this was sad for basically he was a most loveable character, undone by marrying the wrong wife.

Two other brothers of mine stayed with us in Cornwall House – the first Osie, arriving from Canada. He had heard of the scarcity of hard liquor in England and so arrived with a case to help in meeting his requirements, after he had drained my small stock. He was an interesting companion for his experiences had been great – never working for longer than six months in any one job and mixing with millionaires on some occasions and on others living destitute. He finally married very happily, but on his wife dying from a brain tumour he settled in Rhodesia and died there.

Later my younger brother Bill arrived from Rhodesia accompanied by his wife Elf and four children. These, having spent all their lives in the wild, were close on totally uncivilised by western standards – they were a delight but at the same time destructive, swinging on chairs and jumping on beds to their detriment and kicking holes in the cupboard. The room they occupied was so messy that Nanny refused to make any attempt at cleaning or keeping it tidy. If I should happen to tell them off over something or other they would mutter to each other in the Shona language, leaving me to wonder what abuse they were uttering.

As their stay came to an end Elf was worried over how her strict Victorian parents would take to the children, but she need not have done so, for when on being introduced into that holy of holies the Drawing room and immediately started turning somersaults on the sofa, Mrs Hingston told Elf to let them enjoy themselves. It was interesting to see Bill and Elf under these conditions, for our previous glimpse of them had been before the war, when confusion reigned as to whether the marriage was on or off, until final agreement was reached when the outbreak of war led to the need for a speedy return to Africa.

Shortly after the end of the war my cousin Fay van Rechteren arrived to ask us to look after their son Dolph, who was being sent to school in Bedford. Dolph's father, Willem, served in the Dutch diplomatic service. Dolph disliked boarding school life; as a result of which, while in England, we saw a lot of him as he turned up at our house whenever the opportunity offered. At the end of school life he returned to Holland, but frequently flew over to see us.

Another visitor was Asya Cantacuzene who came to England to marry Terence Roddy. Immediately a difficulty arose as the Roddy family Catholic Priest refused to marry Terence to one of Orthodox persuasion. Immediately an appeal was made to Barbara, who got into touch with our local much loved Father Hogan, who agreed to marry the couple, with the result that the wedding took place from 1 Finchley Way. Asya subsequently gave birth to a son Nicholas with further trouble over his baptism, Terence under threat of excommunication if this were not Catholic and Asya threatening to leave him if the child were baptised a Catholic. A masterly compromise solved the problem – Nicholas was baptised Anglican and by a Bishop to ensure validity.

An ever welcome visitor was Nicholas Arsenieff, a professor of theology and a most loveable man. His one defect was that he took his baths in a strange manner – always leaving the room flooded. At breakfast one day I happened to mention that I knew the opening verses of St John's Gospel in Greek, which started him off carrying on in Greek until I thought he would never stop. As I have said a most loveable individual, who regularly sent us copies of his writings, which, to us, were totally unintelligible.

In contrast to him we had Maritchka Vsevoldskaya, who came to us for a weekend. I could not stand her and after a fortnight of her company I told Barbara that either she left the house or I did, this after she had taken out her false teeth at the luncheon table for us to admire. She left and sent me a present of dates, the first mouthful of which led to an intense stomach upset. At a later date she gave Barbara's name as a reference when applying for a job with friends of ours. They did not take up the reference but were furious over Barbara having allowed her name to be used and were only pacified when Barbara assured them that Maritchka was the last person on earth she would recommend for a job.

Family-wise our children played their part in the way of visitors. On one occasion John ordered us two to leave the house as he was entertaining a detachment of French parachutists. They came and went and we returned home, expecting to find the house in disorder, to find it left in perfect order, except for a mass of empty beer bottles in the back yard. Maya used to bring home friends after dances, some to sleep, but most to have breakfast. The depredations on food stocks as a result of this led me to labelling my intended breakfast "Dad's breakfast" to save it from consumption. She also introduced a black Kenyan boxer, who haunted the house for a few days.

We also had a succession of American and French youths either staying with us or haunting the house. These varied in quality and in some cases Barbara had to tell them "your bath is ready" to assure personal cleanliness. One day we had three from Baltimore to lunch, they were of different social and financial grades, but all showing enormous appetites. But at then end of the meal, all three produced small pill boxes, varying from plastic to silver according to status and each took a pill, which, to our surprise over what they had consumed, replaced an element which was missing in the diet.

One young man was of different character. He had arranged to meet Arkadi in London, but the latter did not turn up. Clearly short of money he fed with us, but insisted that he had somewhere to sleep, which we suspected was the park. In due course he left, finally to turn up again a year later when he explained that on his way to take up a job in Rome, he had deliberately travelled via London in order to thank Barbara for her past kindness to him.

We also had three French youths sent to us. The first, Francois Lemerle, had a job and was no problem, the second Jean Giraud, was sent to learn English. He philandered and spent his time enjoying life, but apart from winning a prize for the Cha-Cha in a night-club achieved nothing. The third, Jean-Philippe de Coet-Logon, a Marquis, was the son of an old friend of Barbara's and held the unfortunate position of being the youngest of seven children, all six preceding him being girls. He was a great joy and was introduced to the dancing season with great success. He was invited to a dance in Scotland, but had no money to pay for his expenses, so Barbara advised him to follow in the footsteps of others and take up a part-time job. This he did to have a great time. A year later Barbara met his mother, the Marquise, who enquired as to how Jean-Philippe had been able to afford to go to Scotland. Barbara explained the situation, to shock his mother, who could not understand how her son, the Marquis, had undertaken menial work and could have been received in society after having worked as a waiter.

Then there were Dicky and Kika van Damme, war refugees from Belgium, whom I came across before my call up. Young and miserably depressed we tried to cheer them up with little success. Kika was a French speaking Walloon and looked down on Dicky who was a mere Fleming. Dicky had been born in England during the course of the First World War, when his mother was a refugee. So he was immediately collared by the British Army but he was so inefficient and miserable that he was transferred to the Belgian Army. After the war we met them in France for lunch, at which the wine they served thoroughly upset me. A strange couple.

On our return from holiday one year Barbara, on entering the house immediately said "someone has been sleeping in the house." I could not see any reason for this statement, but when we next saw Richard, my nephew from Africa, he confessed to having done so, having no lodging. He managed to get in through a lavatory window, slept in the house for several nights and on leaving made certain that all was secure.

Outside of these we enjoyed the company of numerous visitors and especially so in Park Road. All our houses were always open to members of the family and friends on passage through London or in the case of Barbara's mother residence for longer periods. An interesting life never knowing what was to come next.

Part IX

MILITARY SERVICE

CHAPTER I

England & North Africa

England

When I was called up in 1940 I was sent to Aldershot to learn how to be a soldier. I was fitted out with a uniform and generally taught the elements of my future work in such compressed style that I did not remember much. More importantly, I was allowed home each weekend.

From Aldershot I was sent to Cardiff to a camp which took in new recruits, all of whom had to be fully examined and given protective inoculations (under not very sterile conditions). All the recruits were Welsh, with some from the North unable to speak any English. My orderly, who boasted of the un-Welsh name of Quinn, spent his civilian life on the dog racetrack and from him I learnt much about its inner workings. With his inner knowledge he also laid some very good and successful bets in which I participated at times. In the mess I shared a room with a young man who boasted of his lordly connections, which did not prevent him stealing a bottle of sherry off me – a rare luxury at the time.

Following my first year's military service in Cardiff, I was posted to Leeds, where I was informed that I was to be sent overseas and given a fortnight's embarkation leave. Our destination overseas was not disclosed and led to much speculation among the seven of us. On my return to Leeds I found myself attached to a unit known as a Reception Camp with a total strength of some seventy. Its purpose in life was to be mobile and at all times prepared to take in men and troops on passage, up to the number of 2000. Usually no notice of arrival was given except in the case of large numbers, so that all eventualities had to be catered for.

During our two or three weeks we got to know each other and collected our equipment, mine consisting of a large chest containing a bottle of South African brandy and a large supply of amphetamine tablets.

Our Colonel was a genial soul, with whom I got on straight away. He liked his drink and, having heard that all troop ships were dry, as soon as he was told that our destination was Algiers, he amassed a large stock of spirits to keep us in comfort on board ship – and how we blessed him for his foresight.

North Africa

On arrival in Algiers, he asked me to take control over the Officers' Mess, and the NAAFI and, although these normally did not fall into the sphere of the medical officers, I decided to take over these jobs.

My medical duties, apart from the normal ones, included giving advice on sanitary arrangements and supervising their proper maintenance. I enjoyed being in charge of the Officers' Mess and in collaboration with our cook ensured that we had interesting food. As for my medical work, the volume of this varied from day to day.

What I did find interesting was that passing through the camp I met a large number of interesting people, while the variable nature of things allowed me plenty of time to indulge in other interests – but there were periods of boredom.

Our intake showed some variety and at odd times included a couple of Arabs, a German prisoner-of-war, two dogs, and an Irish Catholic Padre, who was as confused over his presence as we were. Why the German arrived was never explained – he was a plain simple youth as bewildered as we were.

CHAPTER II

Sicily

Syracuse

On August the 8th 1943 we embarked on a small troop-carrying ship for Italy, with me delighted at the prospect of returning to Europe, having had enough of Africa, although I would not have missed the experience of going there for anything. Embarkation proceeded smoothly, with only a slight contretemps when it was discovered that we had not been issued with any food for the journey. This omission being remedied we set off in intense heat, the ship resembling an oven. Some relief was afforded by the generous offer of gin and water by the ship's officers, but I spent the night hot, sticky and restless. A cooler morning, a good breakfast and the sight of land helped to revive us, with excitement increasing as we approached Syracuse with its warm-coloured houses and churches set on a headland projecting into the sea.

Once landed, I was overjoyed at being back in Italy and appreciating everything I saw including the large-lettered Fascist inscriptions on walls, such as "Credere, Obbedire, Tacere" "Believe, Obey and Keep Silent". Our camp site was under a grove of tall trees skirting a main road on the outside of the town. How pleasing it was to see tall, green trees again after the endless, low, grey olive trees of Sousse. So, our tents being pitched, we made ourselves comfortable and once again I admired the Army Supply Services which provided us with food, water and all necessities without delay. The Colonel wanting to make some purchases, we went into the town that evening only to find all shops shut, it being Sunday, and with me airing my immature Italian on every possible occasion.

Next morning we woke to bright sunshine, with the road busy with passers-by and gaudily painted Sicilian type carts, whose horses were equally gaily got up. There being no cover I had to have my bath in full view of the road, over which I cannot say I was disturbed for I felt that anyone seeing me would be more astonished at the idea of taking a bath than at any display of nudity.

There being no work to do, I started immediately on sight-seeing and made my way to the Greek theatre which lay close by. This proved a revelation and I could only marvel how a structure of such simplicity, consisting of totally unadorned, rising tiers of stone seats could produce such an effect of grandeur and harmony, enhanced by its position, overlooking a lagoon and the green hills in the distance.

But all was not always peace and quiet here, for during the war between Athens and Syracuse, the army of the former was heavily defeated and those soldiers who were unable to get away to the safety of their ships were incarcerated in a huge underground cavern, close to the theatre, and left there to rot while their captors looked down on them from above, a truly terrible story. It is happier to remember Archimedes, who having made a momentous discovery while in his bath, ran naked down the street shouting "Eureka, Eureka." ("Eureka" in modern Greek is "I have found it").

The other great relic of these times is the Cathedral whose florid baroque exterior offers no clue to its interior in which the colonnade of the former temple of Athena, dating back to 1000 B.C., forms the nave and remains unspoilt by excessive decoration. It is good to feel that the site has been used for religious worship for over 3,000 years. I wonder whether such a span is exceeded anywhere else in Europe.

Syracuse has further claims to interest in its baroque architecture. Sadly at this period of life I had not been brought up to appreciate it and, in consequence, some of the impact of the town was lost on me. Nevertheless I found it most interesting to wander through the narrow streets lined with shabby tall houses and occasionally coming across a tall grand portal giving access to the courtyard of a large house or palazzo, with usually at the far end a fine staircase leading to the piano nobile, the first floor housing the reception rooms etc. I would have loved to have seen the inside of one or two, but as things were it was difficult to make out whether any were still occupied by the family or converted into offices or flats. The larger palazzi stood alone with their proud facades clearly exposed and highly ornamented in true Sicilian fashion.

Then of course there were the people. With my Italian improving every day I talked to all and sundry, while watching the local life. We English were well received and everyone seemed glad to see us, though whether we were personally liked or only preferred to the Germans it was difficult to say. Anyhow I found it difficult to believe that we were in an enemy country. Everyone complained about Fascism, some with reason, some without. One of the former complained bitterly "Why, you had to work to get a ration card." But the main complaint was of the vast numbers of highly paid officials, who occupied the best flats and increased their incomes through sidelines such as the black market. One man referred to a large hospital for tuberculosis and to another one for mental patients built under Mussolini, and said: "That is all he did for us. He filled one hospital with those who developed tuberculosis from starvation and the other with those who went mad over the payment of taxation."

Although by British standards food was reasonably cheap and good, especially local produce, there was still quite a lot of evidence of hunger and we were constantly asked for biscuits or any kind of food even by quite well-dressed people. Rationing had been severe. No flour, eggs, pasta and little oil and sugar. No milk, rice or fish and little meat. Bread was black and the ration was 5 ½ oz a day, in the winter recourse had to be made to the black market in which it cost the equivalent of 2/6 a kilo, little enough one might say but with the average wage 15/- to 17/6 a week a lot. No wool, no cheap clothes, little other cloth (and very expensive), no cigarettes or matches. On the other hand at this season vegetables and fruit were excellent and far cheaper than in England. Lemons were 40 a shilling, tomatoes and aubergines a few pence a kilo. But this was summer and in Sicily winters can be cold. Nevertheless people did not look too bad; the situation was improving and, of course, allowance had to be made for exaggeration.

With everyone most friendly and helpful all I had to complain about was the local accent which at times was difficult to get to grips with. But one day I had a stroke of luck. Wandering round a pound containing abandoned enemy vehicles, I found one full of coffee and this proved to be immensely helpful for coffee was unobtainable and was the most welcome of gifts. Incidentally another truck was full of cigars and these were dished out to us through NAAFI.

In the town I made particularly good friends with one elderly lady who ran a shop selling clothing. Initially she sold me some silk stockings to send home and in the course of so doing we got onto other subjects such as families, children and so on. I enjoyed her company, she was a very decent, simple soul and one day I took her a parcel of coffee. This opened the door to many further purchases, including silk and other materials, as well as a complete set of aluminium saucepans, unprocurable in England, which on arrival back home, became much prized wedding presents. Here also I bought a wonderful pair of pyjamas for myself, all purple and gold, described as being of "Poplino Super Lativo". I became very attached to the good lady, a delightful personality and different from the average local. My initial concept of the Sicilians was not too favourable, finding them rather severe and coarse. Young girls could be very attractive, but their good looks fade rapidly. To generalise one could say that the local women could be divided into those too young to have a baby, those about to have one, those who had just had one and finally those too old to have any more. With their mixed blood, including Arab, the Sicilian is very different from the North Italian and is despised by the latter in consequence. As an example of attitudes I once heard an Italian Officer prisoner ask one of the locals for a glass of water. He turned away and the officer exclaimed "This is how we Italians treat each other", to get the immediate response "no sono Italiano, sono Siciliano"; "I am not Italian I am Sicilian."

The immediate surrounding countryside was in no way dramatic, being mainly devoted to plantations of oranges, lemons and almonds, interspersed with vegetable gardens and vineyards. One interesting fruit growing there was the bergamot, a powerfully scented sort of orange used in perfumery. All these were irrigated by streams brought down from the hills in channels of considerable antiquity and complexity and in places running some 15 feet underground.

The following extract from one of my letters describing a walk I took will give a good idea of the countryside: "Yesterday we had a grand walk to a castle some five miles away. Most of the time our path took us through lemon and orange groves, meeting streams bordered by blackberry bushes every 100 yards or so. Every now and then we came to a farm at which we stopped to have a chat and a glass of water. In places we got lovely views extending over the plain and the town and harbour. Eventually we reached a hill village with narrow streets and small one storied houses, on whose roofs trays of tomatoes were drying and getting ready to be made into paste. Most front doors were open giving access to large front rooms, many containing beds, and through them to the kitchen beyond. In most houses the owners were sitting on the doorsteps, gossiping, while half-naked children were running about all over the place. The village centered round a sort of square which housed the church and a café. Further on we climbed up to the castle and from it we got the most glorious views in every direction. We returned by a different route passing a large fortified encampment with walls of stone. This I learned later was a fortified Greek outpost of the town."

The countryside was well cultivated and the farms looked prosperous, with livestock of cows, pigs, chickens and turkeys. Here in the country there was less evidence of hunger. I had a very pleasant experience in a small township. My watch stopped while out walking and seeing a small shop selling watches I showed it to the man, asking if he could do anything about it – I may add that this had occurred twice in England and each time I had taken it back to Benson's in Bond Street, from whom I had bought it, to be charged a couple of guineas for their services. My little man opened the back, picked up a needle, did something with it and returned it to me going. Very surprised I asked him what it was all about and he told me the hairspring tended to stop and all that was necessary was to touch it with the point of a needle. He refused all payment. This incident set me wondering about different standards of commercial morality, to the advantage of the Italian.

An amusing incident concerned a man who came to me asking for an injection of Vitamin C. I pointed out to him that right across Sicily there were miles and miles of orange and lemon groves, whose fruit is packed with the vitamin and all he had to do was to eat more of them. But this did not satisfy him, he wanted an injection. This I refused on principle, although with a bit of pure water in the syringe I could have satisfied him.

After a little time we received instructions to move on and the Colonel took me with him to reconnoitre the proposed site on the outskirts of Catania. Roads were so bad that the forty mile journey took us three hours. I was very surprised that, apart from a bit of barbed wire, there was no evidence of any defences. There was an occasional pillbox to be seen but no bridges had been destroyed. There was, however, plenty of evidence of our bomber activities and one aerodrome was a complete shambles of broken buildings and destroyed planes. In Catania the Colonel went off leaving me sitting in the car to be pestered by people asking for biscuits or anything to eat. I became very annoyed and I wondered whether this was due to my becoming hardened or to the fact of being sorry for the poor wretches and being unable to help them in any way. The town itself looked depressing with a good deal of damage. Despite what was happening at home I derived no pleasure from seeing the damage done to enemy towns.

I loved Syracuse with its echoes of past history, the tragedy of the Athenian army, Archimedes and Eureka

Catania

We moved to our next camp site on the outskirts of Catania towards the end of August 1943. We travelled by rail, loaded into open goods trucks, and the journey took us twenty-four highly uncomfortable hours, involving a nine hour halt in one spot. However, we eventually arrived at our destination. This proved highly satisfactory, being set among lemon groves and vineyards, although offering little shade.

Living and working conditions in Catania were poor and among other troubles we were landed with the riffraff from the 51st Highland Division who had been seeded out prior to the Division being returned home. Some of those men proved a confounded nuisance to my department in the way of over drinking, injuries and general complaints both by day and night. Their departure was greeted with general rejoicing. I also had my first experience of Africans who were well behaved.

Our camp abutted on a vineyard and once settled in, I went over and talked to some men working there. I asked one youth why he was not in the army and he told me that strictly speaking he still was but had deserted. He was in a unit guarding the coastline from which he had a good view of the allied ships approaching, whereupon his mind ran as follows: "If the Germans win the war we Italians will have lost out and the same will apply if the Allies win. What then is the point of risking death if Italy is going to lose the war anyway?" So he escaped. Not exactly a brave attitude, but to my mind showing a lot of sense.

As usual we suffered from one of the inconveniences of life in these parts, namely incessant demands for biscuits, cigarettes and food in general, even from well-dressed people. I began to believe that with us having taken over the country, the Italians thought they were entitled to be handed out such "luxuries" as food and cigarettes, of which we had unlimited stocks. Despite the part the Italians had played in the war, the Germans were being blamed for everything, the Italians being entirely guiltless. I contained myself, remembering that most of the people I met were entirely uneducated.

A few days after arrival I found myself in hospital, feeling ghastly and depressed and with my skin of a bright yellow colour: Infective Hepatitis. But, despite the discomfort it was a joy to lie on a proper bed, between clean white sheets and to get excellent attention from nurses and doctors. My first meal was a disaster as having no appetite I could not face up to the cold bully beef and tinned potatoes offered me, but thereafter I subsisted mostly on fruit, of which there was plenty. To add to my sense of well-being I heard that a large draft of men had somewhat unexpectedly arrived at the camp which consequently was in a state of complete shambles.

There were about fifteen of us in the ward. One patient was a young and very handsome naval doctor, and it was amusing to watch the nurses buzzing around him and entertaining him with their chatter. Listening to them made me realize how far removed I was from my normal world and how long it had been since I had last listened to good female chit-chat and gossip. The bed next to me was occupied by a German officer with whom I got on well and I enjoyed hearing descriptions of his experiences in various sectors of the war. In Russia he was horrified by the conditions under which the peasants lived, their huts made of clay and wattle with a central stove for heating and cooking. All were bare-footed with their clothes in tatters. This was in White Russia and things further South were little better. He also said that he never saw anyone laugh or smile unless drunk. The absence of churches made a great impression on his fellows, such as still stood being used as offices or stores.

I also heard an interesting account of our landing in Taranto from an English officer. This was unopposed until the advance guard came across some stiff resistance which flummoxed them as they had no artillery. However on noticing the state of affairs an Italian Colonel offered them the use of his guns together with some men to help out, and these Italians fought very well indeed. One of them enjoyed the situation as he had been imprisoned by the Germans and felt he was getting his own back. He told me that to judge from the way German wounded were treated by the Italians there was no love lost between them. He had been the first man to enter a newly captured town and in so doing had been kissed by about a hundred people, including the Mayor. He said it was pathetic to see how delighted the inhabitants were to see the British.

Meanwhile the jaundice was slowly subsiding, but to add to my discomfort I developed a corneal ulcer in one eye and also a carbuncle. But in recompense my appetite was improving and the main inconvenience arose from frequent stoppages of the water supply interfering with washing and toilet facilities. Incidentally my gay pyjamas of Poplino superlativo were much admired in the ward.

After a time I was allowed out for walks. Initially I was too weak to go far but I managed to get some glimpses of the town, whose chief son Bellini, the operatic composer, is highlighted everywhere. The town itself was mainly modern and unattractive though possessed of some good baroque buildings, some fine palazzi and churches. I did not feel up to doing any serious sight-seeing but did a bit of shopping for clothes. I also sent home parcels of lemons which arrived safely and were welcome, being unobtainable in England at that time.

Prior to leaving there was a new arrival in the ward, an officer who before the war had managed an estate of some 12,000 acres, spending most of his day on horseback and who had now been blinded. There was hope for one eye but the other was a total loss. What an utter waste of a good life.

I was eventually discharged from hospital at the end of September, having lost a lot of weight and feeling very weak and under strict instruction to keep off alcohol for at least two months. In hospital I had become very friendly with the physician who looked after me, and met him again in London where I used him a lot for consultations. He was a grand man and a great help to me.

Riposto

While in hospital the unit had moved up the coast to a small place called Riposto. Also the Colonel had returned to hospital, which was good news as he had become very tiresome. The journey to Riposto proved interesting. Firstly we passed a fantastic, highly ornate baroque church in the township of Aci Reale, in which I should have loved to have spent some time. Then, once out of the town we saw a number of islets and rocks out to sea, which, by repute, had been thrown by the blinded giant Polyphemus at Odysseus when escaping in his ship. In this neighbourhood too (one amongst many) Pluto is said to have abducted Proserpine and taken her down to Hades. Nearby there was a church dedicated to Santa Venere, built on the foundations of a temple to Venus, which made me wonder how that somewhat adventurous lady took to being converted to a Saint. It is difficult to escape from the past in these regions.

Riposto stretched along the sea coast and its front was lined with pleasant villas, one of which had been taken over as our mess, offering us such luxuries as a piano, a gramophone and armchairs. At the back there was a good sized garden while from the front one got a fine view covering the coast up to Taormina and then across the water to the mountains of Southern Italy.

The mess being full, I was found a room in a neighbouring house, whose high vaulted ceilings conduced to coolness in summer, but made no concessions to warmth in winter. My room was simply furnished, its great asset being a balcony on which to take my morning bath. This afforded a superb view over Etna arising cone-shaped from its lower reaches to its full height of 10,000 feet. Up to about half way up, its slopes are green and dotted with houses. Higher up it is bare, rocky and forbidding, covered in ashes.

Etna has periodically had its days of glory as when some centuries ago it overwhelmed Catania. With us the only sign of activity was an occasional whisp of smoke rising from its summit. But I came across evidence of previous activity in the shape of a river of lava, some forty yards wide and forty feet high snaking down the mountain-side and ending as a high wall in the middle of a field.

My house was well up-to-date with indoor sanitation and a plug and chain. I was a bit astonished however, when one day, standing in the vegetable garden by a small reservoir of water, I heard the sound of flushing in the house followed by gurgling and commotion in the water at my feet, clearly fertiliser is too valuable to be wasted.

The camp itself lay among orange and lemon groves and the site proved to be the best we had so far had. The cookhouse stood out in the open, covered with sheets of corrugated iron. These were struck one day by lightning and hearing the report and the clatter I rushed to the scene expecting to find mangled corpses, only to be disappointed, no one suffering anything worse than shock.

Here at Riposto the surrounding country was flat and not of much interest. This suited me for, in my then state of weakness, I was quite happy to confine my walks to the sea-front. But lovely as the sea was, Etna dominated the scenery at all hours and in all weathers, with its vast cone rising directly from the surrounding plain, particularly so of an early morning when the rays of the rising sun were reflected off the windows of the houses on its slopes in countless pinpoints of light. The more I saw of the mountain the better I began to understand how in the past humans endowed it with an almost God-Like character.

The actual sea-shore was very stony and rocky and not suited to comfortable bathing, but the men made full use of it. Sadly on a stormy day one man would not heed advice but tried to swim and was drowned.

With the arrival of our new CO, Major Horn, or rather Trader Horn as he was generally known, there was a complete change in the atmosphere of the mess. Trader was very much of a buccaneer, missing no opportunity for bettering his condition in life or for amusement. On the other hand he made an excellent CO and proved of immense help to me as I faced the shambles left me in the camp, nothing for example having been done about sanitation and other matters. So everything had to be started from scratch with the possibility of large numbers of men arriving with very little warning. Thanks to Trader too, I was also able to set up a small sick-bay in a neighbouring house, sufficient to lodge ten men lying on stretchers, a facility which proved of great advantage in that I had the sick under one roof and not scattered all over the place.

This was as well, as before we knew where we were our first intake of some 3,000 blacks arrived, men of various tribes recruited into the labour force, including a number of Mauritians whose French dialect proved most interesting.

These men gave little trouble and I found them pleasant to deal with, they were always cheerful and ready for laughter. A particular favourite was a young Zulu who was incorrigible in vaunting the superiority of his tribe over all others, each such occasion ending in a fight with him in the minority always coming off the worst. He would then come to me for repairs, to return undaunted to his former practices with the same results. So I saw quite a lot of him. To help out I selected a Basuto, with some pretence to being a medical orderly and attached him to my jurisdiction, a good man who was very useful in handling his colleagues. Their idea of a really good medicine was a strong purge. Had I succumbed to their demands, I would have been cleared of castor oil and No 9 pills within a day or two and would have had the whole lot reporting sick.

One regular task in the army was the monthly F.F.I. (Free From Infection examination), an external examination associated with the inspection of clothes for the presence of lice, which occasionally turned up in the most unexpected of places. With the ordinary soldier the inspections were matters of bored indifference, but the blacks, keeping their eyes well open took delight in the exposure of any physical abnormality, all the more so should this prove to be of a sexual nature, such as overgrowth of breast tissue, the sight of which would lead to hoots of joy and merriment. Simple minds and simple pleasures.

Once my work was organised I set about getting to know the local population and paid my first visit to the Parish priest, a fat and jovial man boasting of the name of the Revd. Pasquale Sciarcella, with whom I got on well from the word go and we became good friends. Later I suggested that, owing to the nearest doctor living some way away, I would gladly see anyone in trouble. As a result of my offer I soon found myself running an Italian clinic, refusing all payment. A few days later a boy turned up carrying a basket of fruit and fish, sent me by the priest, who on being tackled said that as I was helping the villagers they would like to return the compliment by helping my sick. With the baskets continuing to arrive, occasionally including fish, my sick did not do too badly.

My next move was to invite the priest to dinner in the mess, to the consternation of all but Trader, with whom he got on very well, not surprisingly since they were birds of a feather. He had never tasted whisky and pooh-poohed my warnings regarding its strength; at the end of the evening he had to be taken home safely by myself and another officer, each taking him by an arm.

Some days later he invited the mess to his house, where we sat down in a simple room before an array of bottles of local wine, each one of which had to be sampled. After this each one of us was asked which of the wines he had preferred and got a glass of this. We all staggered home decidedly cheerful. On the following day I met the priest in the street to be greeted with a huge smile and a "Ah, Signor Dottore, I am one up on you," and to my query as to what he meant he replied: "You made one parish priest drunk but I did so to a whole Officers' mess," which was of course not far from the truth.

I liked him enormously. Although in no way well educated he was very down to earth and sincere in his simple beliefs, which were untouched by any profound theology. He knew his flock well, and was the ideal man to be in charge of such a parish. In the pulpit he was magnificent denouncing those who had strayed from the narrow path and not hesitating to address them by name, with particular emphasis on any girl who had been seen consorting with one of our men. The more I saw of him the more I liked and respected him and wished there were more priests of his type, though I could not see him hitting it off in an English village.

One day I was buying some fruit in a shop on the front when a boy sitting at a table asked me to help him over some English he was learning. So I sat down and gave him a lesson and afterwards talked to him and his mother. I subsequently took to dropping in to help him over his English and to get him to help me over my Italian...a very satisfactory arrangement. Angelo, as he was called proved to be a very pleasant young man and I soon became friendly with the whole family, who were a cut above the average Sicilian. On one occasion I was invited to dinner and was introduced to sweet potatoes and to a salad of leaves picked that morning in the fields, a most delicious assortment. Madame also offered to wash my clothes for me, but refused all payment which put me in rather an awkward position.

I also got to know a number of local fishermen, most of whom used bombs to get their catches, despite the danger of having a finger or so blown off. I went out on a couple of occasions to catch octopus and sea-urchins, of which latter the eggs alone are eaten and taste somewhat like caviare. In pursuit of these the sea-bed is scanned with the aid of a glass-bottomed box which is held over the side of the boat in the water. Octopuses are speared with a barbed trident, urchins caught up in the split end of a long bamboo.

Interestingly many of the local names of fish and vegetables are identical to those used in the Near East, these including 'Kefal' for grey mullet, and 'agombro' for mackerel. Strangely 'anguri' here stands for a melon and not for a cucumber as in Greece.

On one occasion I had helped one of the fishermen and he made me the present of a magnificent lobster. This gave a good excuse for a dinner party at which the menu consisted of hors d'oeuvres, soup, lobster, curry and crème caramel, all derived from army rations, except for the lobster.

As the only Italian speaker I was constantly in demand as an interpreter and had to answer some very peculiar requests. The most amusing one came from a man who, in return for the concession of running a stall in the camp perimeter, offered me unlimited supplies of fruit and vegetables and also the full use of his daughter. I never actually saw the girl but occasionally lay awake, wondering whether I had missed the chance of consorting with a Sicilian beauty.

Taormina lay some ten miles away up the coast, and proved to be a most enchanting place, built on a hillside running down to a rocky coastline with sandy beaches. The old part of the town was made up of narrow streets and low houses while in the modern part there were elegant villas and smart hotels. From these a funicular runs down to the sea, and in peacetime this place was a great resort for naval honeymoon couples from Malta. Up above the township there is a magnificent Greek theatre offering spectacular views over Etna in the distance, and said to be particularly lovely in the early part of the year when the intervening plain is painted pink with the blossom of innumerable almond trees.

Here we found a tea garden run by an elderly couple and their son-in-law.

He, having been a Socialist, fled to Paris when Mussolini came into power, but was repatriated by the Germans and imprisoned by the Fascists. We talked in French and had a most interesting discussion. Strangely enough there was a distinctly Russian atmosphere about the family. Otherwise there was little of interest except for a first class bookshop from which I stocked up my library with both Italian and English books, buying amongst others the poems of Leopardi, of which more anon.

The hills above the town looked most inviting and I would have loved to be able to climb them. In the spring they must be ablaze with flowers. In a way Taormina depressed me, not through any fault of its own, but being clearly meant to be a place for sun and laughter it now appeared empty and deserted, entirely as a result of man's stupidity, although it was thanks to this stupidity that I was here at all, and in a privileged position, for but for the war I would not have been able to enter into such a close relationship with the local inhabitants of the country.

With Trader Horn in command life was never dull as he never missed any opportunity for enjoyment. We started by inviting nurses from a local hospital to a dance and on another occasion attended another given in a R.A.F. convalescent home high up on Etna. Both these parties were very good fun but I found the nurses, though attractive and possessed of all the virtues, somewhat dull and uninteresting, but judging from the gaiety and the laughter, the fault for this must have lain in my mental make-up. Clearly I was slowly being seduced into Italian ways, although it was a great pleasure once again to talk to English girls.

Meanwhile an old friend had made a reappearance, this time with a car at his disposal in which he used to make frequent trips to Catania on business, although I had my suspicion that they were more closely connected with an Italian singer. She was part of a troupe who called themselves the 'Sicilian Follies' and as soon as Trader heard of them he arranged that they should come down to entertain the troops. The artistes were made up of seven ladies, all of decidedly Rubensian proportions, who were helped out by a good band. Their performance was cheerful but undistinguished and very funny in parts, although so vulgar as to leave nothing to the imagination, which was just as well as none of the audience apart from me understood any Italian.

After the show we entertained the cast to supper in the mess. I don't suppose any of them had had such a good meal for months and it was a pleasure to see them tuck in. One good lady told me a heart-rending tale about her children and I suggested she took back some of the food home with her. She did not wait to be told twice but quickly emptied a dish of sausage rolls into her capacious handbag.

This was the first occasion on which I had an opportunity to talk to Sicilian women of this class and I was struck how one and all had refreshed their poor and worn dresses with touches of colour, each giving a touch of self-regard to the scene. To stop any misunderstandings I impressed on them that I was 'un uomo serio', a serious man, blessed with wife and children. This fact being accepted, we were able to converse in complete freedom and without any inhibitions. I also had to act as general interpreter. This was great fun as I turned rather banal English compliments into much more flowery Italian phraseology. It was also very amusing to understand our guests' comment on the company and the proceedings, they finding the British somewhat strange. On leaving they all told me that they had enjoyed themselves thoroughly and whatever else, they all, for a change, had been able to fill themselves with good food.

These women led lives of great poverty and deprivation and especially so in wartime, but made no complaint over the hardships of life and were full of fun and laughter. No doubt little could be said about their moral approach to life, but I felt an enormous admiration for them and enjoyed the evening enormously, with little occasion to talk to the men. (The food situation in Sicily at this time was very poor with mainstays of life, such as pasta, in very short supply).

On another occasion when a dance was proposed a friend offered to bring some girls from Taormina. These arrived in the care of an elderly and respectable looking lady, who immediately posed the rather ominous question of: "Are we here on business or pleasure?" in answer to which I reassured her that the party was purely for pleasure. Meanwhile another officer had invited his beautiful girl-friend who, to his horror and to the general amusement, arrived complete with Husband, Mother, Father and Great Aunt, who throughout the proceedings sat silently in one corner of the room. Such chaperonage inevitably gave rise to a certain confusion and dismay in British male breasts as they were totally unused to such conventions. It suited me for I tended to find the younger girls, however attractive, rather dull and I derived a lot of pleasure from chatting with the old ladies. Another source of pleasure on such occasions lay in watching our guests tuck into the food. Poor wretches – home supplied food could never be very ample.

Another friend used to boast of his Diana, who, one day to my great amusement, arrived at a party we gave complete with an insignificant husband and three daughters, the youngest of whom, aged 16, was in advanced pregnancy. On this occasion the husband looked on completely unconcerned while his wife flitted about. She had a lovely face, offset by a very large body and carried on dancing like a two-year old. I found her far and away the most intelligent of the various women I had met, a really charming personality.

Whatever the background of these ladies, with certainly none coming from the higher grades of society, I thoroughly enjoyed their company. None were of any education, but all were simple, good-natured and lively, as well as always ready to laugh. I had a lot of fun with them, and learning about the lives they led, and the hardships and difficulties they had to contend with, I grew to like them more and more and to admire them for the spirit in which they faced the ups and downs of life. In addition they never missed being thoroughly feminine and always made the best of their appearance with whatever simple means they had at their disposal.

My early impressions of Sicilians were not very favourable, but on closer acquaintance these changed. My stay in Riposto allowed me to come into contact with ordinary Italian people, and but for the fact that every move forward was a step nearer home, I would have been sorry to leave this part of the world.

I enjoyed my stay in Sicily for a number of reasons, first among which was my happiness over being back in Europe again. Africa had its points but apart from a few ruined Roman sites, there was no sense of tradition. Here in Sicily, I was among people of my own type, while at the same time, derived immense pleasure from being once again in the normal current of life. I felt at home with ancient Greek architecture and at the same time it was warming to see the rock that grand Polyphemus had thrown at Odysseus, as also to think of – was it Archimedes – who came out with his famous "Eureka". In Syracuse I also learnt to appreciate Sicilian baroque, a most attractive variant. But above all we had fun, although the wine was foul and most of the new acquaintances I made would not be acceptable in English drawing rooms.

CHAPTER III

Naples

We set off from Riposto on December the 12th 1943 taking the coast road, running north. Once we had passed Taormina the scenery became more and more magnificent, with steep, rocky, scrub-covered hills dropping down to the deep blue sea below, their lengths broken in places by torrent beds carrying a lot of water after the recent rains. Such shoreline as there was was narrow and built up with houses wherever there was sufficient space. The consequent long line of houses made it difficult to distinguish one village from another.

The scenery followed this pattern until we reached Messina where we were offered an appalling picture of poverty, malnutrition and general misery amidst the havoc wreaked by bombing. The state of the children was particularly sad and pitiable, bare-footed and with almost non-existent clothing. Here we only stayed long enough to board the ferry and I was glad to get out of the town and land in Reggio where we were billeted in a fine school. One can criticise Mussolini over many things but the schools and hospitals he had built were very fine.

We spent three nights here as the road to the North was broken as a bridge had been washed away so we were forced to while away time as best we could. I tried my hand at fishing, with no success and otherwise walked about the town, searching for books to read. Amongst others I found one in Italian on the poetry of Alexander Pope, published in Bari. I was surprised that he had ever been heard of in these parts. In between times I accompanied our fat major shopping. He added to his already vast impedimenta by purchasing a large vacuum flask, which lasted ten days, and a set of glasses. I fared better through finding a small hurricane lamp, which became my most treasured possession, as it enabled me to read at night in my tent.

As soon as the road to the North had been cleared we set off along the coast. The road first of all skirted the hills; a bit later, as these became steeper, it was cut out of their sides. We passed some fine sandy beaches and some picturesque villages in which the women still wore the local costume with very full skirts of red and black, with a distinction between the married and the single. The views in all directions were superb with occasional glimpses of snow-capped Etna in the distance. The road was terrifying as it zigzagged along precipitous drops to the sea, with some of the bends seemingly impossible for our heavy transport to manoeuvre. After a time we reached the river, the cause of our delay, and this all but one of our vehicles managed to ford, the odd one having to be towed across. The river had cut its way through well-wooded heights and after sitting in the truck I would have loved to do some walking, but this was not to be. Later I saw a stretch of bright yellow flowers which I thought might be Sternbergia, a supposition I was unable to verify. But in general, what with the nature of the road and the rugged beauty of the scenery with its rocks, forests and scrub running down to the sea, my mind was too fully occupied to think of flowers.

We spent our first night in a hotel in a sort of Spa, offering hot sulphur baths. Here we enjoyed the perfect bath, with hot, natural, sulphury water running out of the rocks into a sunken basin at one end and out at the other. It was such a joy to lie in a bath in which the temperature of the water never altered and to this were added the luxuries of a book, a bottle of wine and my lamp to illuminate the scene. Prior to so indulging myself I had met the local doctor who invited me to dinner at his house where, together with some friends of his, we spent a very happy evening.

The following day was similar with further twisting, turning and zigzagging and ended in a series of terrifying hairpin bends which brought us down to another hotel, which provided us with baths and a good dinner. How much pleasanter was this kind of bath to my usual practice of sloshing cold water over myself in the open air.

Our last day proved more peaceful as we crossed a plain which offered us a fine view of the temples of Paestum in the middle distance. During the lunch time halt, I bought a turkey off a passing vendor, in anticipation of Christmas dinner. In its company we arrived at the transit camp in Naples, on a hilltop overlooking the city and set in the grounds of a Royal Palace.

Judging from Byron's experience, little bother was experienced in travelling with his gaggle of geese, but with my turkey things were otherwise as he started to prove a nuisance at an early stage. I had him tethered outside my tent on a lead sufficiently long to enable him to wander about to some extent, this extent unfortunately allowing him to reach my bed which he tried his best to share with me. As time went on, I began to be fonder and fonder of him, and the ruder the comments I had to undergo the more attached I became, although any feelings of this nature were very one-sided.

On Christmas morning I went to the Anglican Church with the Colonel, to find it beautifully decorated with flowers and to enjoy a simple service of readings and carols. During this my thoughts inevitably turned to family and friends scattered all over the world, but such thoughts were dispelled on returning to the camp to find a sherry party in progress. This was followed by a luncheon of pork, turkey and Christmas pudding, washed down by lots of wine. In the evening we went to the Officers Club, where a so-called dance was in progress, 100 men to 5 girls. One of these was quite lovely, but sitting in a corner was her husband, a miserable looking specimen, keeping an eagle eye on her. But although dancing was out of the question, the music was good, as was the wine and the evening passed very pleasantly. This Club was a great asset offering peaceful surroundings, English newspapers and good meals to the accompaniment of a good local band who sang local songs very well. The opera had also opened and I went to the Barber of Seville, such a joy to hear decent music again.

Most of my time was spent in pottering about the town in which I had last been in 1915 on our way to Greece. My chief memories of that visit covered the Aquarium and the freedom with which small children performed their natural functions in the gutters. This time however, all was different, and I was appalled at the sight of a town in such a state of degradation. True there was quite a lot of bomb damage, but this one took for granted in wartime. What struck me was the poverty, more marked than ever before and the hunger showing on people's unsmiling faces, drawn and concentrating on how to get hold of enough food to keep them going for another day. The bread ration was 4 oz a day, with no cereals available. Every other form of food was scarce, except of course on the Black Market which sold food at prices far beyond the means of the poor. Outside the town there was a huge dump of army litter. This was searched by men, women and children for any discarded tin or other package offering any vestiges of food, so replacing the crows and seagulls of our own rubbish heaps. Of course prostitution and venereal disease were rife, with poor prospects of treatment and one got used to being accosted by children offering to conduct one to a 'bellissima signorina'. In fact it was said that for a bar of chocolate a man could have almost any woman or boy in the town.

Clothing shops in the Via Roma were reasonably well stocked but at unaffordable prices. So-called jewellers were doing good business, especially with the Americans, selling valueless knick-knacks at high prices. I wanted to buy a coral necklace for Maya, but only succeeded after a long session of bargaining, which I enjoyed so much that I did not grudge the vendor his excess profit. Everything was much more expensive than in Sicily. To my joy the Aquarium remained open. Here I bought a dried sea-horse for luck and was delighted to see an octopus so replete that it refused further food and to feel that there was at least one inhabitant of the town so happily well-fed.

Otherwise I became fascinated by the local accent and by the wealth and picturesqueness of current forms of abuse and swearing, which I studied wherever I could. With the accent I could not get to grips, but with the swearing I made some progress. My moment of triumph came when on one occasion I was nearly run down by a cart and turned on the driver to leave him gaping with astonishment at hearing such language coming from the mouth of a respectable looking British Officer.

With the museums all shut there was little for me to do in the town except for walking and so I was not sorry when after a few days we moved further north to the Volturno river, in which area former marshland had been drained and laid out into small-holdings. The river crossing had been the scene of bitter fighting, leaving villages completely destroyed and vestiges of war left lying about, including the bodies of civilians, which made one wonder how they got mixed up in it all. Even at its best this could not be considered very attractive country, especially as we found it covered in mud and stagnant water. Nevertheless, in bright sunshine and with the distant hills covered in snow it held a certain attraction.

We were lodged in a solidly built house, with a good roof, but our sleeping quarters in the attic could only be reached by means of a rickety ladder and as a result sleeping quarters for the fat major had to be found elsewhere. My medical department was well housed in another building which boasted of an open fireplace. Fortunately, on the Italian grapevine, I heard of the presence of a dump of coal not far off and this being raided my office was kept permanently warm, to become a popular rendezvous for morning coffee.

What with the mud, the wet and the possible presence of minefields there was little scope for serious walking. To amuse myself I set about getting to know the surrounding small-holders, who turned out to be a very decent lot. I made particular friends with one from Tuscany and to him I presented the turkey, which by now had become a confounded nuisance. He accepted it with pleasure and promptly invited me to supper, in which I was glad to see the bird did not feature; instead we had rabbit and polenta, which I had not tasted for ages. In view of the local food situation I never ate out without taking a quid pro quo, usually in the shape of tinned meat or coffee.

Such people helped to save my reason, for in their company I forgot about the army and the constant criticisms of all and sundry to be heard in the mess. With such decent folk it was a joy to talk about family life and the welfare of children, farm animals and crops. What a relief.

With the departure of the fighting forces the villagers started to return to their ruined homes, bringing with them building materials, drawn by hand or by horse-drawn carts to set about reconstruction. There was something awe-inspiring about their courage, endurance and patience as they set about converting piles of rubble into some form of living accommodation, with me looking on in admiration. Slowly Italy and its people were getting a stronger and stronger hold on me as I felt more and more happy to be where I was. Earlier on I had written home: "The people are charming, often quite irresponsible and not always to be trusted, but cheerful and smiling and always willing to help, although their efforts in this line may not always prove successful. They love a bit of flattery and will return compliments with interest, making it difficult in some ways to take them seriously, especially as their attitude to life is so different from ours."

With the passage of time and greater experience these somewhat superficial impressions changed and the more I saw of the Italian countryman the more I came to admire and to love him. Of course I was immensely lucky in that under wartime conditions I enjoyed full freedom of movement amongst the local population. What with this, a total lack of formality and freedom from inhibitions there was no bar to mixing and talking with everyone. It is true that on their side they may have been actuated by curiosity about these Britons who had invaded their country, but be that as it may, throughout the whole of my stay in Italy I could not have been more kindly received by all and sundry.

Our next move, after a couple of weeks or so, was down to Castelammare on the bay of Naples, where we only spent a few days, but long enough to enable me to visit Pompeii twice and to call on the Scala brothers to taste of their Lacrima Christo wine, but how I managed this I cannot remember. Our next move was to embark for the bridgehead at Anzio.

CHAPTER IV

Anzio

Late in January 1944 we learnt at very short notice that our next destination was to be the bridgehead at Anzio. Here we landed on D Day + 3 after an uneventful journey in a small craft. The main harbour being crammed with all manner of craft, we were disembarked on a sandy beach, already littered with cases and packages of all descriptions, including broken cartons of American cigarettes to which all helped themselves freely. Then, once collected, we set off on a two mile march to our allotted camp site, carrying as much of our personal kit as we could on our backs.

The site lay alongside the main road to Rome at a point where some largish fields separated it from an area of extensive low woodland. Here we settled down for an extremely uncomfortable night, lying on hard ground under the trees and exposed to the cold and drizzling rain. However we rose to a warm and sunny day which soon dried us off. The arrival of our main equipment kept everyone busy, pitching tents and laying out the camp. A small house was taken over to house the Colonel and H.Q. while a neighbouring stone built shed became the Officers' mess. My Medical Inspection (M.I.) tent was placed in a prominent position under cover of a large, solitary standing tree. In the meantime, with usual army efficiency, we had been supplied with water and food and all seemed well.

We were only about two miles behind enemy lines. With none of us ever having had experience of warfare, least of all the Colonel, we were all caught napping and unprotected when we were subjected to shelling and air raids, the latter involving the dropping of anti-personnel bombs whose shrapnel travelled a distance of about 100 yards horizontally above the ground, thus endangering anyone standing, sitting or lying down. It took a rather frightening night exposed to such activity to persuade the Colonel that it would be safer to sleep below ground level. Once he had grasped this all hands were set to dig away the soil under the tents to about 3-4 feet below the surface. Fortunately the soil proved light and sandy and offered no great difficulty and the only casualties were a number of cyclamen corms uprooted.

As it happened however, I was exposed to far greater danger from our own troops than from the enemy, when under cover of darkness, a bevy of Irish soldiers arrived and dumped their ammunition about ten yards from my M.I. tent. This, all packed up in cartons etc., seemed perfectly safe when I turned up for sick parade in the morning. I carried on normally until suddenly there was a loud explosion and we were all hurled to the ground on top of one another. Extricating myself as quickly as I could I rushed out to see what had happened to find the ammo had blown up and the ground up to a distance of 60 yards was littered with bodies, scraps of clothing and other debris. Fortunately only one man had been killed, although there were several wounded. It was only later when the excitement was over that I realized how lucky we had been in the M.I. tent, for had the blast come our way we would all have been killed. So with this lesson in mind the M I. tent was moved to safer surroundings on the edge of the woodland, well away from the paths of incoming troops.

Once well protected in our tents the next important matter was to make ourselves as comfortable as possible. In this aim we were helped by the fact that all civilians having been evacuated, their houses stood there unoccupied but fully furnished. This raised a ticklish point in the army code of behaviour, for whereas looting, i.e. the acquisition of articles of value was taken seriously, a blind eye was turned on the taking for use of simple and utilitarian property and so I acquired a wire spring mattress and a small deal table and chairs for our tent, and one or two chairs for the M.I. room. The mattress was a joy, so much more stable and comfortable than a camp bed and later it accompanied me wherever I went.

I shared a tent with another officer and we decided not to have the whole dug out, but only a sufficient area to accommodate our beds, with space for a chair to be let in at one side to serve as a step-down. Under this there was a can let into the ground to act as a sump and to catch any water oozing into the cavity. In view of all the rain we had this proved of great value. The sides were shored up as best we could and for further protection a wooden canopy overhead supported a layer of sandbags as a safeguard against falling shrapnel. By the beds there was space for tin hats and torches and our clothes were hung on nails, trusting that we would be luckier than a colleague who had all his blown away by the blast.

As for the M.I. tent, this was well dug down to allow of more standing room, the corporal having one end for his bed and, with a table to work on and several chairs, we made ourselves comfortable. Once again I was grateful for army efficiency in the provision of supplies, for my corporal was immediately able to be issued with a can of paraffin, ostensibly for use in the primus stove to sterilise instruments, but more usefully turned to providing boiling water for making tea. Once the presence of this facility became known the other officers would turn up daily for elevenses.

Life thus soon settled down to a routine – up early, then breakfast followed by sick parade, after which elevenses helped to fill up the morning. In general there being no work of an afternoon, I used either to sleep or go for a walk. Of an evening the bar generally opened at about 6.30, leading to supper and then bridge till bedtime.

The principal interruptions to this routine resulted from enemy action which took three forms. Firstly there were some big guns on the Alban Hills which periodically shelled the shipping and harbour, but apart from making a lot of noise did not disturb us. Then the main road alongside which we lay was an important line of communication and so was open to spasmodic shelling both by day and by night, but never at any fixed times. Then finally there were air raids which were mainly limited to nights and to fine ones at that. Of these the shell fire was the most unpleasant as one could hear the approach which aroused suspense until one actually heard the explosion. During these attacks everyone went to ground until peace and quiet were restored. Interestingly I had always thought that the expression "shivering with fear" was a manner of speech, but during a prolonged bout of near-by shelling I found out that it could be very real. On the other hand shell fire had its uses for anything unwanted could be written off in the books as "destroyed by enemy action".

It did not take me long to realise that there would be very little work for me to do in the camp, so I decided to offer my services to the neighbouring Casualty Clearing Station (C.C.S.), which, with an attached Field Ambulance, provided the main British Hospital services on the beachhead. My offer was immediately accepted and I was asked to attend on the following day for my initiation. I started work at 2 p.m. and was certainly thrown in at the deep end for with a lot of activity at the front things were hectic and I was at it continuously. A constant stream of wounded flowed in and by midnight I began to feel desperate, I was so tired and hungry and with no apparent end in sight, but with a bite and a drink and an hour's peace I felt better and carried on until 6 am. Above all I was impressed by the way the orderlies and stretcher bearers worked, some having already been on duty for 36 hours but carrying on without grumbles or relaxation.

The procedure over casualties at the front roughly followed these lines: all received first aid at the front at a field ambulance and were then sent back to the CCS for further treatment. From the front which was only a few miles away the wounded were brought in by ambulance either on stretchers or walking whenever possible and taken into the reception tent in which I was working, the stretchers being laid on supports and the walkers on benches. Any man complaining of cold was immediately given a hot drink and extra blankets (it was certainly cold that night), with the padres wandering round, ready to give a cup of tea or a sandwich or cigarette and carrying the sacraments on their persons for immediate administration to men of all creeds in case of need.

Each man was made as comfortable as possible, the walkers sitting round a stove and helping themselves to tea etc. and offering a sight which often was both comic and tragic at the same time. The fitter ones sat munching, drinking, smoking and talking, happy to be out of the line and only lightly wounded, while others lay or sat doubled up, utterly exhausted and totally indifferent to what was going on around them, just longing for sleep and peace. It was a great relief to see these packed off to bed.

I was immensely struck by the spirit shown by the majority of the wounded, cheerful, laughing and joking, with the place taking on the atmosphere of a club as new arrivals were greeted. But of course there were others...

My job was to see and catalogue all new entrants as they arrived and to pack them off to the right department for further treatment. Most importantly this applied to cases of severe shock and haemorrhage, these being immediately dispatched to resuscitation, from which it was astonishing how quickly an almost pulse-less and seemingly moribund case could be revived and rendered fit for operation.

In general policy was as follows:

1. All minor cases of flesh wounds and injuries were packed off to bed after these had been dressed, and these were shipped off the beachhead as quickly as possible.

2. All cases whose treatment could wait for a time were packed off to bed and seen to later.

3. All those in need of immediate operation were sent to the theatre to await their turn. These comprised all abdominal and chest wounds and all those of similar gravity. In emergency four fully staffed theatres could be in action at the same time but there were no facilities for the treatment of a highly specialised nature, such as brain surgery, such cases either being transferred to the large American hospital by the sea or evacuated by sea in the hope that they would survive the journey.

The amount of work to be done varied from night to night depending on what was going on at the front. Some nights I was at it the whole time while on others there was so little to do that I could cover myself with blankets and get some sleep lying on a stretcher. But, of course, when cases came in at sporadic intervals, sleep could only be obtained in snatches if at all.

Together with our men a few German wounded might be brought in. To help with these an English speaking German orderly was attached, a very pleasant fellow with whom I had long conversations and who was accepted by all as "one of the gang". He told me that very few had any hope of the Germans winning the war. Whenever possible I made a point of talking to all of them. Many were young and frightened for who knows what stories they had been told about us and a bit of reassurance did no harm. It was strange to see them sitting there over their cups of tea and to think that a few hours previously they had been doing their best to kill our men. Incidentally over treatment no distinction was made between them and our men, all took their priority from the severity of their wounds.

That first day I got back at about 8 a.m. and then carried on with the normal day's work. I was lucky to have been thrown in to the job on such a busy night as I was given no time to ponder on the horror of seeing men suffer. Thenceforward I was on duty from 10 p.m. to 7 a.m. on alternate nights and was very happy at last to be doing some useful work. The general atmosphere was most congenial, with a total absence of grumbling however hard the work. A Pole manipulated a villainously dangerous stove, burning petrol of all things, which I hourly expected to explode. This it did not do but it provided us with cups of tea at all hours and it was fun to sit together and chat over a cup. Incidentally all personal belongings were taken off those unable to look after them themselves and stored away in safety, to follow them wherever they were sent, thus disproving the cheerful jibe that R.A.M.C. stood for Rob all my Comrades! At night the reception tent presented a somewhat eerie and dramatic picture with the dark and low roof of the tent above, the dim lighting, the rows of stretchers and with men huddled into a corner or moving about on their work, the whole a scene worthy of a Rembrandt.

Back in the mess, life apart from bridge tended to be very dull. The Colonel, although very pleasant and easy-going was a man of no interests, of no outside resources and in many ways had the mind of a school-boy of fifteen or sixteen. The other officers, except for the Major, of whom more anon, and one other, were young and inexperienced in life. Conversation in consequence tended to be stilted and dull and mainly devoted to gossip, sex, to running down senior officers and rejoicing over their mistakes. The fat Major contributed no joy, his talk being confined to the First War and to how he stood up to things without feeling any fear. The odd man out was connected with a university in civil life and with him it was possible to discuss such matters as music and ballet and so on. He introduced me to a study of philosophy which certainly distracted my attention from other matters but at which I made little headway.

He would find fault with me for reading and enjoying a paper called "The Magnet", intended for school children and full of the doings of such characters as Keyhole Kate, Desperate Dan, fat boy Billy Bunter and his mates at Greyfriars School. I was derided for reading such tripe until one morning I heard chuckles coming from Hatchett's bed (for such was his name) and I found him reading a copy. Having thus started on the downward path, he became an avid reader taking in all copies before they were passed over to the mess and to the staff in general.

Circumstances were such that long periods of boredom were inevitable, especially in view of periods of total lack of work. On former occasions we had had a constant stream of officers passing through our hands who relieved any monotony. Here no one stayed with us longer than 24 hours and so there was no distraction from their company.

The Major was a tiresome old man and one of the crosses we had to bear, but he did afford us a moment of great excitement on one occasion. He had been posted to us as second-in-command, but being lazy and totally incompetent, he did nothing but bore us with endless tales of his heroism in the face of danger, in spite of which he was always to be found in the safest corner of the mess during air raids. He also took no chances over his tent which was dug down to a depth of 6 feet and covered with a strong layer of sandbags. Entry was effected by means of a ladder down which he sped at the first sign of any danger, burying himself like a mole and emerging after all was over to tell us how he had felt no fear. He was caught napping one day however for an air raid surprised him as he was sitting in the large metal bath he had acquired from somewhere. With a tin hat on his head and fat spilling over the sides he made a ludicrous sight. His kit was fantastic and how he got it transported remains a mystery. It comprised the following:

12 pairs of boots	1 carpet
15 shirts	1 typewriter
50 handkerchiefs	1 writing desk set
2 chairs	1 table cloth
1 table	8 Pillow cases etc. etc.

And to add to his other disadvantages he was a poor and slow bridge player and as his hands were always dirty it was an offence to see him handling the cards. One day he came out in spots on his face which developed so fast and became so widespread that it became necessary to send him to hospital for the treatment of what was now frank impetigo. So off he went and was struck off the strength of the unit.

Some time later picture the Colonel's dismay when a message came through to announce that the Major was sitting on the docks and could transport be provided to return him to us. The adjutant was promptly sent off to point out to the Major that he was no longer on the strength of the unit and so there was no place for him, and also that he had better return to Naples in the boat that had brought him unless he preferred to spend the night on the dock without shelter, food or water. Loud protests followed together with the threat of appeal to higher authority with all blame being ascribed to the Doctor who had conspired to get rid of him – anyhow we saw no more of him. A few days after his departure I wrote: "We are still recovering from the dismay and consternation aroused by the possibility of the Major's return and I am not exaggerating when I say that a division of Germans marching down the road could not have caused more of an upheaval."

The woods round us also formed the refuge of a number of deserters whose main difficulty of course lay in getting food. Some of the brighter ones solved this problem by joining the queues of our men and intakes at mealtimes, getting away with this ruse for some time until the police got wind of it.

Although life was very restricted it had its amusing moments. One day one of our men, one Gilham, who ran a garage in private life, approached me with a request for a bottle of whisky. Now as whisky was not being issued to other ranks I was somewhat surprised until he told me that an American had offered to exchange a jeep for such a bottle. As we had no unit transport a jeep would obviously be worth its weight in gold, and with the Orderly room proving agreeable although unwilling to take any responsibility, the jeep appeared on the scene and was hastily put into good order.

Transactions of this nature were by no means uncommon, for the American troops were issued with no alcohol and of course there was no wine available here, so it was possible to acquire almost anything in exchange for a bottle of whisky. The British soldier also got a regular issue of beer and in this respect he was better off than his American counterpart.

Thanks to my interest in natural history and arriving on the beachhead as winter was coming to an end, I always found plenty to keep me occupied and I spent a lot of time walking about the small area at my disposal keeping my eyes open. Without these walks I do not think I could have kept my reason.

Of mammals the only ones I came across were mice which entered our tent at night to get at our chocolate. Before taking to wrapping this up securely I laid a trap and caught a field mouse, a delightful little animal, which I let go. There was an abundance of snakes, mainly of the grass variety and harmless. I caught a four-footer and kept it in a pit, but, not being quite certain as to what to feed it on, and finding frogs and lizards far too difficult to catch, I eventually let it go. Lizards were common and included one magnificent bright green one, nearly a foot long.

Once the warmer weather set in the frogs came into prominence with their croaking at night, a sound that took me back to my childhood. Waking at night later on in the season was almost a pleasure for the croaking of the frogs rivalled the song of the nightingales, of which there was an inordinate number, to such an extent that after a time their song began to pall. But they had their uses, for as soon as shelling started their song would cease, to resume as soon as no further action was contemplated. So reliable were they in this respect that one could almost imagine they were in telepathic communication with the German gunners.

Insect life was of course present in abundance, especially prominent being some superb large beetles. On one occasion I collected four large praying mantises and took them back home in a jar to see whether they were any good at catching flies. I put them aside for an hour or so but when I came to look at them there was only one, with the remains of the other three lying about. My most intimate contacts, however, were made with ticks of which there was abundance on the low bushes, so much so that on my return home I invariably took off my clothes to remove any that had attached themselves to me.

I only took a casual interest in birds, of which, apart from the nightingales, I kept no notes. I did look around for nests, but found none, although a friend showed me one of a long-tailed tit. With one small bird I became quite well acquainted. Gilham, the mechanic who had got hold of the jeep had also somehow acquired a motorbike, which he proceeded to take to pieces to put into order. In so doing he left the petrol tank lying about and this was immediately taken over by a blue tit as a fine nesting site. When the day came for him to fit the tank to the bike, the tit was already sitting. Public opinion meant that there was no possibility of disturbing it until the young had flown. So, to his great annoyance, there was nothing for it but to exercise patience.

Later in the season I came across some fine caterpillars and kept a selection of these outside my tent, without realising in what I had involved myself. Not only did I find that they had voracious appetites, but that they were also so fussy about their food that they would only eat particular leaves and fresh ones at that. In consequence I was kept running to and fro collecting their fodder, some at quite a distance. However they gave me a lot of interest and amusement, but as we moved before the chrysalises had hatched, I unfortunately never saw what they turned into, as I had to leave them behind.

These were all sidelines however, my chief interest lying in flowers. I was very grateful to the Army for having selected the month of January for the landings, for the timing allowed me to follow the whole succession of flowers from late winter to early summer. Once we were well settled I started to go for walks and explore the surrounding countryside. This was generally quite flat with fields extending from our woods to the coast and town, although in one area the land rose in a series of hummocks with patches of marshland and streams running in the hollows.

To the east I was cut off by the firing lines, with beyond them the Alban Hills, only a few miles away, but entirely inaccessible. These I used to look on with nostalgia, for to them, during the First World War, when we lived in Rome, we used to go for walks and picnics, returning in the spring with bunches of narcissi, cyclamen and anemones. Now all I could do was to gaze on them and wonder what our former haunts such as Rocca di Papa, Grotta Ferrata, Lake Nemi and Monte Cavo looked like now.

I found no narcissi round us, but the woods in season were carpeted with cyclamen, growing so closely that one could not avoid stepping on them. As for anemones, initially I only found scattered patches, although eventually I came across a sheet in full flower late in the season.

As time went on I developed a routine, and on my return from walks would sit at the table, preferably out in the open, study my findings and try to classify and identify them. Life would have been easier had I had a suitable book to help me out, but as it was I managed reasonably well. Later on I took to drawing any flowers that proved particularly interesting in the hope of being able to identify them on my return to England. My drawing was not particularly impressive but it amused me and gave me an insight into details of flowers which I otherwise would have missed and also revealed a number of hidden beauties. Most important of all, this occupation kept boredom at bay, and boredom was one of the worst of enemies. With flowers I only suffered one disappointment. One day, not far from the tent, I noticed a thick purplish spike emerging from the ground. I had not the least idea what it was and pictured something like a gladiolus or a lily. So I protected it from harm by surrounding it with thorns and watched it daily. Eventually the stem grew up to a height of about 18 inches, but the eventual flower turned out to be a very drab and indifferent orchid, of which I subsequently found several specimens.

My favourite haunt was a small, shallow valley in the hollow of which ran a small stream, in which there was a patch of marshy ground. One slope was grassy and full of flowers, the other covered in broom and a white cistus. What particularly excited me was a large growth of the Royal Fern, a plant I had long wanted to find growing in the wild and here it was resplendent. I used to sit on the grassy bank, in the sunshine, and forget all about war and soldiers and rejoice in the peace and quiet. Only once was I disturbed here. I saw an officer approaching, leaving me wondering what he was up to and feeling annoyed at his presence. Just at that moment there was a bang as a shell fell close by, causing us both to fall to the ground. This I felt was a sufficient excuse for an introduction, so when all was quiet I went up to him and found he was after birds, and we sat down and compared notes. During all my years in the army he and another were the only two men I found with any interest in natural history.

As fighting at Cassino intensified we enjoyed a lull. Life took on a more peaceful aspect with more being done in the way of entertaining the troops. One of the first fruits of this policy was a football ground laid out in the fields nearby and on April 5th 1944 I was able to write home: "There is a football match in progress, we are now very smart with a proper ground and goal posts. There is a lot of noise going on, and, judging from the whistles, there is also a referee, an unheard of luxury." A fortnight later there was an excellent match between Basutos and one of our teams. Half way through the Basutos started discarding their boots and playing barefoot. The highlight of the match came when one of them kicked the ball, stopped to pass water in midfield and then carried on with the game. This of course brought the house down. On another occasion while a match, watched by a large crowd, was in progress there was a terrific bang just off the road, and in the twinkling of an eye the field was empty. I have never seen a crowd run so fast. Play was resumed when nothing else occurred.

By the end of April I wrote: "The whole place is now covered in football grounds, six within 600 yards of the camp, and all constantly in use. We run two teams who are a constant source of argument and every morning at coffee we have a grand discussion on the composition of the teams. Considering we only have 50 men in the unit, and all of low category, we do not do at all badly. The Yanks of course play baseball, but in addition to football our men also play cricket and hockey and I have even heard of a game of rugger. Netball, quoits and beetle-racing make up the list and all are popular, the latter complete with bookies.

At the same time a theatre of sorts has been set up in the camp, and a Y.M.C.A. tea stall. The latter is very useful as I can now complement morning coffee with a bun. The theatre is a doubtful proposition. On the one hand it is pleasant to get some form of entertainment, but on the other it has involved us in an awful lot of noise, not only during performances but also when the bands practice. The noise of the band reminds me of the horrors of civilisation and we have quite enough noise here without adding to it." To this a few days later I added: "An E.N.S.A. party has just left us and we are now spared the strains of hot music for which we are all grateful. Still there are pipers knocking about and they could be worse. We have been promised a swing band. In the M.I. room I now have white and yellow iris, orchids, white-flowered garlic, blue lupins and a pea with blue flowers.

Outside the trees are turning green and the broom and hawthorn are in flower. Add to that that the birds are singing all day and the nightingales all night and you can imagine how pleasant it all is. The only trouble is that in the morning the water is warm and I can no longer enjoy a cold bath. How I love it of a morning, walking straight out of the tent into the woods and washing and bathing in the open. I love this life and will miss it when we settle into a house...I have lived in a tent now for 18 months. With all the drawbacks I am enjoying myself and am so happy to be in Italy in which the climate, the sunshine and the beauty of the air make one feel cheerful. What I really enjoy about army life is that in a place like this one becomes part of the country and really lives in it. In this respect I will be sorry when all is over."

In the meantime the C.C.S. had left, leaving behind a Field Ambulance which had no use for my services, there not being enough for them to do. I was very sorry to give up my job, which was fascinating and which I enjoyed. It was good to feel useful again. Fortunately hitherto there had never been any trouble in the mess, which, considering the fact that we eight had been cooped up together for three months, reflects a lot of credit on the Colonel, who kept things in order very successfully.

Some of the men started going on leave and it was a pleasure to hear how they fared. Morning tea in bed, a huge breakfast, and excellent food throughout. Transport to carry them to local beauty spots and to the neighbouring town in which all prices were strictly controlled, and with a man to make boxes in which to pack presents for home. Proper baths, old clothes replaced for new and so on. One man who had been in the army 15 years told me it had been the best leave he had ever had. It was good to hear of such a place, with the only snag that it will be a long time before all the men get there.

On May the 3rd. I wrote: "We have been having a lot of rain and it is good to see the sun again. Two recent army orders have given rise to a lot of amusement. One runs: 'In view of the contamination of water supplies no water will be drunk except that passed by the M.O.' The second runs as follows: 'It has been found that chambers, Army, rubber, deteriorate if kept in an upright position. In future they will all be stored in an inverted position and to obviate any possibility of error their bottom will be marked 'top'.' The officer who issued the first order has never been able to live it down. These remind me of an occasion in North Africa when an order was issued to M.O.'s. A fortnight later there came a circular. 'Order No.... has not been complied with. Will M.O.'s see to this matter.' This was followed by another some time later. 'With reference to order No...Medical Officers are reminded that orders are meant to be obeyed.' The next step was another circular issued a little later. 'Order No.... has been rescinded.' The original order had comprised a whole lot of totally unnecessary paperwork, the concept of a bureaucratic mind." As a superior, I always found that the regular Army Medical Officer was infinitely preferable to the ex-civilian. The former's attitude was "Get on with the job and only come to me if you are in trouble," whereas the latter tended to poke his nose in where he was not wanted. I well remember one of the latter being horrified on learning that to obtain drug supplies I never filled in forms, and in fact did not know which the requisite forms were. It was much easier to approach a hospital dispensary directly.

All sorts of rumours were circulating that we were alternately in the process of moving to England, Corsica and the Balkans. How these rumours arose remained a matter of doubt. In the interim I was told that there was a fine tulip to be found some two miles away, but on getting to it found it was an orchid which also grew some fifty yards from my tent. In the course of the walk I visited the Borghese palazzo, superbly situated on a hillock overlooking the sea, but possessing no qualities as a building. The grounds were drab and uninteresting, making no use of the opportunities offered.

At about this time my boils started to return so I went off to the Field Ambulance for advice, which I got in full measure, every member of the staff suggesting a more lurid treatment. Finally a regime was decided on which involved my spending two hours every day over my toilet and covering myself in Elastoplast. At the same time I was given masses of yeast to eat, which fermented inside me. But all went well and in a few days I was all right again.

On May the 10th 1944 I wrote: "To-day is beastly, clouded over and muggy and it has been like this for the past three days. Still my boils are O.K. and I feel fit again and have restarted walks. Things are extremely, almost unnaturally quiet, the lull before the storm no doubt. My corporal has been very busy making himself a wireless receiver out of a razor blade, some copper wire and a set of earphones. This works very well, getting the local station, mainly broadcasting in German. Hitherto their only communications with us have been by means of leaflets dropped from the air, showing our men how their wives are carrying on with the Americans at home."

On the 11th I received letters from Mother in Turkey and from my brother Hugh in Eritrea. There had been news from Lorna in Rome who seemed all right and who I was looking forward to seeing in the near future.

On the 15th I wrote home: "Reading the papers from England and listening to the wireless makes one realise how out of touch we are with home affairs. When we hear statements like: 'All soldiers abroad are burning for reconstruction after the war' one realises how little people at home know about our soldiers here. If you ask any out here what they would most want in life, the answer would be to get into civvy clothes, have a few pints of beer at the local with a good night's loving to follow. No one cares two hoots about reconstruction, all they think of is peace, beer and lovemaking. When men live like animals, as they have to, it is absurd to expect them to think of any but animal matters. The intelligent are no different and not one of us will be able seriously to think of the future of England until we get home."

From now on I will quote from letters as I wrote them.

May 19th. At long last the period of waiting is over and things seem to be moving at Cassino. What particularly pleases me is that the French have done so well. I am so fed up with hearing our allies run down, and I get so fed up with the perpetual English attitude to others. We have been having it very quiet here and I rather think the Germans have had it, although one can never be certain with them. But we have the benefit of superior forces and overwhelming air superiority.

May 22nd. There are times when I dread the thought of returning to the English climate and wonder how I will be able to stand up to an English winter. At present I still have six blanket thicknesses on my bed and the daytime temperature is that of a warm day in July in England. After Africa this country is delightfully cool although there I only once felt really hot and that was when the temperature reached 110 degrees in Sousse. One of my staff has just had a nasty shock in the form of a letter to say that his girl friend is having a baby and that will be 7/6 a week please. One more Anglo-Sicilian.

May 24th. It is exactly four months since we landed on the beach-head, four very pleasant and happy ones, far better than I had expected. Altogether, despite moments of tension and fear it has been a pleasant experience. Certainly it has been a revelation of army organization. It is months or even years since I have had so much entertainment, and food has been absolutely first class throughout, with the only lack being that of wine. But I now feel that I would rather have the Germans some 30 miles away rather than 3 or 4 as hitherto. At the moment my only grouse is the cacophony of a jazz band in the camp. Anything more revolting it is difficult to imagine. This and the bagpipes form our major inconveniences.

News is good and long may it continue so. The French Moroccans, the Goums, have made a great name for themselves and it is said that their wives and children follow in their footsteps robbing the dead and wounded, though this is, I believe, an exaggeration. They have become a legendary force. They can move about at night making no noise and terrifying friends and enemies alike.

May 26th. The long-hoped-for day has arrived and we are no longer a beachhead and I am not certain whether to be sorry or glad, for whereas it is good to be free from anxieties we are now merged into much larger forces and no longer have any individuality. It is true the early days were very anxious and the proximity of the enemy never very pleasant, but at least we saw something of the war and were able to appreciate in very small part what the infantry have to go through. Meanwhile I hope we will be in Rome by the time this reaches you.

May 29th. Events have brought a slackening of tension and in consequence a sort of mental and nervous collapse. Formerly there was always a certain strain and anxiety which kept one's mind alert, for to give in would have courted disaster. Now that we have been relieved and the strain has been dispelled we are all 'flopping' and the absence of work has left us bored and dissatisfied. Heaven alone knows how long we will stay here but I could do with a change. I know the country all about only too well and with summer approaching flowers are losing their charm, being chiefly confined to thistles and the like.

On June the 5th, I wrote that after the nervous strain of the past months it felt a bit flat at first, but after a few days I learnt to appreciate the change and the ability to walk about without fear of bombs and shells. All the same the past four months have been very happy ones, experience of which I would not like to have missed despite the at times intensive air raids and shelling. Over air raids I felt safe in my dug out, but with shelling it was otherwise, the actual shells making a filthy noise going overhead, a sort of whining whistle and not giving any indication as to where they would land. I ended this letter by stating that the caterpillars were flourishing and that my copy of the White Paper on Medical Services had been eaten by a mouse...a fitting fate.

On June the 7th I managed to go to Rome where I called on my cousin Lorna (van Heemstra) and her husband Mario Hodler. There being no lift working I had to climb four flights of steps carrying a heavy bundle of foods to get to their flat and it was a wonderful moment when the door opened and I saw Lorna, very pregnant and dishevelled as we fell into each other's arms. After all these months of expectation it was grand to be together. Both of them looked very tired having had a pretty hard time of it. For example there had been no electricity for some time, and latterly no water so Mario had had to carry it all up the four flights of stairs. Food also had given problems. Butter was only available on the Black Market and cost 860 liras a kilo. No margarine or sugar, flour 200 liras a kilo, oil 1000 liras a litre and shoes 2000 liras a pair. With Mario's salary of 5000 liras a month how they managed I did not go into, but both seemed well fed. Fortunately they were able to get plenty of milk. Mario, being Swiss and with a wealthy father, no doubt had outside resources, but how the ordinary Italian managed was beyond my ken. Lorna had heard I was in Italy from her sister Ailsa in Holland. It was extraordinary how news got about despite the war.

Rome itself I found very clean and well kept and it was lovely to see a town not touched by war. Despite my twenty-six years absence I found my way about quite easily and it was a joy to revisit old scenes. Anzio is now deserted and desolate, after the past four months the contrast is awful.

Later on the 15th, I wrote: "All the local populace is returning and along the main roads there are processions of people carrying bundles and returning home. Why they are so doing heaven alone knows as there is little left. Half the houses are destroyed and all destitute of furniture etc. The land is neglected and the crops destroyed. It is a pathetic sight but I get very angry to see the women carrying enormous bundles and the men nothing. All the dugouts and camp sites are being systematically searched by the Italians, who in addition are firing any weapons they find, there being a lot of ammo lying about. They are like the Arabs, totally impervious to danger and walk gaily over minefields etc."

Some weeks prior to this date I had been on a walk in the woods and had come across a large dump of American rations, all in tins, in an isolated spot far from any of their stations. What the dump was doing there I could not make out, but presumably there must have been some sort of a deal with the Black Market. Anyhow I rushed back to camp and returned with a truck to carry back such items as we lacked, mainly tinned fruits and fruit juices, to make a welcome addition to the unit's diet.

On June the 18th, I wrote: "The weather has been lovely and quite cool. I have been back to Rome on semi-business and dropped in on Lorna to find her and the boy looking much better. It was such a pleasure seeing her and I hope to be able to drop in again in the near future. I did the necessary work which consisted of ordering 72 pairs of silk stockings for the mess and for the rest of the time wandered about revisiting old haunts. The town has changed comparatively little and such changes as there are are improvements. It has been opened up and the old ruins made more visible. The only snag is that there are too many uniforms about and I am longing to stay in a hotel without a soldier in sight. The shops are full, at least the luxury ones, and one can buy any article in that category, but useful things are scarce and dear. Materials are impossible, 20 to 30/- a yard for art silk and so on."

I returned to Rome on the 19th with two objects in view, to buy more stockings and pipes for the mess. Of the latter I was able to buy quite a number of Dunhills at a price of about 25/- which pleased everyone. I saw some lovely dress shops with, in the windows, some beautiful underwear which gave me quite a thrill...all frills and ideal for a young girl. What is more in one shop I met a most beautiful lady, a Princess and the first real lady I had come across since leaving Tunis, this cheered me up. Otherwise I revisited old haunts and revived many memories. Rome is such a lovely town and I have spent so many happy days here. Fortunately, unlike so many other towns it had been improved, with so many former slum areas cleared and the ruins opened up. In general the town looked clean and well kept.

On the 24th I was back in Rome having lunch with Mario and Lorna followed by a good gossip. Urs, the boy, had had an attack of diarrhoea and was not looking too well, but Lorna herself looked better. Mario was thin and finding life difficult, food being an awful worry and being difficult to get. With most of it having to be obtained from the Black Market it was very expensive. The cost of living had gone up 1000% in the last 3 years. He had got hold of a Prince Wiazemsky who gave him addresses of Russians for me, and of the church to which I will go on Sunday. Lorna told me that the Alliottis, the family of Aunt Alec's sister, having been great Fascists and full of enthusiasm for Mussolini, fled to Smyrna as soon as the war started in order to avoid military service.

My letter carried on as follows: "Lorna heard from her sister Ailsa in Holland that things there were very bad. When the Germans arrived there was at least a chance of reconciling the Dutch to their fate as they were bewildered by the Queen's flight. But instead of supporting the moderates the Germans put all power into the hands of the Dutch Nazis, with the result that the country is united in its hatred of the Germans. Typical German psychology. The husband of a cousin of Lorna's, a German Colonel, visited them in Holland told them that after the war there is one country he would never visit again, namely Holland, for the Dutch hated the Germans too much. Lorna also told me that all educated Germans and officers of the old army had no hope of winning the war... only the younger ones steeped in propaganda had hopes of winning. Everything in Holland was taken away, and all train loads were labelled 'Gifts from the Dutch people to the Germans in gratitude for our liberation.' With regard to Italy, when things were going well everyone supported Mussolini, and there was enthusiasm over the declaration of war and over the move into Libya and the threat to Alexandria. As soon as things started to go wrong however, Fascism became anathema and everybody blamed it for the results. No individual stops to think whether he profited from Fascism or to what extent he is to blame. They only think of themselves. There are some 30 political parties, all at loggerheads with each other and Mario thinks that the Italians are totally incapable of ruling themselves." This letter ends with a request for some coffee beans....the most welcome form of gift in all walks of life in Italy.

A few days later I was back in Rome with the Colonel, he was after Vermouth and Pâte de Foie Gras. Unfortunately all shops were shut as it was a holiday, so we called on some Russian friends, the Pavlovskys, and spent a very pleasant afternoon listening to our host discoursing on politics. He came out with a most involved story of how he was about to be arrested when the Allies took over and about all the proofs he had shown of his sympathy for their cause.

Apparently there was a spy in the colony who had come from Germany and was most pro-Soviet and a watch was kept on Pavlovsky, who however, was warned in time. From him I also heard all the news of the Russian Colony. He told me that the Germans had behaved well apart from the secret police who were most brutal with tortures, murders etc. He now believes all the stories of German atrocities, whose cruelties were only exceeded by Mussolini's Republican army, whose excesses even horrified the S.S. With further talks on Italian politics we spent a very enjoyable afternoon.

I was back in Rome again on July 1st. to see Lorna. Both she and the boy I found looking much better and as usual we had a good gossip and what a pleasure it was to be back in a family atmosphere again. After supper I was collected and taken to some Italians where I sat and talked to an old retired Colonel, chiefly about shooting, wine and politics. We had brought some biscuits with us and it was pathetic to see how they wolfed them down. People would do anything for food but fortunately the situation was improving. One trouble is that while the Black Market flourishes food is always available, at a price, but as soon as it is stopped food will disappear. No measures would be likely to succeed in stopping it as here it is possible to do anything by bribery, a relic of Fascism. In those days everyone who wanted to get on had to belong to the party, but now that it had failed, everyone was trying to find a scapegoat and to emphasise their hatred of Mussolini. So to-day there are some 39 political parties but no leaders as all liberal minded men were done away with or were tainted with Fascism. In consequence there was no one capable of government and the moral sense of the people had been destroyed by years of self-seeking, bribery and by the police system of denunciation. The Royal Family were most unpopular as, of course, everyone blamed them. A tragic situation with literally hardly a single honest man left in the country.

CHAPTER V

Callese, Assisi & Pesaro

Callese

Our next move on the 11th July 1944, took us to the village of Callese, North of Rome and not far from the small town of Civita Castellana. Here our camp was set in a field on rising ground, offering us a lovely view from the mess tent. I was glad to be away from Rome, which, with modernisation and growth was quite different to the town I knew in World War I. Also after the seclusion of Anzio I was glad to be back in open country and free to move in every direction and, above all, once again to be free to mix with the Italian population.

We had hardly settled down when an old friend turned up complete with car and took me for a superb drive which led me to write home in these words: "I have just had one of my best days since the war started, as we drove through incredibly beautiful country, very similar to the landscapes to be seen on Italian pictures, with wooded hills, deep ravines, limestone crags, olive groves and vineyards, with villages perched on the top of the most inaccessible hills, often walled and battlemented with their grey stone houses topped by a round-towered castle. Their streets narrow and cool, lined by tall houses, some of magnificent style, clearly belonging to some noble family, some of these latter even having small gardens, a sign of luxury in these closely packed townships."

Each village had its own particular character, with its site and walls reminding one of the days when it took a foolhardy man to live outside its protective walls. Most of the hilltops were covered with woods with olive groves often encroaching and vineyards everywhere else. How I longed to have a car of my own to enable me to explore more of the country, although, in a way being confined to one small area enabled one to enter more closely into the spirit of the country. How happy I was to be in Italy and in such country, even though, in view of the war, my feelings about the Italians should probably have been different. Later on I wrote of the countryside surrounding our camp: "The Tiber winding in the valley, the wooded hills, the villages perched on their tops, the green fields, little would seemed to have changed over the centuries.

In these parts there does not appear to have been the same shortage of food as elsewhere and people looked fit and well. All are poor as is to be expected, but perhaps this helps them to remain as hospitable and welcoming as ever. Yesterday I approached one house to enquire whether they had any fruit for sale and I was given a whole lot of Morello cherries for which payment was refused. At another they insisted on my being served an omelette and at yet another I was given a huge bunch of onions, which are precious commodities these days. Wherever I go I meet with the same reception and I believe this to be due to a genuine feeling of hospitality, coupled of course with relief at the departure of the Germans."

From day to day I carried on with my normal task of shopping for our mess and for that of the men. Here I could do so with no qualms of conscience for there was an abundance of fruit and vegetables on the market on which the needs of our small numbers made no impression and which, owing to lack of transport, could not be sent on to Rome. To satisfy my personal needs I came to an agreement with a farmer to be allowed to eat as many peaches as I wanted in return for a small payment, while I was also able to buy ten gallons of wine, which it was such a joy to drink again after six months of abstinence.

The weather remained hot in the middle of the day, encouraging the taking of a siesta, but nights were cold and required three blankets on my bed. Sleep was encouraged by the chirping of the crickets. There was not much work and that mainly was in connection with some Cypriots, involving the speaking of Greek and Turkish. It felt quite like home again.

The village of Callese stood about half a mile away from us, as usual on the top of a hill, where it was dominated by a fine castle. As is customary the village church was sited in the main square, and there was another one some 600 yards away. This was a fine Romanesque building and, as luck would have it, I met the priest who related the following story. Some 800 years ago the future Saint, to whom it was dedicated, lived in the village where he performed several miracles in the way of saving people from drowning in the Tiber and, in one year of extreme drought, emulating Moses by striking a rock to give rise to a spring of fine, clear water. Before his death he had requested that he be buried, not in the village church, but on a bare piece of land lying outside. After his death the villagers decided to ignore this request and all was made ready to bury him in the church. But when they came to the point of so doing, it was found that his body had disappeared and it was later found resting on the piece of land the holy man had chosen for his grave. The villagers were not prepared to put up with this insubordination, so back he was taken to the church, whence once again he disappeared to his chosen resting place. So back to the church again but when he went off once more the villagers gave up the struggle and he was finally buried where he wanted to be, with the present church later erected on the site.

The Saint was canonised later and has continued to save men and women from drowning in the Tiber. The number and nature of ex-voto tablets had worried the priest, who found them unsuitable company to a Romanesque church and he had been trying to reduce their numbers, slowly and quietly. The embalmed body of the Saint is preserved in the church and on showing it to me the priest bent down and kissed it, whereupon feeling it was also expected of me I followed suit, which gave the delightful old man evident pleasure, especially on hearing that I was a Protestant.

Some days later, when sitting at tea in the mess, I saw a smart dog-cart approach and a lady step out. I walked to the bottom of the hill to greet her. She told me that she was the Duchess of Callese and that as we were encamped on family property she had come to see what it was all about. She spoke perfect English and I invited her to the mess for a cup of tea, over which we had a very pleasant chat. On leaving she asked whether any of the officers would like to see over the castle and this we did on the following day. The castle must have been some 5-600 years old, but its interior had been refurbished and modernised and made most comfortable, each bedroom having its own bathroom hollowed out of the thickness of the outer walls. The Duke spoke French and he and his wife could not have been pleasanter, although he was clearly under her thumb. As we were leaving the Duchess asked whether any of us would like to come to dinner, this being arranged she whispered to me: "Could you bring some salt when you come?" In answer to my surprise she told me that at the start of the war she had laid in huge stocks of everything, except salt, feeling safe in this respect with Italy surrounded by water and sea. And now they had had none for five months!

Later I heard that in his younger days the Duke had been very much a man about town and had even kept a private doctor to keep him up to the mark. But financial troubles intervened and he married the daughter of a wealthy Milanese industrialist and, though this led to the castle being done up, an eagle eye was henceforward kept on him, only allowing him to escape during any absence of his wife.

Both were charming and the dinner excellent and a great success, in part thanks to the bag of salt I had brought with me. The Duke had known Felix Youssupoff and when I mentioned that his daughter Irina, was one of Barbara's oldest friends, I was socially well away, so much so that shortly after I was able to write home: "I have now become très snob, having dined with a Duchess, a Marchesa and a Contessa in the past week. At one of my visits I met a young man who had lost an arm and also spoke beautiful English. On my asking him he told me that his arm had been shot off by his uncle, in explanation of which he told me that it had been shot off in a naval engagement in which the British Admiral in Command happened to be his uncle. What a joy it was to be back in such surroundings again."

At the same time I was making friends at the other end of the social scale. Out walking one day I came across two boys paddling in a stream and grubbing about under the banks. I asked them what they were up to, to be told that they were fishing in the manner of tickling trout, i.e. by moving their hands slowly under the bank until they felt a fish, and then with a sudden movement jerking it onto the bank. This intrigued me, so off went my shoes and socks as I stepped into the water (and onto very sharp stones), when after a short time, to my surprise and delight I landed a fish all of six inches long. This proved such fun that I arranged to meet the boys again in a couple of days. On this occasion I was invited home to their house to partake of the catch, which ended up as a fine frittura. I spent a delightful evening, meeting some neighbours and after this I was accepted in the village and was never at loss for someone to talk to.

Through my walks I also got to know several farmers. What a joy it was after the long seclusion of Anzio to be able to talk in Italian again, and to meet simple people with whom to discuss matters of family and country life. Being made welcome everywhere after this manner, I felt so contented that at times I began to wonder how I would settle down to life in England again.

From time to time I was able to return to Rome to visit Lorna and Mario and Russian friends, and was lucky enough to be able to take a small sack of potatoes to the Orloff-Denisoffs, who had not seen any for months. I also called on a former C.O. to find him installed in luxury in a hotel in the Via Veneto, together with a most attractive secretary, with whom he seemed to be on the best of terms. Trader always knew how to make himself comfortable. He was dealing in food for the civilian population and told me a story. The Americans had devised a superbly healthy form of sausage made from soya beans and these were distributed to their forces, who flatly refused to eat them. They were then passed over to the British, with the same result, and so finally were turned over to the Italians, who apparently after sampling them said they would rather die of starvation than eat such things. Here in Rome, I also met an old colleague, who immediately asked me to cash a cheque for fifty pounds for him. His optimism I could not but admire, having been in the same unit for several weeks.

Early in August I wrote home: "We will soon be leaving these parts to go on to Assisi, a town I have always longed to visit and in which I will be able to enjoy some sight-seeing. But I shall be sorry to leave this place where we have made some very good friends thanks to the Duchess being in need of salt. But joking apart she has been most charming and through her I have met others living in the vicinity. With such aristocratic connections you won't know me when I get home but how wonderful it will be to be all together again. Still this is a wonderful country and I am so happy to be in it. All and every day I thank God for having brought me here."

Assisi

We arrived in Assisi in mid-August 1944, after a pleasant journey which took us past the Roman town of Tarquinia. For lunch we stopped in a small town, which had suffered from bombing. Here we settled down by the roadside in the main square, with an audience of small boys who grabbed at every morsel of food offered them. Some wit organised a race, with the prize a tin of bully beef laid on the pavement, the course being some 50 yards. There were seven contestants and in the excitement the tin was knocked over and spilled its contents, which however were quickly picked up and eaten. This was the first occasion since leaving Naples that I had come across real hunger. At a party in Rome, at which were present several fairly highly placed Italians, the tin of biscuits I took along disappeared very quickly. It always upset me to see hunger in any form, particularly so as we, as individuals, could do so little about it.

We settled in a field surrounded by vineyards below the town, not far from the church of the Porziuncola, built round a small stone house in which St.

Francis is said to have either been born or lived. Up above us on a hilltop lay the town itself dominated by the huge monastery at one end and a large castle at the other. With its grey stone houses and its many church steeples it appeared most attractive and promising. In these parts vines are trained from tree to tree along ropes, with a fifteen foot interval between the rows. When in fruit they must present a fascinating sight.

Fortunately the town had not suffered from the war, although when we arrived it was full of soldiers and even boasted of an Officers' Club which offered glorious views but pretty filthy wine. Here my love of sight-seeing was fully satisfied as I pottered about. At this time of the year there was no competition from flowers, the land being too dry. In the Great Monastery there are three churches, one built on top of the other. The top one holds the famous Giottos depicting the life of St. Francis. These I found interesting, but far preferred the primitives in the lower churches and especially a Cimabue in the lowest. I also visited St. Francis' "country retreat" and of this I wrote: "I have just been for a lovely walk to a monastery on the mountain, tucked away among trees on a hillside, to which the Saint used to come to do penitence and to fast, and in which one can still see his cell and his chapel. It is here that he is said to have preached to the birds, stopping a stream from running as it made too much noise. The stream bed is still there and as one would expect, completely dry at this time of the year. The small monastery itself is a delight, so quiet and peaceful and isolated from the world, that I should not mind staying here for a few days to get away from the army."

One day when walking in the street I came across a nun carrying a heavy load, which I took off her and carried it to her convent. When about to enter she turned to thank me, asking if I were a Catholic, and to my answer of "No" she said "Peccato... What a pity" in a lovely soft voice, and with such a sweet smile, that I have never forgotten the incident, which has remained one of my happiest experiences in Assisi.

Back to more earthly affairs, I had not been settled long when a man came to me seeking advice, feeling weak and lethargic and not up to the mark. On going into his history I found that a wife and a mistress and of course the occasional pick-up were making heavy demands on him. Hearing this, my first inclination was to congratulate him on his stamina, but contented myself with telling him that there was only one answer to the problem and that was a period of total abstinence. This he told me was not possible as it would lead to impossible trouble with his women-folk, so I offered to give him a course of injections which might help. In these, such as they were, I had no faith, but the psychological effect was good and he claimed to feel much better. In due course we became the best of friends. He was, I was certain, up to his neck in the Black Market, as well as every kind of devilry, in fact a thorough rogue, but he was cheerful, gay, fun and very good company, and, like so many disreputable men, far more entertaining than the respectable.

He put me into the way of getting wine, but I also made this question of getting wine an excuse to visit a friend living some twenty kilometres away. He had organised himself well in a superb house, set in a fine garden, complete with bathroom, sitting room and two attractive girls to look after him. He had, if I remember rightly, something to do with organizing food supplies for the civilian population. The sight of this luxury gave me hopes of spending a few days with him, but this never came off, but I did return from the visit laden with excellent wine.

Otherwise in the evening I used to go with a friend and talk about England and home. He had already been away for three years and this made me realise I had nothing to grumble about, except for having missed so much of the children's lives.

Pesaro

For our next move in September 1944 we crossed the Appenines and settled outside a small township near Ancona. The journey was fascinatingly beautiful, though alas, too late for flowers, and took several hours. On arrival at our destination nobody knew anything at all about us and we were offered the prospect of returning to where we had come from, but were told to settle down until something definite had been decided. So we sat there with no work to do and with everyone getting bored, with bridge as the only relief. The Colonel in particular grew more and more tiresome so I sought for my usual relief among the local population.

We had one excitement. A very secret convoy was due to pass along the main road and all military and civilians had to keep away for the space of a quarter mile or so. The officers in charge of the convoy lunched with us and I casually asked one of them where the amphibian tanks were moving to. He looked at me in absolute horror and asked where on earth did I get this information and the reaction when I told him that one of the farmers had asked me the same question was most amusing. Apparently the whole movement was intended to be top secret.

Otherwise my main objective was to get hold of some decent wine. A friend had advised me to go to a village in the hills not far from the small town of Jesi. Arriving there in a jeep with a couple of empty demi-johns I was made welcome and immediately ushered into one of the cantinas, a large cave artificially hollowed out of the soft rock and lined with rows of vats, containing about 20,000 litres of wine. So we sat down, about half a dozen of us now, wine was produced and we started chatting. We tried the wine from several vats, but after all these glasses of wine, my choice, when it came to the crunch, was rather haphazard. Anyhow, having settled the financial aspects, the party sadly came to an end, with me being invited, and I promising, to return. As it turned out the wine was excellent and must have been what is sold under the name of Verdicchio di Jesi in England.

After a few days we finally received instructions to move on to Pesaro, further up the coast, where we were comfortably installed in a small house, complete with bathroom. Pesaro was the birthplace of Rossini and of this one was left in no doubt, with a conservatory named after him. The old town was very pleasant with some fine old houses and palazzi. On one occasion I was in the courtyard of one of these when large stones started falling about me, leading to a quick flight. I was glad to hear later that the cause of the trouble was men working on the roof and not due to any animosity over me. The sea coast here was also lovely, with broad sandy beaches, and the sea still warm enough to bathe in.

Our men were billeted in a field, together with my medical tent. One day a man came and asked me whether I would object to his digging near the tent and this of course I allowed. My corporal and I stood idly watching when to our surprise he unearthed a box full of silver. Corporal and I kicked ourselves over having missed such lovely loot, but talking to the man I was told that most people had hidden their valuables in this manner for fear of the Germans. I then asked him whether it was not unwise to expose his treasures to the eyes of the British. To this he replied “No, for with them he felt absolutely safe,” an answer which gave me great pleasure.

The town possessed a fine library and I had just got permission to read in it, when I was offered a week's leave in Rome. This was not to be refused. The journey there was pretty awful, twelve hours in the back of a truck, and it was a relief to find ourselves lodged in a comfortable hotel in the Via Ludovisi, my room being complete with private bathroom, a box-spring mattress and clean sheets. After washing we went downstairs and were delighted to find a bar, well stocked with a most reassuring array of bottles and here we settled down, until dinner was served. And so to bed and an excellent night's sleep.

Next morning we went for a stroll and then sat in a cafe in the Via Veneto, watching the passers by. A sleep after lunch was followed by a visit to Russian friends (the Pavlovskys), and the ensuing evening was marked by the discovery of a 'strong drink, very reminiscent of vodka and also pure alcohol'. (grappa).

Of the town I wrote home as follows: "Our hotel is in the best part of the town and very comfortable and quiet. Rome is looking lovelier than ever and greatly improved since I was here last, what with the weather being much cooler and the town emptier with fewer troops milling about. I had intended to do some sight-seeing, but doubt whether I will do any, it being too tempting to sit in cafes and watch the street life. The shops are better stocked, but prices are terrific. Women are still well dressed but, in general, not as good looking as further North."

I made the usual round of visits in the Russian colony and of course saw Mario and Lorna. Her baby, Fay, was now a month old and had gained 1 kilo in this period. Nevertheless she told me that 1) it was not eating enough, 2) that it was dying of diarrhoea, 3) that her abundant milk did not suit the baby, and 4) it cries for about 2 hours a day.

I went to the small Russian church, to find curious characters similar to those in London. There was great excitement as a senior Soviet Official had called on the priest to give him official thanks for all the help he had given Russian prisoners. I also visited an exhibition of paintings which had been brought out of hiding, in which it was a great joy to see Piero della Francesca's Flagellation from Urbino, the great Velazquez Pope from the Doria gallery, and Giorgone's Tempesta. Mention of Piero reminds me that at some time we passed through Arezzo only to find his frescoes boarded up and invisible.

Meanwhile the country was still in a state of chaos, with many people regretting the passing of Fascism, while back in camp the Colonel was as tiresome as ever and of him I wrote home: "Besides being stupid, he is extremely self-centred and his table manners are vile and worse than those of any Italian.... he is the son of a Lord."

The absence of work in no way saved me from masses of paper emanating from medical H.Q., most of which went to scrap. I had early learnt to take no notice of most of such stuff and to have as little to do with higher medical authorities as possible. In North Africa, in my innocence, I once reported several cases of fever in my unit and was then bombarded with such a host of demands and instructions etc. that thereafter my monthly reports made no mention of anything out of the ordinary in the state of health of the unit. Thereafter peace reigned.

In my description of North Africa I forgot to mention that we were instructed to issue a new anti-malarial pill to all members of the unit. After my first one I retired to bed, feeling like death and running a very high temperature. Quite a number of men were similarly affected. In this case I did report the matter and stopped the issue of the pill, later to hear the whole army had been similarly affected. On hearing about this the General in charge of medical affairs, pooh-poohed the idea, took one of the pills himself and. to everyone's joy, promptly went down with the same symptoms. The whole batch of pills was withdrawn and the ensuing one gave rise to no side-effects. There must have been some impurity present.

Before leaving Pesaro I had to go to Rimini and there visited the Malatesta temple. We also called in on a hotel and met a number of members of Popski's Private Army, an irregular unit which had worked behind enemy lines in the desert with considerable success. We had a good evening.

To-day this area is tourist ridden in summer, and the beaches lined with big hotels. Rimini, Cattolica and Pesaro are especially affected. In consequence I would not like to return.

CHAPTER VI

Ancona – "U" Prisoner of War Camp & Home Again

I took up my new post as Medical Officer to this camp on the 14th of April 1945 and arrived to find everybody in the throes of settling into a new site, which was on a hill-top overlooking the Adriatic and about a mile or so outside the town of Ancona. The location was superb, open to all the winds that blew and offering fine views over the sea. Here it was much cooler than in Chiuravalle and free from the flies which were beginning to make an appearance there. Heat I was able to stand up to, but a combination of heat and flies was too much for me.

I was equally pleased to return to tent life. Solid walls and roofs were all right in winter time, but in the warmer weather it was a delight to be able to wander out into the open air early in the morning and enjoy the cool, fresh air, while still clad only in pyjamas. However this was a pleasure to anticipate, for after settling into my tent, the next job was to meet all my fellows in the Mess and to learn what was expected of me in the way of work, which was to organise medical care for a possible ten thousand inmates, and to supervise the general hygiene of the Camp. Fortunately the Colonel proved first class and most helpful, more than can be said for my immediate Medical superior who proved to be a total wash-out.

The job of the Camp was to hold up to ten thousand prisoners on their way down to base camps in the South, with most only staying a few weeks or so. The Camp was made up of ten heavily wired pens, each provided with full washing and toilet facilities, the men sleeping in low tents, a new experience for many of the Germans. Food was brought in from a central kitchen, and the rations supplied, as I saw for myself, were of good quality and in good quantity.

My medical department had been allotted a small fenced in enclosure within the main perimeter of the Camp, with adequate space for all needs. Here a fifty-bedded hospital was housed in marquees and there was adequate tentage for other purposes. But all this, together with all the medical equipment, had to be indented for and set up on arrival, which required the dickens of a lot of work, in which I was ably supported by my British staff.

By the time the first 5,000 prisoners arrived on the scene all was in order and we were ready to face up to the worst. Fortunately by this time another British doctor had arrived on the scene. From the mass of prisoners, three German doctors and a dentist were picked out, together with a number of men from the Medical Corps allotted to us, but with none of these speaking any English I had to act as intermediary. Fortunately the other British doctor proved to be a very pleasant companion, who had never had any experience of this type of work. We therefore agreed that he should supervise the purely medical work, leaving me to see to all else in the way of Camp hygiene and organising our German staff. This worked very well, and never gave rise to any disagreement.

In a Camp of this nature, with large numbers of men closely herded together, general hygiene and the prevention of the spread of infections were subjects of the greatest importance, calling for close supervision of cooking and toilet facilities and the immediate isolation of any infective or potentially infective case. In consequence I covered the whole camp every day, inspecting all installations and insisting on the maximum of cleanliness, backed by the Colonel, whose ideas on the subject coincided with mine. He had had considerable experience of such camps and one of his introductions was the use of five gallon petrol tins cut and beaten out into sheets and used for lining the walls of the kitchens, thus allowing them to be easily cleaned, and for lining the ground around the washing facilities and the runnels for carrying away the waste water, thus keeping the surface dry, and preventing seepage into the soil.

On the purely medical side there was accommodation for three doctors to see patients simultaneously, the only difficulty arose over the question of language. Harry, my colleague, knew no German and the German doctors no other language. One of the staff who spoke German helped Harry out of his difficulties, but on all other occasions I was called in to sort matters out. This I found great fun, having to use my full range of languages.

Nothing was known of the quality of the German doctors when they were picked out and they proved to be a varied lot. The oldest, a Doctor Kaiser from Hamburg was first class in every respect. I had the greatest liking for him and trust in his ability and his attitude to the sick. He had been trained in pre-Nazi days. The second had only partially been affected by Nazidom. His attitude to medicine was more scientific than human and he expressed a great interest in herbs. The third and youngest had been entirely Nazi-trained, which had left him ignorant and unfitted to take responsibility. He was hard and somewhat indifferent to his patients. He was removed from general consultative work and limited to the treatment of minor conditions only.

A friend of mine of some considerable experience had strongly advised me to leave the care of hospital cases in British hands. He had had some unfortunate experiences with German treatment, telling of one occasion, when doing a hospital round, he had come across one German, severely ill with malaria, who had not been put up for transfer to a base hospital, the German doctor in charge saying: 'What is the point, he is going to die anyhow?', thus depriving the poor wretch of any hope of survival. After seeing the likes of him I was not surprised, after the war, to be told that the best doctors in Germany were women.

I had also been advised not to treat German soldiers in the same manner as British, but at all times to insist on the strictest discipline, failing which they would become unhappy and obstructive. Initially I took no heed of this advice, but experience soon taught me of its wisdom, and at the first sign of any slackness or disgruntlement I would summon the Sergeant and go round the compound finding fault with everything, indicating deficiencies and pointing out spheres for improvement. Results were invariably excellent, with disgruntled looks giving way to smiles and the general status of the compound improving in all directions. Smiles returned as I offered my congratulations and told them what a fine lot of men they were and all ended happily.

On occasion prisoners in the main camp organised a Concert Party and these we always got to give a performance in our compound for the benefit of staff and patients. Some of these were of a high standard. As for the doctors I got permission to take them out for walks to return each time with large bunches of medicinal herbs. Usually I took them to a farmer friend to treat them to a glass of wine before returning home, but I never found out to what extent the herbs we gathered were subsequently used.

The amount of work that fell to our lot varied according to the number of prisoners in residence, and an intake of 5,000 or more would keep us well occupied, as many arrived in poor condition, with the number of skin infections suggesting somewhat of a breakdown in living conditions behind the German lines. Mentally most arrivals were in a state of apathy with a considerable percentage relieved to be out of it all, with only a small number still waving the flag. But glad as I was at the prospect of victory and of a return to normal life, as in North Africa, the sight of an army in defeat was a sad one. In the treatment of skin conditions the German doctors were constantly asking for a special coal-tar preparation which was unobtainable from British sources. This saddened them, although to my mind rest and cleanliness played a far bigger part in cure than any ointment.

In the course of work I met a number of interesting men, both pleasant and unpleasant. Of the latter I remember a Frenchman, suffering from lung tuberculosis, who annoyed me with his constant complaints over how he had been mistreated and mishandled by the Germans in hospital, complemented by horrifying stories. Unfortunately for his credibility he had brought with him his medical dossier, which indicated that his treatment had been all that it should have been, and his physical condition certainly bore this out. I so often heard tales of this description from non-Germans that eventually I never took heed of them and in a way I felt sorrier for the Germans who had lost and whose dreams of world conquest had ended in a prisoner of war camp, worrying over what had befallen their families at home.

Fortunately men like this Frenchman were few in number. One man I greatly admired was an elderly Italian, who in reply to my query as to what he was doing here, said that the reason was that he was a Fascist. At this I expressed surprise, saying that during my two years in Italy I had as yet never come across a Fascist. He then told me that he had always been one and still was, firmly believing that Fascism was the best form of Government for Italy. It was such a pleasure meeting a man of this calibre that I got him to report sick on the following day to be able to continue with our conversation.

Another interesting man was a Greek who struck me as being an appalling old rogue, and who had somehow got mixed up in German affairs, although in what manner I could not make out. But despite not being able to believe any of his stories, he was cheerful and very good fun and no doubt fully prepared to carry on with his roguery as opportunity offered. In contrast was a pathetic Italian who asked me what the P.O.W. camp down South would be like. "Will there be any pasta?" "Doubtful." "Will there be any wine?" "No." "Any Women?" "Certainly not." ..."Then I will die."

In contrast was a young German officer, of the name of von Bock, presumably a relation of the Marshal. A very good looking man (speaking excellent English, learnt from an English governess), who, unlike so many others, faced up to events without making excuses. I enjoyed talking to him, but like all the others off he went. About a month later he reappeared on the scene. I asked him "What the devil are you doing back here?" He replied, "I have had some bad luck." The story he told me was a sad one. Having managed to acquire a British Officer's uniform he also managed to escape from the camp, then posing as an allied Yugoslav, he thumbed lifts to the North. The last one took him to near the front line, but as luck would have it, the driver of the jeep turned out to be a Serb, and gave him away. And so back to us again.

Encounters of this kind made all the difference to life as one never knew what lay round the corner. They also made up in part for the comparative dullness of the medical work, covering, in the main, only minor illnesses. The other relief I found lay in talking to Dr. Kaiser, who viewed the world and what was going on in it in much the same light as I did. I was very glad to have him at hand to talk things over and to express my feelings to someone of my own profession, age and background, leaving me happy to feel that there still remained some Germans of this quality. Once things had become well organised and the staff knew their jobs and could be relied on to get on with them, it became possible to relax more and more and as fate willed I chose this moment to become a hospital inmate.

At the top of a hill the brakes of the truck in which I was driving gave way and we careered down to crash into the back of a ten-ton lorry. With the doors jammed I had to climb out of the window (I was sitting in the front seat) suffering no further damage than a pain in my right foot. This I ignored for a couple of days, but with things getting worse I went to hospital where an X-ray revealed a fractured metatarsal. So I was put in plaster and admitted. All hopes of a life of indolence and ease were soon put to rest, for after a couple of days I found myself giving anaesthetics every morning. After lunch I was left in peace to read (the library having produced The Three Musketeers and Prescott's Conquest of Peru) and also to sleep. Then after tea I would walk or rather hobble about in the grounds, watching the fireflies which appeared at dusk to remind me of early days in Moda.

I shared my room with a young German doctor and found it interesting talking to him and to any other German officers in the offing. Some of these still refused to admit that they had been beaten in the War (and seemed quite ready to start up again, especially against the Russians).

But my room-mate was quite different, he belonged to a Christian sect which had fallen foul of the Nazis. Two years of service had been spent on the Russian front, where he had been greatly impressed by the extreme poverty and the appalling living conditions of the local population and the lack of necessities such as clothing. In the way of fear and repression of thought he found conditions far worse than in Germany. "Moralisch", i.e. from a moral point of view he thought the Russians to be the best people in Europe and their language the most beautiful. In his view the Germans could have won the war in Russia in a few months if the occupation of the territories taken over had been free and liberal, whereas, instead, the people were ground down to be worse off than in their former state. Had their lives been improved they would have flocked over to the German side.

Later I was put in charge of one of the German wards and this work I enjoyed, being able to talk and listen to the men's tales. These three weeks in the hospital opened my eyes to conditions present at that time in the German army, with their wounded often arriving in an appalling state, with wounds neglected and with only paper dressings, suggesting that medical services had broken down. On the other hand it was satisfactory to see that in the way of treatment no difference was made between the handling of British and Germans.

I was formally discharged after three weeks in hospital, my leg in a walking plaster, delighted to return to work and to find everything in the camp running smoothly. Initially, doing the rounds was slow and cumbersome but the worst inconvenience was that of taking a bath without having water run down inside the plaster. Life once again ran pleasantly and quietly, without much of interest to cheer me up. Fortunately the mess was totally free of sex talk and we played bridge and poker and talked. Whenever opportunity arose I used to return to Chiaravalle to visit old friends and was sad to learn that my erstwhile German teacher and her family were returning to Venice. Of course there were other changes afoot, sadly I was unable to get in touch with my farmer friends as they lived too far out of town.

However I got to know some people locally. On one of my walks I noticed some shotguns on display in a window and on entering the shop I asked whether I could just handle them for a minute. Conversation ensued and I was invited into the house to talk about shooting. The establishment was run by two brothers, both champion clay pigeon shots, who introduced their families, and what with presents of cotton and sweets for the children I was always made welcome when passing that way.

I had also met one or two girls living in Ancona, and took to visiting them, naturally always under the eagle eyes of their mothers, as always I enjoyed the company of both and had lots of fun. I found these elderly ladies always delightful company and it was such fun teasing and at the same time flattering them and their daughters. I had also got to know a local farmer of whom I wrote to the children: "There is a lovely farm near here, all smelly and dirty, which has eight cows, seven calves, four large pigs and eight little ones, as well as lots of rabbits, although sadly all the chickens have died so there are no eggs for my breakfast. As for children I am not certain how many there are but all run about barefooted and dirty and play in a muddy pond. They have no toys but make do with sticks and stones, and one girl has wrapped an old rag round a stick and calls this her doll. Children here start work very early in life and at seven they help in the cooking and on the farm."

I often used to come here to sit and watch the children at play and also the work in progress, and in the intervals discuss farm life and the world in general. It was always such a pleasure to be welcomed by the children, though this I suspect was more in honour of the sweets I carried than of my good self. All these farmers grew lots of hemp for making binding material. Today I wonder whether this hemp has any relation to "pot".

Another farmer, a far more prosperous one, invited me to the wedding of his daughter, to, I think, a soldier. I did not attend the service but arrived at the house later to find a large crowd assembled, including some of my men, with the young couple seated, silent and rigid, on a couple of very upright chairs at one end of the room. Wine and food were served and what with the former, the smoke from the countless cigarettes (British mostly) and the noise of countless voices I packed up after two to return to my tent for a sleep. I returned at about five-thirty to the same pandemonium, with the young couple still unmoved on their chairs. How they stood up to it all I could not make out. By nine o'clock, what with the wine and the talk I was completely exhausted and this time made no further return, later to hear that the party broke up soon after. I could only hope that the couple were allowed to recover in peace the following day.

Having, in conversation with my staff, persistently heard about the deficiencies and iniquities of the Italian population, I one day asked: "Why, if you dislike the

Italians do you spend so many evenings in the local farmhouse?" to get the answer that the people there were different. I used to get very bored with all this kind of ignorant talk about the locals.

On one occasion some thousand S.S. arrived with everyone expecting trouble. But far from it, these proved to be among the best disciplined men we had to deal with and far from causing trouble turned out to be ideal inmates. Their pen adjoined some fruit trees and the farmer owner complained that his fruit was disappearing. It was thought that some of the S.S. were getting out at night and helping themselves, to do which they had to find their way through an entanglement of barbed wire. Anyhow the matter was discussed with their man in charge, a sergeant, who offered to put up guards to prevent any further raids and there is no doubt he would have done so if asked. Instead the barbed wire was strengthened.

Most trouble came not from the disciplined but from the more simple-minded and especially the Southern Italians and Sicilians, whose ideas on hygiene proved somewhat rudimentary. Used in their part of the world to the Eastern hole in the floor for toilet purposes, they did not know how to cope with the seats provided and used to squat on them instead of sitting, with frequent unfortunate results, but apart from easily remedied matters of this kind I experienced little trouble.

Both we and the prisoners were especially lucky with regard to the weather. True it was hot, and most downfalls of rain were of short duration. The winds were more tiresome, rising suddenly with considerable force and blowing up clouds of dust. On one morning I was woken up by a particularly strong gale and got out of the tent to make certain of its security, when happening to look across the valley I saw the hospital tents collapsing, one after the other. Fortunately there were no inmates there at the time, and I, biding my time, retired into my tent, leaving it to the staff to mend matters, which fortunately they did very successfully, so that by the time I crossed over to work all was in order again. One of the lessons one learned in the army was to keep away from trouble.

Normally a gentle breeze would get up of an afternoon, cooling things down, the temperature in the tents at midday being about 90 degrees. This did not worry me, except for the fact that all the herbage was dried up and there were no flowers, except for thistles. The early mornings were lovely, with the air cool and inviting, and lying in bed at this time, looking out into the open was an ever-recurring pleasure, especially when I heard the strains of Ritorna Sorriento approaching from the distance, a sure sign that my batman was bringing me my tea. In rivalry to him, other sounds of singing also came from trucks passing by, taking loads of Italians to work.

We also had under our care a number of scattered small units in the area and these often involved a certain amount of travel, by this means I was able to visit Loretto, with its Cathedral and House of the Virgin which miraculously flew over from Palestine. I also went to Recanati, the town in which the poet Leopardi was born and here I visited the Palazzo, containing the rooms in which he lived and worked. Outside the town was bedecked with placards bearing quotations from his poems which made sad reading as one remembered what he had to say about the town and its inhabitants and the way these treated him:

Ne mi diceva il cor che l'eta verde
Sarei dannato a consumare in questo
Natio borgo selvaggio, inta una gente
Zotica, vil; cui nomi strani, e spesso
Argomento di riso e di trastullo,
Son dottrina e saper; che m'odia e fugge,
Par invidia non gia, che non mi tiene
Maggior di se, ma perche tale estima
Ch'io mi tenga in cor mio, sebbn di fuori
A personne giaramai non ne fo segno.
Qui passo gli anni, abbandonato, occulto,
Senz' amor, senza vita; ed aspro a forza
Tra lo stuol de malevoli divengo; ….*

For my heart never told me my green age
was doomed to waste here in this barbarous town
Where I was born, with a cheap boorish people,
Who hold in no repute learning or knowledge,
Often indeed their jest, a thing to laugh at
A folk who hate and shun me, not from envy
They do not judge me better than themselves
But they suppose that in my heart I think so
Although I never showed it any man.

And so I pass the years, alone, obscure,
Loveless and lifeless; and I am forced to grow
Bitter myself, with this malignant crowd…

Fortunately the hill which Leopardi loved and to which he used to repair when in search of solitude has been preserved from building to become a public garden, bearing a line from his poem I'Infinito: *Sempre caro mi fu questo ermo colle* (*This lonely hill was always dear to me*) and on it I found myself alone. Poor man, what a life he led, but what a poet.

Once we were under peace time conditions leave was easier to get. Hearing that Masha was in hospital in Rome after an operation I applied and was granted a couple of days off. I arrived to find her in good form, what a joy it was to have news of home at first hand, (she having just arrived from England) and to have a good gossip about all our friends. She, together with some other acquaintances, was attached to the Austrian Commission. Of them I wrote home: "You cannot imagine the difference between people fresh out from England and those who have been here some time. They have no idea of how we feel nor of the relative importance of different things in our minds. The atmosphere of the Commission made me feel rather sick, as does that of Rome in general. These people come out here when all is quiet, live like Lords, get extra pay and every comfort and facility, promotion and God knows what else, while the wretched men who have done all the hard work are treated like dirt. Despite all this (and to be honest), I have enjoyed the life I have been leading and would not have had it changed in any way, given that I had to be away from home. But no doubt there will come moments at home when I will long for a return to Italy."

The increasing number of prisoners passing through our hands and their general condition left us in no doubt that the end of the war was at hand, so when it was announced it came as no surprise. No doubt in Rome it was duly celebrated with champagne and the like, but here our men were not even issued with an extra bottle of beer. But despite the general relief and rejoicing the atmosphere changed, for, thanks to the removal of tension and the cessation of the need to work for a definite purpose, everyone became somewhat demoralised, fortunately without affecting discipline in any way, and, with thoughts tending to be concentrated on returning home the former spirit of general cheerfulness started to disappear.

In actual fact we in our camp were luckier than most others for, with an increasing number of prisoners passing through, we were kept busy and hard at work, while I was probably luckier than most in having a number of interests, especially my love of the country. As I wrote home: "Lying on my bed I can see the sea as a background to a couple of haystacks. It is cooler at this hour; I am tired after a good day's work and am proposing to spend the rest of the evening reading. However much I may grumble I continue to enjoy the life I lead here and always feel content. In fact, on looking back, I do not think I have ever felt otherwise, except perhaps when thoroughly frightened at Anzio."

Meanwhile the German Adriatic fleet, such as it was, arrived in Ancona and I was told to go and collect any medical equipment on board which would prove of use in the camp. So off I set and the first treasure to come to light was a large container of the coal tar ointment the German doctors were hankering after. Then in addition to other medicaments there was a fine array of beautiful surgical instruments in fine cases, a joy to look at and handle but of no use to me. So reluctantly I let these go. Then I was told that there was a case of bottles of unknown content standing by. I opened this up and my eyes fell on the label "Slivovitz" whereupon these valuable medicines were immediately and safely placed into my truck, to be later highly appreciated by a few connoisseurs in the mess.

In the intervals I continued, whenever possible, to visit friends in Ancona and Chiaravalle, attending the occasional party. But things were not as in the past and I wrote home: "I sadly miss the old life in Chiaravalle, during which I was able to go to parties almost every night, while here I am out of training, with only the slightest of hopes of a return to the good old ways. I have become so fond of Italian women of all ages and of all types, and it will be hard getting back to English attitudes. How I love this country, and every evening I sit outside my tent, watching the sunset and feeling how lucky I am to be here.... a perfect part of the world and even the counterpart of Turkey."

Nevertheless life began to get a bit boring with no real incentive and things were not helped by a constant stream of papers from Headquarters referring to demobilisation but offering no definite dates. Newspapers from England were also full of talk about the coming election and the introduction of the Welfare State and of the future Paradise, matters in which no one was in the least interested, what was wanted was a return home. But the "News of the World" was refreshing in that it was good to hear that people continued to be normal enough to commit murders and robberies.

Letters from home were also depressing with Barbara and the children continuing to be ill off and on. Barbara had been advised by her Doctors to apply for my early return home. At my end I had filled in all manner of papers to that effect, without any hope of anything resulting. So August set in with great heat and winds whose continual moaning did not add to the joy of nations. Work also was reduced to a couple of hours a day, the only highlights were a couple of invitations to the Sergeants' Mess, with the usual devastating after-effects. The morning after one of these I was summoned to condemn some stinking meat, including, to my anger, some lovely looking hams, the like of which I had not seen for years.

Then suddenly, out of the blue, I received orders to repair to Naples, from which after a couple of days I was able to write home: "I am leaving for England tomorrow and hope to see you in a fortnight." And so on board ship, the old *Georgic*, a former transatlantic liner, to land in Liverpool ten days later.

Home Again

So, after four years abroad, I returned to England, where, after two weeks' leave, my next move was to a small prisoner of war hospital in the Chilterns near Wendover. Here John joined me for a few days to be made much fuss of by the men, while I was taught the elements of carpentry by my batman and constructed some toys for the children's Christmas – a train for John, or was it Michael, a doll's cot for Maya and a third piece, the nature of which I have forgotten. From here, after two months, I was finally demobilised. I was one of the lucky ones for we slipped back into family life without the least difficulty. Even Michael, who had never set eyes on me, accepting me without demur.

What with this and the fact that we had all come through unscathed, I felt immensely grateful to God for that fact, and where better could I express my gratitude than in Church. So after a few days, I dropped in on our local church, and there met the clergyman, Michael Ridley. I had an encouraging talk with him which led to the development of a great respect and friendship for him and Betty his wife. So back to normal life, with the children attending Sunday school and I, on my free Sundays, taking Barbara to her Church.

Men and women seek impact with their God in different ways, and in this story, I have tried to relate mine.

CHAPTER VII

Military Service – Reflections

My first year in the army was spent in England during the course of which I was able to see the family at regular intervals. I was then drafted to North Africa, an event which left me with conflicting emotions. On the one hand, regret at leaving the family coupled with anxiety over Barbara being left on her own to cope under wartime conditions, while on the other there was excitement over the prospect of seeing new lands and meeting with new experiences and possibly adventures. How lucky it was that, at that point of time, I did not know that four years were to elapse before I would see my family again.

The War introduced me to hitherto inexperienced situations; fear, boredom, idleness and frustration, but also others such as close contacts with nature and human beings. Nature offered me a new open air activity in generally beautiful countryside with possibilities for long walks, centered in one season on a search for wild flowers which led to temporary complete forgetfulness of War and all other anxieties.

At the same time, wherever I might happen to be, my command of languages allowed me to come into close contact with the local population, mostly simple town and country folk, with whom it was a delight to escape from military matters and talk about cows and pigs and crops and children and domestic affairs in general. I met a variety of people for in North Africa, apart from the French and Arabs, I came across Italians, Maltese, Armenians, Turks, Russians and even some Anglo-Dutch relations of mine.

My medicine brought me into touch with the local population but everywhere I never hesitated to talk to anyone I met. In this way, both in North Africa and also later in Italy, I met a variety of men and women from the lowest to the highest ranks, making many friends and enjoying fun and laughter even though conditions of life were deplorable in so many cases. I can honestly say that I was welcomed in all quarters with kindliness and this factor coupled with the way people stood up to their difficulties and troubles with only rarely a complaint, helped to strengthen my feelings of liking and respect for the majority of human beings. I will restrict myself to a few incidents.

In North Africa, I was touched on return to my tent, to find a small parcel of eggs, surreptitiously left by some grateful and impoverished Arab patient. The French in general looked down on the Arabs, but I made a number of friends – with some of whom sadly, there was no language in common, only a bond of sympathy. The contrasts in life were also startling. I was asked to visit a dying old man, in his hut to find him lying on the ground as a cloud of flies rose from his exposed face and hands. Conditions in the hut were indescribable, even I was glad to see that he had not long to live. In contrast, when I had tea with my relations in Tunis, I was ushered into the garden – white table cloth, porcelain cups, and silver teapot – no change from former days. Enough to make one think and especially so after receiving kindness from "a pack of ignorant Moslems".

In Italy, standards of life were higher and here I moved with the highest and the lowest, but principally with the latter. I talked to all and sundry everywhere to be welcomed and received with kindness. This enabled me to keep my outlook in balance and to dispel the horrors of war. I have always enjoyed the company of men and women of all classes, and Italy and the War offered me the opportunity to indulge in my pastime – for here again, there was lovely countryside – beautiful flowers and delightful people.

On one occasion, we were told to requisition a house and I, as the only Italian speaker in the unit, was deputed to tell a man that his house was to be requisitioned and that he and his family would have to move out. He became angrier and angrier over the matter, I followed suit and told him where he got off in no polite terms and we parted in no friendly fashion, leaving me wondering whether I might get a knife in my back. But far from it, I met the good man in the street a couple of days later and he greeted me like a long-lost brother. "Ah, Signor Capitano, what a pleasure it has been to meet an Englishman who speaks our language so well, and who likes and understands us Italians. Will you come and have supper with us?" Naturally I accepted, to find the family well installed in a large barn. We ate outdoors, under some trees, and had a most cheerful and enjoyable meal. I had taken with me a parcel of sweets and chocolates for the children and it was a great pleasure to see their looks of happiness at the sight of something so rare. To complete my enjoyment, although I was called "Signor Dottore", the old Mother refrained from discussing the state of her liver with me. The past was forgotten, relations were of the friendliest and I enjoyed myself enormously.

Later, in Assisi, in the course of a search for wine, I met the Head of the Black Market, a thorough rogue in every sense of the word, but he proved good company and with my natural liking for cheerful rogues, we got on well and he invited me to a family meal. Here, to my astonishment, he appeared in a totally different guise as devoted husband and father – Judge not.

My last story is of a different nature. I dropped in on what was a very poor farm and in the course of talking, saw a small girl, scantily dressed in little better than rags and with bare feet, playing with her doll, a stick round which some rags had been tied. The sight of her as she unconsciously tended to her toy transfixed me in a welter of emotions – and how glad I was that I had a packet of sweets in my pocket.

CHAPTER VIII

Warfare

The four years I spent in North Africa and Italy gave me an opportunity to observe the effects of war on human beings and the environment.

The area in which fighting mostly took place in North Africa was only sparsely inhabited so physical damage was not great. At the same time, in so far as I could see, there was no lack of food, the main deficiencies being in the line of clothing, manufactured goods and tea, the Arabs' favourite drink. I saw no sign of suffering except in the case of eight largish groups who, in fear of bombing, had left their village homes to take shelter in some caves. There were some sad stories of course, a French farmer had had his farm destroyed in the First World War and had moved to Tunisia in search of future safety, only for his son to see it all once again destroyed. It was on this farm that I witnessed the sad sight of a field of ripe corn on fire.

In Italy conditions were somewhat different. I mixed with the civilian population wherever I happened to be and so heard complaints, which in the food line were in respect of periodic shortages, especially of pasta. It is true that most of my time was spent in country districts, in which, as in Britain, things were easier than in towns, but by and large, I heard few complaints and in fact the most appreciated contributions to domestic economy that I made were of salt to farmers to help preserve their pig meat, pepper and reels of English cotton, the local variety being too fragile.

Conditions in towns like Naples and Menina were very different with clear cut hunger and distress. In Naples I saw men, women and children scouring piles of discarded tins for any scraps of food left behind. The town was also in a state of moral degradation, though I had no personal experience of this, and of course the Mafia and the Black Market flourished allowing some to live in luxury while others starved. It was pitiful to see gaunt and haggard men, women and children begging for food, especially so with the knowledge that round the corner there was a solid meal waiting for me. Here I saw more evidence of physical destruction, especially so in Naples and Cassino and in a number of villages. However, it was sad to see Horace's Mount Soracte filled with gun emplacements.

In North Africa, I only met with results of actual warfare on two occasions. The first, when as we moved forward, I came across the grave of a man with whom I had been drinking a short time ago. On the other occasion, an Arab was brought to me whose leg had been shattered by a landmine. There was little I could do, save relieve some of his pain and send him on, on horseback, on the five mile road to hospital, his uncomplaining attitude making me feel for him all the more.

We arrived at the Anzio beachhead within a day or two of the original landing. Here life took on a different aspect. Our camp site lay along some woods, bordering on one of the main roads to the front and situated some three miles in its rear. Its disadvantages were rapidly exposed, for that night enemy planes flew over and henceforward we were subjected to shelling and bombing at odd intervals, forcing us to sleep as much as possible below ground level – cowering in a slit trench with shells falling about. The place was no pleasure, and I never quite conquered fear on such occasions. After a time I got used to the state of affairs which eased matters to some extent, though I never quite disposed of feelings of anxiety.

Having offered my services to the adjoining CCS (Casualty Clearing Station), I approached this work with misgivings initially as never in my life had I been in contact with active war and wounds of such possible severity. I need not have worried for, on my first night I was kept so busy that I had no time to think.

The general atmosphere was one under which everyone worked wholeheartedly, uncomplainingly and always in good spirits, however exhausted they might feel. I enjoyed working under these conditions and with matters helped by the attitude of all those of the wounded who were capable of showing any feelings. Sadly there were those who were too shocked to show any sign of consciousness, while most tragic were those for whom I felt there was little or no hope of survival.

Fortunately I was able to find relief from this restrictive life mainly in the lovely countryside. My walks covered a large area of the bridgehead and I was able to watch and study the arrival of flowers as winter months passed into spring. The flowers were glorious, with many in view and hitherto unknown varieties appearing in conjunction with old friends. The nightingales were also a source of joy and never have I heard such numbers in song. This would immediately stop at the onset of any noise from bombing or shelling only to resume as soon as peace was restored.

With the fall of Rome, my experience of actual warfare ceased, and from now on life resumed its former peace and quiet.

CHAPTER IX

Germans

Despite past associations I entered the war with feelings of intense dislike and distrust of the Germans believing the worst of them. Then in Algeria for some totally unfathomable reason a young German prisoner arrived in our camp, nobody knowing why or how. I had a chat with him to find a perfectly normal and pleasant youth utterly confused by the turn of events. I did my best to reassure him but next day he left us. After this I saw no more of Germans until the end of the campaign in Africa, when I happened to see a long line of dejected and ill arrayed prisoners marching on their way to detention. On the one hand this was a happy occasion, but on the other it was tragic to see the remnants of what had been a fine fighting force reduced to the status of sheep being herded into their pens by dogs.

Then no more until some months later in Italy, I picked up an unposted letter written by a German soldier to his wife. This thoroughly upset me for it exactly followed the sense and words of my letters home to Barbara and led me to wonder whether the poor wretch ever got home alive.

A couple of months later, I was in hospital with a fractured foot, sharing a small room with a young German officer, a delightful, well educated man and a fervent Christian, of a sect which had fallen into disfavour with the Nazis. He and I held long discussions and talks in the course of which he mentioned his experiences on the Eastern Front. Here the military and the native Russians got on very well, but all changed when civilian administration took over, successfully, converting potential friendships into pure hostility. He deplored the conditions of life of the Russian, but had the greatest admiration of their spirituality and attitude to life.

After this, no more Germans until I was appointed to a Prisoner-of-War camp, a small one of a transit nature. Here my working life was spent entirely among Germans, but of these the only fixture was my orderly who boasted of the name of Siegfried. Young, handsome and speaking some English he had the run of the camp being utterly reliable. He was anxious to clothe himself as an English Tommy, and soon had somehow scrounged a battle dress. His next ambition was to collect "flashes" but was never, to his disappointment, able to acquire one of the Desert Rats.

By this stage, all feelings of hostility towards Germans had vanished and I began to enjoy and be interested in their company, and this was as well as I was then placed in medical charge of a unit housing 10,000 prisoners. Here all my energies were devoted to the welfare and well being of so called enemies. The medical unit was made up of a medical colleague, three German doctors and some twenty other ranks, with a 60-bed "hospital" at our disposal.

From now on I spoke German and mixed with Germans for most of my working days enjoying the work and the company except on those rare occasions on which I had to cope with an ardent Nazi, all others being ordinary human beings anxious to get back to their wives and families or else to their girlfriends and to normal civilian life. At the same time it was interesting to have three fellow doctors with whom to enter into discussion. Perhaps my happiest moment came when on Christmas morning, I found on my table a note from some of my patients in one "hospital". "Five unhappy German prisoners of war would like to thank their doctor for his care and his treatment, as also to wish him a happy Christmas and a speedy return."

Part X

BARBARA (Vava) WHITTALL Née POUSCHINE

CHAPTER I

Alexandra Pouschine 1890-1982

After our formal engagement I started to call my Mother-in-Law "Mum" instead of the formal Mrs. Pouschine so as to avoid any confusion between her and 'Mother' in Turkey. The children always knew her as Bunny, which presumably arose from putting together the Russian Babushka and the English Granny.

With work and getting myself adapted to married life I did not get to know Mum well in the early days of our marriage, also our house was too small to allow her to stay with us. But once we had moved to No. 1 Finchley Way I got to know her better.

She never talked much of her married life and all that I know about it was picked up from odd scraps of conversation and from her memoirs. On the surface it would appear that she and Lawrence made an oddly assorted couple, she being very young and innocent, coming from a puritanical and intellectual background, while he was much older and very much a man of the world, enjoying a gay and social life and anxious to present his lovely wife at Court. She had other feelings on this point and was saved from this experience through having a steady sequence of children. Then the War came and with it separation, as Lawrence was put in charge of a hospital train, leaving her behind to look after a hospital set up in the family house in Orel.

Prior to this Lawrence had made one attempt to introduce her to a gay life by taking her to a sort of night club. This ended in disaster as she was so upset at the sight of the gypsy girls and the thought of the sort of life they led, that she burst into tears and had to be taken home.

Then followed the Revolution and the family's emigration to England. To begin with all went well but with the passage of time, hopes of a return to Russia fading and family resources starting to fade away, Lawrence set out for the States to make his fortune, leaving Mum to cope with the five children.

In Russia she had never had anything to do with money and in fact had never even handled it. Now she was faced with the problem of caring for the family on small and dwindling resources, at the same time having to learn English as she only spoke Russian, French and German. The future looked decidedly bleak, especially as at that time there was no form of Social Security. But an old friend, the Russian Consul, stepped in and offered her a job in his office. Here she taught herself shorthand and typing in all of her languages. So, thanks to this experience, once the Consulate had closed, she was able to get a job in the City as a foreign correspondent at a modest salary. Then two Anglican convents each offered to take in two girls from the poorest of the Russian émigré families and Mum's daughters were chosen unhesitatingly.

All was now well in term time with the girls at school and Ivan at Sherborne School. Lawrence, while he still had money, had paid for his full education there. Provision had to be made for the holidays and to ensure this Mum had to scrape and think of every penny, taking on extra jobs wherever she could. From time to time she was invited to stay in houses to give full-time Russian lessons in her spare time, but essentially, although still young, attractive and intelligent she had to give up all social pleasures in order to be able to manage. All this she did without regard for herself.

At one point she experienced a breakdown and had to enter a sanatorium in Baden-Baden for a year or so. Here she was joined by Catherine and Masha, while Natasha and Barbara were left behind in England, to spend holidays in the school and only to see their mother during the summer. How all this was paid for I do not know, presumably Lawrence had a part in this.

All this took place before I got to know her, by which time she was in better health, although the occasional headache of a migrainous nature kept her in bed over the weekend, which in those days started at midday on Saturdays. At this time the three eldest, Ivan, Catherine and Natasha were all in the United States and with Masha at Oxford, only Barbara was at home.

Once settled in Finchley Way I saw much more of Mum and with John's arrival she joined us to help Barbara. Then Masha left Oxford and took up a teaching job at Northwich in Cheshire, where Mum joined her. With the advent of war both returned to London, Mum joined the American Red Cross to appear very smart in a new green uniform and Masha worked at Reuters monitoring Russian broadcasts, later to join the Army as a Russian interpreter. She was sent to Vienna where she met her future husband Alan Williams. By this time I was in the army.

The war being over and the American forces returning home, Mum was put in charge of the department looking after the interests of the illegitimate children they left behind. She continued this until retiring on pension, when, with Masha away married, she came to live with us. When Masha and Alan were in England, either en poste or on holiday, she stayed with them and also made annual trips to America to see the family there. After a number of such trips she got so well known to the air crews that each time on taking flight a hostess would bring her a glass of port, her favourite tipple, 'With the compliments of the Captain'. So as time went on I got to know her better and better and at the same time became more and more fond of her.

She was a most interesting person to talk to and we had many long discussions, during which she often told me that she felt much happier in England than in Russia. The only explanation of this that came to mind was that in this country she had found a concrete objective in life, as opposed to her previous aimless existence. Totally inexperienced when married, she was taken to live in a large house with elderly in-laws, in which there was nothing at all for her to do except have babies, which on arrival were immediately taken out of her hands and placed in those of competent nurses. Her only duty in fact was to play the piano to her father-in-law every afternoon, but when on one afternoon she omitted to do so and went for a walk with her husband, the old man was so upset that he packed up and moved to another house on the estate.

Life in England was quite different for her, inexperienced as she was; she had to cope with a job, to earn money and to take care of five children on altogether very slender resources. Hard as this was, in comparison to her previous life, there now was a real purpose in life and how successful she was in this is borne out by Barbara who told me that the family home life was so happy that she never experienced any sense of deprivation, not even in relation to her far better off English friends. In fact, so happy was she in her home life, that there were times in which she felt she was luckier than some of them. Even with their poor conditions of life and their very simple diet in which herrings and macaroni played a major role, she never felt she had missed out on anything except perhaps in the matter of clothes for it was only on rare occasions that it was possible to buy new ones and reliance had rather to be made on other people's cast-offs. What did help them out came from the marriage of an uncle of friends of theirs, the Zvegintzovs, to Alice Astor in America, who periodically sent them bundles of clothes for which she had no further use. When such clothes arrived, the Zvegintzovs made their choice and then summoned the Pouschines to make their. In this way it became possible for one of them to appear at a dance wearing a dress made by a world-famous couturier.

Mum's influence on her children was profound, especially so in her attitude to life and the way she took it without any trace of envy or complaint. I never once heard her grumble over the way life had treated her, least of all over the loss of status and possessions she had enjoyed in Russia (in all fairness the same applies to almost all members of the émigré community whom I met). In the same way the question of money was never raised in the family. In consequence the children were brought up in a placid atmosphere of normality, to feel that the life they led was quite a normal one and they accepted and enjoyed what came their way as fun.

She was also very religious and the children were brought up to attend Church regularly. She herself at one time sat on the Church Council at which she occasionally caused trouble by, in her innocence and practical good sense, coming out with some remark which exploded idealistic plans and speculations propounded by others. In this way bringing matters down to earth and restricting discussion, which did not meet with everyone's satisfaction.

The Church was one of the last connecting links with Russia and so meant a lot to people outside its spiritual significance. But, whereas this had followed her into exile, the countryside was lost for ever. She loved talking about this, to wax lyrical over the coming of spring when in the spring sunshine the snow began to melt and bushes and trees to burst into bud. This was the aspect of Russia which she most missed.

Mum, of course, had received a first class education and was always a most interesting person to talk to and we had lots of discussions. These revealed one aspect of her character, namely the clear and abrupt division between her attitudes to those persons she liked and those she did not. This came to light when we were discussing Charles Dickens and she was extolling his high moral character; at which I made mention of the fact that in his old age he had a girl friend. At this she exploded and I was accused of wicked and slanderous gossip, for how could a man who wrote such wonderful books descend to such depths etc. etc.? True as it was she could never believe it.

This attitude came into real life also, when at one time, one Ivan, a very worthy young man of decent family and with a good job, was in love with Masha. Mum, on meeting him, had taken an instant dislike to him and nothing he could do or say was right. Whether this attitude was due to Mum having grander ideas about the man Masha should marry, or whether she was alarmed at the idea of losing Masha, remains unknown. Maybe also this harsh black and white attitude may have stemmed from her Puritan up-bringing. But strangely enough, when Felix Yusupoff, of whom normally Mum had not a good word to say on account of his reputation and connection with Rasputin, came to the house, Mum fell to his charms.

She also caused Barbara endless annoyance through taking a dislike to our marvellous Nanny who looked after the children beautifully. She was always accused of not feeding her charges properly, mishandling and generally neglecting them. In fact in Mum's eyes she could do no right. In reality she spoilt the children as the following story shows. One day Barbara, on entering the nursery, found Maya lying flat on her back on the bed, with one leg raised vertically into the air. Asked what on earth she was up to, she said that she was waiting for Nanny to put on her socks. Nanny came in at that moment and Barbara told her that Maya was quite old enough to put on her own stockings, to which Nanny replied: "I know that, but I enjoy putting her socks on for her."

Another habit Mum had was to pick up 'Waifs and Strays' and to bring them home for Christmas lunch. On one occasion two girls and a boy appeared, these being of Irish-Finnish parents. All went well until the boy said he intended joining the British army. At this one sister flew into a rage and accused him of being a traitor to his Irish Motherland. This started a loud argument, with her being all Irish and he protesting that he considered himself to be English, the other sister who considered herself to be Finnish not entering into the dispute. Peace was eventually restored but our Christmas lunch had been greatly disturbed.

On another occasion Mum, in a tube station, saw a foreign looking girl quietly weeping in a corner. She went to offer her help and was replied to in Russian, whereupon the girl, on finding she was talking to a fellow Russian fell into her arms with redoubled sobs, this time of relief. Eventually she quietened down and it turned out that she was one of the first Soviet brides and came out with a long story of her misery at being deposited in this country. Mum brought her to our house and then in rather typical fashion, left her on our hands to find that she, her husband and three small children were in a rather bad way. So we felt we had to help them and this we had to do throughout a whole series of ups and downs until the boys were old enough to be let loose on their own. There came times when I felt anything but grateful to Mum, but in the end all turned out well, and with the boys now getting on satisfactorily and the father retired, we have remained good friends.

Mum was always worried about the possibility of a revolution in this country. While living with Barbara, while I was away, she started to hoard away a stockpile of food to act as a reserve in case the revolution should happen and she said nothing about this to anyone. One day when I was back home again and Mum was away with Masha, I was routing about in the cellar and found her store, hidden away in a corner and evidently forgotten. Barbara was delighted, especially as with rationing still in force any extra supplies were more than welcome.

When we moved to St. John's Wood we wondered how Mum would amuse herself. Once settled in, every morning she went out on a couple of walks, with frequently another after tea and all seemed well. It suddenly transpired that she had taken to betting on horses and that these walks were to and from the book-maker... in the morning to lay her bets and in the evening to collect any winnings. Mum was very upset when we got to know about this and implored us not to tell the grandchildren, though they, in the way of children, soon had their eyes opened to their Grandmother's carryings-on. The astonishing thing is that she was very successful at the game and as she gave Barbara half of her winnings she, also, was pleased. Once this became known, at Ascot time all Barbara's friends asked for Mum's tips. She became a great favourite with the book-maker and if ever Barbara or I went to collect any winnings there were always anxious enquiries as to the 'old lady's' health. How and why this puritanically brought up elderly lady took to this pursuit I cannot say, but her home town of Orel having been a centre for breeding horses, it is possible that the air infected her.

Another pleasure of hers lay in bridge which she played very badly. But she had her moments of triumph, as, when staying with her son in Miami, she once called and made a Grand Slam. Immediately her son, a very good player and a stickler for formality, turned on her angrily and told her that she had both called and played the hand badly and that she should never have made it. Poor Mum had done something hitherto inconceivable in her experience and all she got was blame for having done so.

Like most Russian ladies I met, Mum was very well educated. At the same time she was amazingly innocent and in many ways not conversant with everyday life. This led to some concern when I brought my cousin Winnie to the house, to convalesce after a serious illness. Now Winnie was a person of supreme excellence, but at times her conversation could become very racy and her stories not exactly drawing room so we tried not to leave the two alone. But one day this was inevitable and as we returned home we were rather worried, but as it turned out needlessly. For on our return we were met by an enthusiastic Mum (Winnie had gone to bed) who related how well the two had got on and what a wonderful girl Winnie was and so on and so on. We breathed sighs of relief, knowing that once Winnie had passed the test no fault would ever be found with her.

It took Mum some time to decide on taking on British nationality and when applying for this she had to provide a list of all the addresses at which she had lived and these had been so many that such a list was beyond her capability. Fortunately however, as an alien she had had to register each move at the Police, who on hearing of her difficulty, compiled a list for her which helped her to get the desired papers.

Mum and I always got on very well, in part no doubt because she always favoured men as against women and to the end I remained extremely fond of her and also a great admirer. In all the many years together we only had one tiff and that was on the occasion of Alan's death, when Masha rang me up to tell me of what had happened and asked me to go round and help her over the formalities. I asked whether she would like me to bring Mum, but this she did not want as yet. But as I was ready to go, I found Mum, dressed in her outdoor clothes ready to accompany me and I had to tell her that I was not going to take her with me as Masha did not want her at that moment. As I did so, Mum got more and more upset and angry, insisting on accompanying me with me as strongly insisting that I was not going to take her. I had never seen her angry before and to see her in this state, in a way behaving more like a small child rather than an adult, was pathetic and upset me too. But eventually I got away without her and on my return she had calmed down and I later took her to see Masha.

As time went on Mum became more and more infirm and in our flat with steps leading down to the washing arrangements Barbara and I got more and more worried. Later the Health Visitor told us that the flat was now quite unsuitable for an invalid of that nature and advised putting Mum into a home. So we had a family conference, at which Masha decided to take Mum into her large house and here she received every care until she died. In the later stages she knew no-one, but she died peacefully under marvellous circumstances while listening to a broadcast by the BBC of the Russian Easter Service to Russia.

CHAPTER II

England

Once it had been decided to send Barbara and Natasha to St Hilda's Anglican Convent in Whitby, the first question that arose was how best to cope with their religious observances. Mum consulted the Russian Orthodox Bishop in London and he had no hesitation in saying that they must attend Services and instruction and take Communion with the other girls. Simultaneously the school consulted higher Anglican Church authorities, including the Archbishop of York, who were of the same opinion. In consequence the girls underwent exactly the same religious teaching as the other girls, to acquire a detailed knowledge of the Anglican Church. But, so as not to cut them off entirely from their Church, Mother Margaret, the Head of the Order where Barbara and Natasha were at school, took every opportunity of talking about the Orthodox Church and of explaining such differences as exist between the two religions.

Barbara was happy at school, that is in so far as any child is happy away from home, and got on well with the other girls to make many friends. Her only real difficulty arose from the attitude of one of the nuns who disliked all foreigners and resented the presence of the two Russians in the school. She was furious when Barbara won the prize for the best essay and did her best to prevent her being appointed Head of Games. Barbara had the greatest respect and admiration for Mother Margaret, a truly outstanding woman. She had started life as an actress, but, later, getting the call, founded the Order. Brilliantly intelligent and a superb teacher, she had that rare capacity of being able to lecture on a very wide range of subjects, from Greek civilisation onwards, while at the same time totally holding the attention of her audience. And, of course, in view of her past, she was a great proponent of acting in the School.

Whitby offered great advantages as a site for a school and especially for one run on religious principles with its links with St. Cuthbert and St. Hilda and as the site of the great Synod which linked the English Church to Rome. The town itself was also of great interest with its ruined Abbey, extraordinary Parish Church and its old fishing harbour and fishermen's cottages. In addition the surrounding country was of great beauty with the moors stretching close by, interrupted by streams and rivers running through green valleys. And of course there was always the cold North Sea, with sandy beaches running below earthen cliffs in which fossil ammonites and jet were to be found. Early experience of bathing in these chilly waters had left Barbara with a permanent preference for them over the warmer waters of the Mediterranean. The climate was generally cold and there were frequent sea fogs, which led one new girl, unused to the sound of foghorns, to complain that she had been kept awake all night by cows mooing outside her bedroom.

All in all the nuns were very good to the girls, finding clothes for them from those discarded by other (growing) girls and boarding them when their mother could not have them during the holidays. On such occasions they lodged in the school, except in summer when most of the nuns were away, when they were found rooms locally, usually in a cottage. During the summer term, in lieu of games, the girls were often set to help local farmers over hay-making and on one occasion Barbara and two other girls were placed as residents on a farm, where they were expected to help out between lessons.

Natasha's career at Whitby was unusual. The nuns adored her, but she was constitutionally incapable of obeying rules, and at last, in despair, Mother Margaret had to ask for her to be removed as she was demoralising the whole school. After a time she was invited back to train as a matron, but again she came to grief after being caught exchanging dresses with one of the novices. But she was not forgotten and on an occasion when Barbara and I were visiting the school I was warned that the first question to be asked by all the nuns would be "How is Natasha" and so it turned out.

Barbara eventually left school to return to London, having made a large number of friends, most of whom have stood by her for life. Here she proposed studying medicine, and, having won a scholarship, entered the Chelsea Polytechnic where she came into contact with Miss Kempson (the Aunt of the actress Rachel). She was Head of the Women's section and in her found another good friend and one for whom she had the greatest respect. (Many years later we visited her when in a home in Worcestershire). The first year went well but as time went on greater and greater demands were made on her by her mother and family and her courses were so interrupted that she had to give up all idea of higher education.

While still at school a young Russo-American engineer, Ross Nebolsine, (more generally known as Kapa for some obscure reason) had appeared on the scene and was courting Catherine. To enable him to propose marriage under suitable conditions, he asked Mum whether she would allow Catherine to accompany him and his Mother and sister on a trip to the Loire Valley. Catherine, suspecting what this was all about, refused to go and so Mum, in her innocence, told Kapa that Catherine could not go, but that Barbara would love to replace her. Kapa, valiantly concealing his disappointment, agreed to the change of plan and behaved so kindly to Barbara and treated her so thoughtfully, that she became a life-long admirer of him.

They eventually married, children were born and whenever in England Barbara had the task of looking after the youngsters, one of the many reasons which made her give up the Poly. At one stage Catherine had rented a house at St. Germain en Laye, outside Paris, where Barbara joined her. This was in winter and despite the heating being full on the house was always cold and nobody could make out why, until, one day, Barbara went into the attached Conservatory to find it beautifully warm. Further investigation showed that the heating was switched off in the house and was only serving the conservatory.

Barbara grew up with the Russian colony in London and got to know the majority of its members. She also enjoyed the added advantage of spending several summer holidays at the seaside in Normandy with youngsters from the Russian colony in Paris. Her mother used to visit the Grand Duchess Xenia, sister to the late Tsar, periodically and in her house Barbara met Betty Frederici, whose widowed mother had married Prince Andrew, a son of the Grand Duchess. They became great friends and following this Barbara regularly spent week-ends at Frogmore Cottage, the Grace and Favour House in the grounds of Windsor Castle in which the Grand Duchess lived.

Here she got to know all the family, young and old, making further friends connected with the family such as Marie-Madeleine Madvidoff and Irina Youssupoff (Baby), daughter of the man who had killed Rasputin and had married the daughter of the Grand Duchess. Here a simple family life was led with baccarat played for matchsticks as one of the amusements. They had free use of the grounds but care had to be taken to keep out of sight of any members of the British Royal Family who might be taking the air.

Alternately she spent weekends with the Galitzines, who were living in

Chessington Hall, a house rented from my Barker relatives. Here she mixed with the three sons of the house and their cousin Natasha (now Heseltine), all of approximately the same age. The only snag arose as the Prince was customarily known as Vava, as also was Barbara, so that when anyone called for the one the other might turn up. Life here was much more free and easy than at Windsor and more cheerful, despite the fact that the Princess was also of Royal Blood. The boys had a tutor, blessed with a wooden leg and the story runs that when necessary he used to take it off to beat them with.

At the time I got to know the family they were distributed as follows. Mum and Barbara were in London. Catherine and Kapa spent some time in Greece and subsequently in Portugal. Natasha had set off for America, while Masha, having developed tubercular glands in the neck while still at school at Wantage, after an operation was sent to stay with her Aunt Mima Cantacuzene at Glion, where she finished her education at Montreux College. On her return to England she attended Oxford on a scholarship and in consequence of all this she never grew up in the Russian colony.

Barbara was therefore at home, mostly alone with her mother, who, when living in Hampstead, took in paying guests. On one occasion there was a contretemps, when Mum rushed up from the kitchen to tell Barbara that one of the male guests was parading about in the nude and sent her down to cope with the situation. Surely enough, the young man was in the nude and he explained that he had worked things out and had come to the conclusion that a state of nudity was not only more natural but also more healthy. Barbara agreed that this might be so, but that her house was not a proper place to put such ideas into practice and requested him to go and put on some clothes, which he did. I met him in later years, a very pleasant man, now married to a charming Australian pianist.

Barbara in the meantime had to earn some pocket money and fortunately got an introduction to the Housekeeper at Claridge's Hotel who then engaged her whenever any of the very wealthy American guests required help in the way of looking after small children or an elderly lady. She also had to help her mother in talking Russian to their paying guests, most of whom were there to perfect their conversation.

I settled down into General Practice in 1934, and soon after doing so met Barbara through a cousin of mine. We found a common interest in the ballet and off we went once a week, and, in return, she took me behind the scenes.

Things were running smoothly, and we seemed to be getting on fine, as I thought, when Barbara accepted a job to look after and teach English to a French boy in Paris and off she went. Altogether she spent a year in Paris getting on particularly well with Madame Lemerle who had always longed for a daughter and later asked Barbara to stay on as company after Francois, her charge, had returned to school. Barbara also had friends in the Russian colony, including Nicholas Ignatieff who was secretary at the Palais de Sports to which, in consequence, Barbara had free entry.

Although we had kept in touch, I had more or less given up hope of seeing Barbara again, when one day the phone rang and there she was to invite me to a party at her flat in Abbey Road. Here for the first time I met her mother, small and dark, with flashing eyes and the most wonderful of smiles, supervising all and everything, and making all feel at home. I talked little during the course of the evening, in part through shyness, but also because it was difficult to compete with Russian volubility.

After this I saw more and more of Barbara as I took to dropping in on the flat or taking her out on my free evenings, at this time she was working in a shop in the Burlington Arcade selling antique Chinese porcelain, until the day came when I asked her mother whether I could marry her and how happy I was when she raised no objection.

Mum proved the essence of tact and when Barbara and I were together would go out for a walk, with us accusing her on her return, of not having in effect gone for a walk, but over to the Ladies' Room in the pub across the road to have a glass of her beloved port. This was always good fun, but more importantly, the better I got to know her, the fonder of her I became and the more I admired her sterling qualities. In her I found a faithful ally for, in her eyes, in my relationship to Barbara I, as a man, was always in the right, while she as a woman always in the wrong. She always made me thoroughly welcome, and I am happy to say that this close relationship lasted until her death.

As time went on I mixed more and more in the Russian colony and the greater grew my liking and admiration for them. Despite having lost all their worldly goods, they all made the best of their present status in life. I cannot remember ever hearing any complaints over the way life had treated them and the only regrets I heard arose from their separation from the Russian countryside. All retained a capacity to make the best of things, the most of life and were always ready for fun and laughter although, no doubt, in their private moments all were at times subject to fits of depression, in fact it would be hard to think of this not being so, but in company this was never evident.

This attitude struck me forcibly for in my work I was continually forced to listen to the most trivial of complaints and from time to time also indulged in such myself as one does. In particular I admired the women, who, one and all, were magnificent and provided the stability round which family life evolved. I particularly felt this when visiting the Galitzines in their antique shop off Berkeley Square, there to be served tea in cracked cups, in their dingy, small back room, the Princess taking it all quite naturally but at the same time never losing the dignity of her Royal forebears. The same could be said of one and all, to impress me more and more with the value of a background of good breeding. This put me on my mettle – if they could stand up to such vicissitudes in life without complaint, I, who was infinitely better off than many of them could do the same.

Prior to our marriage, Mum, a great believer in the health-giving properties of North Sea air, had rented a cottage in Birchington, on the Kent coast for a fortnight and here I was invited to join her, Barbara and Masha. This stay enabled me to become more closely involved in their family life. In one way Mum was incorrigible, however bleak or wet the day she would cheerfully come out with a 'What a lovely day for a walk' and off we all had to go. Otherwise there was bathing and visitors came down from town for the day and what with all this and the close company with Barbara, whom I now called Vava, life was perfect in so far as I was concerned.

We decided to get married in early October 1936 and so preparations got going with all in the Colony putting in a helpful hand, for Mum had nothing and so today Barbara says that her marriage was arranged by the Russian Colony. For example Mr Sabline offered his house for the Reception, Galia Ampenoff, now Mother Elizabeth, designed and sewed her wedding dress, Prince Galitzine gave her away and the Princess and the Madame Wolkoff prepared the food, with someone donating the wine and all this left Mum with nothing to do.

We were married on October the 5th in the now demolished Russian Church near Victoria Station and we spent our honeymoon in Baden-Baden. And so back to England and a new life.

CHAPTER III

Letters to America (Written to Barbara's Mother and family)

21.11.51. Vava was admitted to a three-bedded ward in Granard House, the private wing of the Cancer Hospital, on Saturday, for the operation on Monday and she was operated on at the appointed time. I visited her that night to find her well but dopy. Vava has never been really fit since I returned from the army, and I hope that this will prove the turning point.

The house is miserable without her, but it has been terribly good of Mercy (my sister-in-law) with Elizabeth her daughter to move in and look after things together with Solveig (our German girl). She will be able to stay until December the 4th. Maya was concerned over the name of the Hospital, but I was able to reassure her. All is well with the children. Maya loves her boarding school and John is well and has got into the XV. I think he is getting reconciled to Eagle House. The family wants the usual Christmas party, and this Winnie has undertaken to organise.

23.11.51. Vava was much better yesterday but complaining of various ailments. Please tell Masha that Vava is almost making as much fuss as she does when ill. I told this to Vava and she replied that it was so lovely to be in a position to make a fuss.

23. 12. 51. Vava still suffering from several complaints, none important, but enough to keep her in bed and make her feel rotten. At this moment she has also taken to vomiting in the morning and everyone is wondering where the baby is hidden. Appetite poor, but she drinks red wine in abundance and keeps bright and cheerful. I was told all this was due to poor health following on the War. She has plenty of visitors and these have included the Bishop and Rev. Mother from Whitby. Daily visitors are Tamara Rodzianko and Natalia Heseltine, (nee Galitzine), both of whom thoroughly enjoy the wine and are cheerful as a result.

Mercy leaves tomorrow and we will have to manage as best we can. I will be engaging two women to come in and relieve Solveig. She is a grand girl and. has turned out trumps.

8.12.51. Vava is better and Mr. McCleod thinks she will be back home in a couple of weeks. By this time she will have been six weeks in hospital. She is not eating or sleeping very well, but is drinking lots of wine to cheer her up.

The day sister is an old friend of Edna Woodman's. One day she complained of feeling thoroughly depressed and Barbara advised her to go out and buy herself a new hat. Following this advice she returned a couple of hours later, full of cheer, having bought two hats. On the other hand the night sister was reputed to be somewhat of a martinet, until, finding that Barbara had a bottle of whisky, she took to visiting her every night for a tot which put relationships on a happy footing.

Matron arrived one day to find the ward full of visitors and decreed that in future two at a time was enough. So, when on future occasions there was a threat of a visitation, surplus visitors draped themselves round the other inmates of the ward to distract attention.

12.12.51. Vava is much better and able to go out and, all being well, she will be back home on Sunday. It is lovely to see her looking like her old self again, if not quite as fit as I would like to see her.

The children will be home on Tuesday and it will be grand seeing them again and having them all home for Christmas. This year Vava will have nothing to do and it should be a good party with Aunt Mercy, her son Charlton with Iris and son Peter and with them a friend from Rhodesia, Vernon, Terence and Asya and possibly Xana.

26.12.51. We had an excellent Christmas. The family all rallied round and Vava came down for lunch and then retired to bed. She had to return to hospital for further treatment of an infection. Scott came on Monday and said she ought to see Mr. McCleod again and he poor wretch was disturbed on Christmas Eve. She will be in for a week or so, although I anticipate two. Asya and Terence will be staying for the rest of the holiday, which will be an enormous help. Vava won't feel herself till the end of the month and by then will be fed up, what with feeling rotten and having nothing to do. Maya has proved an absolute brick and Solveig has also proved invaluable. The real trouble is that all this happened at the busiest time of my year. In the summer things would have been easier.

2.1.52. All is well and Vava is feeling better and may be home this weekend, to fly to Germany next week. It will be good to have her home again. It was an anxious time, although thankfully she is now better. If I can fix up the domestic situation she may stay longer in Germany.

7.1.52. Vava is now in Germany having been seen on Saturday and pronounced fit to fly. She will be staying with the Schlitters, who have given up their castle for use as a Children's Home and have moved into the farmhouse. It is anomalous that of all our numerous friends, they, in a defeated Germany, are the only ones to have a full staff. They live in a small village outside Munich.

20.1.52. The house is empty, John and Michael having gone off to school on Friday, the latter resplendent and terribly proud in his uniform. He made a wonderful picture. There appeared to be no regrets and he jumped into the train, hardly looking at us. Mrs. Wootton rang me up that night from Eagle House to say that he appeared well and happy.... a very kindly gesture. John had a good deal of shooting these holidays and last Sunday had a go at 50 geese, flying overhead, but out of range. To-day Maya went off and I am feeling miserable in consequence. She has been such a help and moral support that I do not know what I would have done without her. She did everything necessary on her own, without question or hesitation, buying Michael's clothes, marking them, seeing that John's were in order, packing the trunks and getting them off in good time. I would never have believed it possible that a girl of fourteen, who had never had to do anything for herself, could do so much and so quietly and efficiently. I feel terribly proud of her and grateful.

Vava appears to be getting on well and will be staying away for a month. I will be glad to have her home again and to throw some burdens onto her back. It has all been something of a nightmare, especially so as work has not been lacking.

During her absence I received regular letters from Barbara, all complaining of pain and of not feeling well, keeping me in a constant state of worry and anxiety. Eventually I consulted Scott, who offered to fly out to find out what was the matter. But before matters came to a head I received an ecstatic letter relating how Oscar having sold a pig, there was sufficient money to allow all of them to attend the Ball of the Bavarian Nobility in Munich, at which she had stayed dancing till the early hours of the morning, to return home feeling wonderfully fit and free from complaints. She returned home a few days later after a harrowing flight in makeshift planes in the middle of a snowstorm, in the course of which she polished off the bottle of German gin, (Steinhager) which she was bringing me as a present.

31.5.55. Vava and I are at the moment lying in bed at Nata's (Sowels), the sun is streaming in at the window, the birds are singing and we have won the election and with nothing to do all day life is perfect. Nata's Father-in-law has been staying here and done nothing but complain of poverty. So, on his return home he bought a new car and a horse and has built a stable for the latter.

Vernon is much better, thank heaven, and is talking of finding a job. Meanwhile I hope he is doing some work in the garden.

1.1.56. Maya looks very well in that black top you sent her, and she is delighted with it. She is still very displeased with the family and gives us all hell.

All the family is at home and very well. Vava is the better for her holiday and looking well. Yesterday I was very pleased for while I was cleaning the car an old lady started talking and asked how Vava was. After an answer she went on: "I must tell you Doctor, that I think your wife is wonderful and easily the most attractive woman in Finchley. When you lived in Nether Street I always used to look out for her, as one glimpse was enough to cheer me up for the whole day. Her expression and her charming manner and her whole attitude are quite exceptional. She and her sister are a constant pleasure to watch."

Christmas went off very well but we were a small party, only 18. Us, Christine and her boy-friend, Winnie and Aunty, the Schlitters and two friends, Mrs Malakoff and the Gagarin and Peter. It went off very well. Soup delicious, Turkey superb and large enough to allow us to pick at it for three days and Vava's usual Christmas pudding. We were all very happy and cheerful and after listening to the Queen we all went for a walk to return all ready for the Christmas tree which, this year, was far better than usual. It was a lovely day and all the more so as Daisy and Oscar looked so well, with Marion as lovely as ever.

On Tuesday we went to cocktails at the Schlitters with John and Maya. John was very talkative, so much so that Vava and I came to the conclusion that he is far less shy than Maya. I do not know what he talked about but his mouth never closed. We also dined with the Bryants, had drinks with Edna Woodman and spent New Year's Eve at the Schlitters and for this occasion we bought John a dinner jacket in which he looked very smart. Half way through the party some young friends turned up and took away the 'Young World' leaving the Old behind. We stayed on until 2 am. to find that neither of the children had returned. Maya had gone off to another party with Lois in Chiswick and only turned up after lunch.

18.6.58. All are well with Vava very worried as phone calls will now cost 2d for 3 minutes instead of 3d for an unlimited time. Michael is said to be taller than me and has just bought a bike. He is very pleased with it and spends his time cleaning and oiling it. It is at present kept in the dining room until I can work out some suitable accommodation.

John's tastes have turned to clothes and in his eyes the correct width of trouser legs and the correct curl of the brim of his hat are as important to him as the smallest details in the getup of a particularly vain woman. He now no longer walks, he glides with an elegant slouch and his hair is just the right length to carry distinction. His mind is now set on buying a small car. His one trouble is lack of work. He resents having little to do and cannot take a life of idleness. But in all armies it is the same for as Tolstoy said, the military career is the only one in which one is paid to do nothing.

3.6.72. Life has been very busy with an influx of invalid relations. My cousin Hazel arrived to have an operation which I had to arrange and she needed visiting. Now James, another cousin, has also arrived and I must see to him. There are also the regulars to see to and what with one thing and another I have been very busy.

Barbara and I have been sitting down to discuss our life and what a wonderful time we have had together and how lucky we have been and particularly in our children. We have had hard times of course, but these have not affected us in any way and we have enjoyed life to the full.

I never arrive at the cottage without feeling how happy Mother, in the next world, must feel that the money she left me was so wisely spent in buying it. She so loved the country and her garden that it must be a great satisfaction that we are enjoying ourselves in the same way.

29.12.72. I suppose you will want to hear about our Christmas. On the Saturday we decided to have a party and when this came to pass about 24 people came to drinks, of whom 18 stayed for supper ... cold chicken and ham, a salmon mousse, salads and a sweet and cheese. (Winnie had given us Stilton for Christmas.) It was very good fun, and especially so as most of the guests were young, Michael having brought in a batch. The nationalities were interesting, two New Zealanders, one Australian, two Americans, a Greek girl, born in Turkey and married to an Englishman, a French girl, born in France, but living in Turkey and married to an Austrian, several Russians and the remainder English, apart from one Scottish lady, a friend of Diana Zvegintsoff who, whenever she was introduced as Mrs. McNab, immediately corrected this to McNab of McNab. The young certainly ate enough, and it was all very successful.

Sunday morning we did nothing but in the evening went to some friends in a neighbouring square in which lighted candles stood in every window. Then on to dinner at the Hapsburgs, a family party at which John kept us entertained with stories of the East. Then on to midnight Service, John with us and on our return he and Vava opened their stockings and we got to bed at about 1.30. Next morning we woke up late but Vava went straight to Maya's to help cook the Christmas lunch. We were a small party, three Hetheringtons, two New Zealand and one Australian girl, friends of Michael's. Lunch was excellent and after this we all went for a walk and then sang carols and played games.

Later. We are now at the cottage and this morning being cold and misty we are thinking of you with envy. I have quite a number of flowers open in the garden, roses, winter jasmine, wallflowers and primroses from Turkey.

This is the peaceful time of the day, with both Vava and John asleep, an hour I look forward to daily. Vava is getting into the bad habit of waking early and demanding conversation and some display of affection, for neither of which I am prepared. I have to push her over and tell her to go to sleep and leave me in peace. She obeys for one minute and then demands coffee and takes most of the newspaper and is altogether a confounded nuisance.

Masha takes after you, for left to herself the other day and having to cook her lunch she burnt two non-stick saucepans and broke the coffee percolator. Excitement as she has just rung to say Natalie has had twins.

16.2.74. John writes briefly and contentedly from Arabia where he is working very hard. Maya and the children are in good form. The children are magnificent, Charlotte being a huge galumphing girl who forgets how large she is and how old I am and wants to be lifted and carried. She spends most of her time reading and is quite happy in a corner with a book. Anne is improving and much less trouble. The arrival of Helen had distracted attention from her and she is losing her tantrums! Both girls adore the baby and quite rightly as Helen is a lovely child and as good as gold, smiling all the time.

Weston is in good form and for a change I have been able to work in the garden, over which I am very pleased, especially having being able to devote a whole day to it. I always say the best three medicines in this World are a long walk, a day working in the garden and a bottle of whisky.

You may remember Kathleen, our old friend who does our washing for us. She has been working for a family who have now fallen on hard times and she told Vava that as they had always been very good to her she will be going on working for them, but without asking for money.

CHAPTER IV

Villa Ribeaupierre

When the Revolution broke out in Russia Prince George Cantacuzene accompanied by his wife, a former Countess Kapnist and their two sons together with his younger brother Prince Constantine with his wife Catherine, née Naryshkin, (first cousin to Barbara's father, Lawrence Pouschine) and their two children, Alexandra (Asya) and Nicholas (Kolya) settled in their old holiday home, the Villa Ribeaupierre, in Switzerland. The house was in the village of Glion, standing on the mountain slopes above the Lake of Geneva. They were joined by two orphan children of a brother of Catherine's, Helen and Alexander (Sasha) Naryshkin.

The latter four children decided that it would be much easier if they all called their Mother and Aunt by the same name and picked on that of Mima, which was then taken up by all her friends, only her husband and close relatives calling her Catherine.

The original house was stone-built with three-stories and housed all the domestic offices, the bedrooms and a large dining room. Standing nearby was a two-storied annex built at a later date. This was more elegant, with its upper floor approached by a marble staircase leading into a large hall and a number of bedrooms, while the lower floor was mainly a large drawing room, with French windows giving onto the terrace which offered a superb view of almost the whole lake, extending from the snow-capped Dents du Midi in the East almost as far as Geneva.

The ascent to the Villa from Montreux by the lakeside was by either of two railways running to Glion station, one a funicular from Territet and the other a mountain railway climbing up to the Rochers de Naye. The Villa itself stood well above the station and village and the hot steep walk up deterred visitors to the Villa from doing it too often.

At first the brothers still had some money, but, as this started to dwindle it was decided to take in paying guests and the house was adapted to that purpose.

I made my first acquaintance of the Villa in 1938 when we decided to take our summer holiday there, bearing one year old Maya in tow. This certainly proved an experience.

We were greeted with open arms by Mima and Uncle Kostya and with them I soon felt completely at home. Uncle George was more reserved and I never got to know him properly. Bearded and short in stature he was very mild-mannered and completely overwhelmed by his wife, Aunt Margosha. They tended to keep apart from the common herd, but every morning we were graced by the sight of Aunt Margosha, of no mean size, proceeding to the bathroom in her dressing gown, followed behind by a much smaller Uncle George, carrying a towel over one arm, with a soap dish and other toilet necessities in hand. After a time they left the Villa to live in a flat in Montreux, to which we used to be invited to tea and to indulge in the richest of cakes which Aunt Margosha adored, despite her weight.

Uncle Kostya was the exact opposite of his brother. Nervous, alert, excitable and always on the move, he saw to the fabric of the house and did the shopping in the Montreux market. He used to enjoy his marketing and the company of the vendors, both male and female, among whom he was very popular. At home he was just as likely to be found mending the roof as sitting in his room playing the zither, at which he was quite an expert. In general he seldom talked in a quiet voice, usually preferring to shout, which made things difficult as one never knew whether he was in a state of excitement or carrying on a placid conversation. He was kind-hearted to a degree, and I found it difficult to get onto close terms with him, but on the other hand it was impossible not to admire his great qualities and to love him.

One thing that always roused him to fury was any breakage of glass. So when one day Pierre, a young friend, and our John were playing, the former put his hand through one of the glass door panes in the sitting room, the whole household fell into a state of frenzy, despite the fact that Uncle Kostya was out. All gathered around wringing their hands and speculating as to what the Prince would say until someone pointed out that while they were all moaning and wailing, poor Pierre was slowly bleeding to death. Immediately all thoughts were turned in his direction and his wounds were seen to. The next thing on the agenda was to conceal the event from the Prince, fortunately the glazier was able to come up immediately to repair the damage, so on the Prince's return the only evidence of the accident lay in Pierre's bandage.

Stories about Uncle were numerous. On one occasion I saw him in the distance shouting and gesticulating, with John standing beside him with open mouth in dumb amazement. I, fearing the worst, rushed up to calm things down, only to find that Uncle Kostya was explaining to John how best to fly his aeroplane.

On another occasion my niece, Noreen Jackson, arrived from Paris. As she walked up the hill in the sunshine with her black hair and red cheeks set off by a scarlet blazer, she looked absolutely stunning. After the usual greetings, she was asked why she had left Paris, to which she replied that she could not stand the attentions men paid her in the streets, at which we heard Uncle grunting in the background: "What the devil does she expect with the face and the figure she has. Now if I had met her as a young man I'd have been the first to......."

The boys had been teasing an elderly and not very handsome lady, and this had upset Mima who told her husband to talk to them and tell them off. She, listening in the background, heard him explain to them how rude such behaviour was and not befitting gentlemen, only to be horrified at his ending with: "Of course, if the lady were young and pretty, that would be another matter, but with one so old and ugly it is not decent."

Uncle Kostya stood out in sharp relief to Mima, she never pushed herself forward and being quiet, patient and understanding and the essence of kindness, always prepared to listen to other people's troubles. Yet she was far from being a weakling, in fact very much the contrary, with a firm sense of duty and of right and wrong, and unhesitatingly outspoken should the occasion demand it. It is impossible to do her justice in words, but with her essential goodness, kindness, tolerance and generosity, she has left an unforgettable impression, almost of saintliness, of one who was loved by all.

She had an amazing knowledge of the Russian nobility, knowing everyone's relationships and family history. A great friend of ours, married to an Englishman, produced a son with bright red hair, over which we used regularly to tease her. They came to the Villa and as soon as Mima saw the boy she came out with: "How wonderful, he has his Grandfather's hair." And this of course solved the mystery.

Outside the immediate family there were two others attached to the household, namely Nusha and Serge. Nusha had been Mima's personal maid in Russia and had followed her into exile. Short, fat, ugly and reputedly ill-tempered, she only spoke Russian and held command over the kitchen. At first I was somewhat nervous about her possible reaction to taking my breakfast long before the rest of the household, but my fears were happily soon allayed, she apparently approving of me and not minding my presence in the kitchen of an early morning. Whatever the state of family finances, she was always paid regularly and so there came times when she, having few requirements and seldom leaving the Villa, was the only member of the family to have any ready cash. So, from time to time, she acted as a banker until things returned to normal. Everyone treated Nusha with great respect, except for the boys who used to tease her, to her delight and at times to her fury.

The other inmate was Serge Sheremetiev. He was born with both speech and hearing defects, and sadly had had to leave his special school in England through lack of money before the course of training was completed. Back in Switzerland he was sent to the Villa on holiday and somehow or other remained on permanently. Strong as a horse he did all the heavy work about the place and made himself generally useful. He adored Mima and Uncle Kostya and nothing was too much trouble for him.

He loved music and somehow or other could hear this to some degree anyhow. Otherwise he could lip-read in Russian, French and English. In the days of silent films he was known to burst out laughing, even in moments of great drama, as he could understand what the actors were saying to each other. He also spoke the same three languages, but to understand him one had to be initiated into his manner of speech. This I could not always understand but on the whole he managed to make himself understood. At one point of time he was given an effective hearing aid, but this was discarded, as, when using it, he found the world to be far too noisy.

Another attachment to the house, though non-resident, was Bobby, pronounced Bobbee, the youngest son of Theophile the farmer next door who had bought it from the brothers. From a small boy he enjoyed doing things for Mima whom he adored. By the time I met him he was in his late ‘teens and applying for a job in the Post Office. To get this he had to pass a medical examination over which he was worried, as there was a vague story of sugar in the urine. So he came to me for advice and I gave him full instructions as to how to set about things. Whether thanks to them, or otherwise he passed with flying colours and I was given the credit. At this stage he was strikingly handsome with a superb figure and to see him stripped to the waist and scything grass in the field below the Villa took one back to the days of the Greek Gods.

We became great friends and used to meet of a morning before lunch for a glass of wine in the Café de la Gare, when I used to be brought up to date with all local goings on, he no doubt reading all the postcards and telegrams. Back in London, whenever we received a letter from the Villa, Bobby would always have a note for us on the back of the envelope.

With his looks he was of course greatly sought after by all the girls both of the village and of the Villa, the latter often to the anxiety of their mothers. It was rumoured that he had been 'caught into marriage' by one Rosa, who, although not physically attractive, made him a good wife, keeping him happy and bearing him fine children, also putting up with his aberrations with a patience which I would consider to be very un-Swiss.

Outside his job, Bobby was a first class skier and a good tennis player, giving lessons in both these sports. In later years he was invited to Australia to teach skiing one winter. On one occasion I taxed him with a lack of ambition in not moving out of the narrow circle of Glion, indicating how well his two brothers had done in the outer world. He replied that he loved the village life and above all his connection with the Villa, from which the example of Mima and Uncle Kostya had given him a good set of values and had taught him to enjoy life in a way totally hidden from his brothers, despite their far greater wealth. In effect his contact with Russian attitudes and ways of life had been more important to him than anything else.

Most guests at the Villa came on holiday and so only stayed for short periods. Regular visitors included Jean Cocteau, Igor Markevitch, the conductor, and Sir Timothy Eden, brother of Anthony. A large proportion however had Russian connections. Naturally they varied considerably in their personalities and attitudes, many tended to return again and again. Amongst them there were of course the odd eccentrics, such as one who considered the local mountain water tainted and preferred to buy his own bottled variety. One elderly Russian Colonel had had an operation in the vicinity of his heart. On leaving hospital he had been given a diagram to illustrate what had been done. He loved to way-lay people and discourse on this at length. His English was not too good and once, to everyone's amusement, having talked at length to a lady, he produced his diagram upon which she turned to him and said: "How interesting, and is this a map of your estate in Russia?"

The Villa was ideal for a peaceful holiday. There was none of the luxury of a Grand Hotel, for, after all, living there was cheap. Provided one could overlook occasional mishaps, especially in connection with the hot water system, life was comfortable and simple and things ran smoothly. Above all one could find absolute peace and quiet, especially as there was so much room for any children to lose themselves. Nothing could be more pleasant than to sit on the terrace and admire the view either in silence or in quiet conversation. For the more energetic there was always a choice of walks, either up the mountain or on more level paths skirting their contours, while down below there was Montreux offering every degree of sophistication and good bathing in the lake.

The principal meals were taken in the dining room, with the more dignified guests sitting at a sort of high table. Mima sat at its head and she often got Michael to sit at her side to amuse her with his talk. One day however I was horrified to hear him in his loud and clear voice coming out with: "And Daddy was so drunk that on getting out of the car he could not stand up but had to hold himself up on a lamppost." Everyone burst out laughing and it took me a long time to live this down, despite giving my version that Michael was repeating an experience I had had when called to the Police Station to examine a man charged with being drunk when driving a motor car. Conversation was generally carried out in a mixture of Russian, French, English and German.

After the evening meal the company would split in two, with most of the guests repairing to the drawing room for coffee, while Mima's intimates, the "aristocracy" as we called ourselves settled in the kitchen to hold conversation while the washing up was in progress. Here, on choice occasions, Mima would produce a bottle of her home made orange liqueur, while Uncle Kostya, when pressed, would entertain us on the zither.

A great change came over the area when Moral Rearmament took over the Caux Palace Hotel, some 1,500 feet higher up the mountain. Prior to their coming, all cars climbing up would willingly stop and give lifts to pedestrians, but members of the Movement were apparently too exclusive to mix with the general public and never stopped. This exclusiveness also caused several shops in Caux to close down, only those showing sympathy with the Movement being patronised.

Their conception of right and wrong was shown up by one incident. After the war a number of British airmen who had suffered extensive burns and disfigurement were sent to Switzerland for further treatment and to get adapted to the outer world. A party of these were being taken out for a drive and the organiser thought that a Movement of such high principles would gladly give the men afternoon tea. But not a bit of it. When approached M.R. bluntly replied that they could not possibly entertain men in such condition in their quarters. After this abrupt refusal contact was made with the Manager of the Hotel Victoria, the best in Glion, who, on the situation being explained to him, promptly invited the whole party to tea as guests of the hotel. He then went round the lounges and explained to the guests what he had done, advising any who might be upset by the appearance of the men, to move into one of the smaller rooms. No one moved and when the party arrived they were greeted with every mark of pleasure, conversation flowed and the tea turned out a huge success.

After this the low opinion in which Moral Rearmament was locally held sank to a nadir. John and a couple of friends once attended a lecture at Caux out of sheer curiosity. In the darkened room the lecturer discoursed on the degenerate state of British youth, with their long hair and scruffy clothes, which latter he described in full. Great was the delight of the boys when the lights went on and they stood up immediately in front of the lecturer dressed in exactly the manner he had so deplored.

Life at the Villa took on a simple pattern. My chief pleasure was to set off early in the morning up the mountains to return at midday, often carrying a basket of wild strawberries or raspberries, leaving Barbara to look after the children and to talk to all and sundry. A favourite excursion for the family was to descend to the Gorges du Chaudron for a picnic. Here a stream, flowing through rocks, left a number of pools ideal for bathing and for sunbathing lying on the rocks.

In order to introduce the children to rich and cream cakes such as they had never enjoyed before due to the war, we all descended one day to have tea at Zurcher's, the town's most famous patisserie. Here Barbara and I almost wept at the thought of what the children had missed when they refused the unfamiliar rich cakes and instead chose simple buns and biscuits.

Visits were also paid to my Uncle Hugh Whittall who was British Vice-Consul. He had a lovely house and garden in nearby Clarens, in which among other things he grew all his own breakfast cereals. He was also very interested in dwarf conifers, but these had outgrown their promise to become so tall as to exclude light from the sitting room windows. So, as to destroy the plants would have been sacrilege, the sitting room was moved upstairs and the downstairs room converted into a bedroom. We always had tea in the garden, which was lovely, except for the tame crow, which, with a beak like a dagger, used to wander around our legs, keeping all in a state of constant anxiety. Uncle's other pet was a chicken with three wings, this one being harmless.

Visits to his office were always fun as Uncle, despite his age, always kept an eye for young and attractive women, as Maya found when she used to slip over from Paris when studying there. These visits were always the occasion for opening the safe to reveal an array of bottles, prior to settling down to talk. On one visit we found Uncle in a very displeased frame of mind caused by the total lack of consideration shown by an Englishman who chose to die on the summit of the St. Gothard Pass, necessitating all manner of arrangements to get him down again, all this falling onto Uncle's shoulders. However we cheered him up and restored him to equanimity. Actually Uncle was the soul of kindness and such moments of exasperation were short-lived.

He related the following pleasant story. The local Anglican Church was holding its annual bazaar and garden party and Uncle asked Charlie Chaplin, who was living in retirement nearby, whether he would attend. Charlie refused saying he no longer attended public functions, but as Uncle was leaving, called out: "One moment Whittall, I did not quite catch what you said. Did you say the party was in aid of the Church, for if so I will certainly attend?" and attend he did.

In the meantime another local resident wanted Uncle's job and kept writing to the Foreign Office suggesting that Uncle was becoming too old and incapable. So a couple of young men arrived to look into the matter, and, after business was finished, Uncle suggested a walk. Off they went, but at the end Uncle returned on foot and in good form, while the two youngsters had to be brought back by carriage. There was no further talk of incapacity. Uncle also proved very useful when shopping, for having a lot of local influence, a recommendation from him ensured that the local habit of overcharging the foreigner was not indulged in.

No sooner had Barbara heard that there was a casino across the water in Evian, than this became an objective which had to be met. On the first occasion when we set off we left the children almost in tears, imploring us not to lose all our money, as they did not want to return to England. Reassuring them to the best of our ability we set off on our trip round the lake. Arrived at Evian, I asked a policeman's advice about a good restaurant which would not ruin our finances. This we followed. Settling down at table I asked the waiter what he recommended us to eat; when he had had his say, our neighbour chimed in with his advice and soon everybody took part in the discussion and practically ordered our meal for us. The end result was excellent and eventually, with thanks to all, we left for the Casino. Here I gave Barbara her allowance and looked on, awaiting the worst, which was not long in coming. But as we were leaving, rummaging in her bag she found a further note and returned to the tables, to come away triumphant having won enough to pay for all the expenses of the evening and leave her a surplus. So we returned home in triumph, with me being reviled for a lack of faith in my wife.

One afternoon we were invited to tea by a Miss Lomas, sister of a former English clergyman in Montreux. On arrival we found the table beautifully laid, with silver and porcelain and plates of small sandwiches and fine cut bread. The children settled themselves down and in no time the table was, to Barbara's and my horror, cleared. Miss Lomas rose to the occasion, the maid was summoned to return with a large loaf of bread, a large dish of butter and a jar of jam, to which the children did full justice, with Miss Lomas evidently recapturing her youth and encouraging them to eat more. The afternoon thus ended most successfully with the children satisfied and us enjoying an interesting conversation.

Of an evening we often used to go round to the Princess Wittgenstein (no relation to the philosopher) to play bridge. Her niece came to us for dinner in London while studying nursing. We asked her about her life in East Prussia, when to everyone's surprise our Swiss au-pair girl chimed in to say that she knew the estates involved and had actually lived on them for her father had worked there as a carpenter. A strange coincidence.

At the time of our first visit clothes were still rationed in England so Barbara took up the opportunity to stock up the children with winter wear. On leaving, to avoid any trouble with the English customs, the children were dressed up in our purchases, to look as though they had just emerged from the North Pole. Arrived at Dover all was going well until John suddenly showed the customs official the new watch which Uncle Kostya, his Godfather had given him. The man was suitably impressed and then suggested that Barbara took the children to the train leaving me to deal with the luggage, which was let through without inspection. Evidently he was a family man.

Our stays at the Villa ended with the death of Uncle Kostya in the sixties. With his passing Mima could not cope on her own and the Villa was sold. Uncle ended his days in glory, for, on the morning of his funeral, the market in Montreux practically closed; with all his old vendor friends turning up at the Church to pay their last respects. Happily too, prior to his death, he got even with the Railway. He had carried on a regular war with them as they would not recognise his right to a season ticket at the reduced price for "locals" as he was not considered an 'indigene' They had built a new station on a level with the Villa and approached him for a contribution to the cost as the station would make things much easier for him and his guests. He in a fury turned on the man and said: "For forty years you have refused to allow me to have a season ticket at a reduced rate and now you come to me as a foreigner to help pay for your station. It is just sheer impertinence approaching me in this way."

After the sale of the house Mima moved into a flat with Serge. During her last illness Barbara came over to help nurse her with Asya. They told the doctor that, being unskilled, it might be better to place her in hospital, but this he refused to do, saying that while their nursing was not up to hospital standards, once admitted, she would be subjected to all manner of totally useless treatments, whereas, as things were, she was at home, among those she loved and could die undisturbed and peacefully.

I last saw the Villa in 1989 when Nicholas drove me up to it in company of Bobby. It had been beautifully done up and gleamed in its new paint, but the occasion was sad, and even sitting down to a bottle of wine in the Hotel Victoria did not cheer me up. But Bobby was in good form, now retired and somewhat heavier, and what a pleasure it was to talk over old days and to recapitulate the happiness of those times.

Talking to Sasha Naryshkin one day I asked him whether a farming life would suit him to get the reply that in view of the difficulties in the way of getting work in Switzerland he would leap at any opportunity of finding any. So I wrote to my brother Bill in Rhodesia and he replied that he would be glad to take on any physically fit young man. So Sasha set off to work some years on the ranch. Then, with the war starting, he joined the army and on his return to civilian life the Government offered him the opportunity of starting up on his own as a farmer. He made a considerable success of this, married and had children, and is now retired in Durban.

Epilogue

GEOFFREY WILLIAM WHITTALL

Geoffrey's life was shaped by his love for and interest in people. Class for him did not exist and whether he was talking to royalty, the fish-monger in Lerwick or the paper seller on the corner of the street, he had the ability to make them realise that he was interested in them as individuals.

This love of people led him to his choice of career as a doctor. He was not interested in becoming a specialist, but in meeting and treating ordinary people. He was a very good doctor and his success ultimately led to his decision to give up the work he loved in order to see and give more time to his family. His new work with the Ministry of Health brought him into contact with doctors, not as an unwelcome visitor from head office, but as a colleague to whom they could relate and who had a wealth of experience. He refused promotion as he did not wish to lose this human contact in his work and he was not interested in the material signs of success which tend to govern peoples lives. He was able to arrange that he could continue this work on a decreasing basis for ten years after his official retirement.

His other love which he shared with Barbara was for their family and friends. The transitions from patient to friend and from friend to family were always blurred and many gradually stepped from one to the other. All his children grew up with and still use the expression "he or she is part of the family", when describing someone who is no actual relation. He kept in touch with most of them throughout his life. Both Geoffrey and Barbara were totally loyal to their families and friends and their house was always a natural port of call. To them a friend was a friend for life, to be kept and supported always. This friendship extended to their children and even grandchildren. It is a measure of the quality of this friendship that at Barbara's 90th birthday party and at Geoffrey's funeral there were so many children of their old friends who came, not out of a sense of duty, but because of their own friendship with them.

Geoffrey was a man of wide interests and culture and with a great knowledge of an extraordinary range of subjects. His great and abiding love was for flowers and he became an expert on them, although he never thought of himself as one.

His faith sustained him throughout most of his life. It even survived him being told by a 17 year old nephew that, as he was not Orthodox, he was condemned to everlasting damnation. (The selfsame nephew flew over from New York to attend his funeral). Brought up in a country where all the major Western faiths existed side by side in harmony, all these faiths were represented at his funeral. He had no fear of death and he said to John many years ago that when he died he was looking forward to seeing his Mother, Father and all his relations again. As his family were sitting waiting for the undertakers to come after his death, they were speculating on the re-union which was going on in heaven at that moment. As he grew older, he gained more and more pleasure from the weekday children's service for St Mary Abbott's Church school, and it was fitting that as his coffin was borne from the church, the children should rush out into the playground to play. Maya hastily reassured their horrified teacher who was trying to quieten them.

Main Articles written by Geoffrey Whittall

The Medical World 1962

Displaced Persons in Germany

Anglo Portuguese News 1970 onwards

A Childhood in Turkey

Kiamil

Letters from Liverpool 1811 – 1813

The Fate of the Apostles

Wine Tour of the North

Lunch in the City

Lady Hester Stanhope

Portugal in London

Our Village Jubilee 1977

Pirates in London

The Lusiad in English I

The Portuguese in Southern Arabia

Buried in Lisbon

Up-Helly-AA

The Lusiad in English II

America Again

Life on Foula

Portuguese Words in English

Eighteenth Century Dreams

Hymns and Hymn-Writers

The Great Earthquake at Lisbon

Drake's Pilot

Turkish Pottery

An Experience of Churches

Family etc.

The Early Whittalls
The Older Generations.
Related Families
General Practice 1934 – 55
GWW & BW 1906 – 1955
The Russian Family